RADICAL

Maajid Nawaz

With Tom Bromley

WH
ALLEN

2 4 6 8 10 9 7 5 3 1

First published in the UK in 2012 by WH Allen

This edition published in 2013 by WH Allen an imprint of Ebury Publishing

A Random House Group Company

Copyright © Maajid Nawaz 2012

Maajid Nawaz has asserted his right under the Copyright, Designs and Patents Act 1988 to be identified as the author of this work.

www.randomhouse.co.uk

Addresses for companies within The Random House Group Limited can be found at www.randomhouse.co.uk/offices.htm

The Random House Group Limited Reg. No. 954009

A CIP catalogue record for this book is available from the British Library.

The Random House Group Limited supports The Forest Stewardship Council® (FSC®), the leading international forest-certification organisation. Our books carrying the FSC label are printed on FSC®-certified paper. FSC is the only forest-certification scheme supported by the leading environmental organisations, including Greenpeace. Our paper procurement policy can be found at www.randomhouse.co.uk/environment

Printed and bound in the UK by CPI Group (UK) Ltd, Croydon, CR0 4YY

ISBN: 9780753540770

To buy books by your favourite authors and register for offers, visit www.randomhouse.co.uk

For my family, my son, and for all my friends.
And for those with whom I started a movement.

Contents

PART THREE: RADICAL

The moving finger writes, and having written moves on.
Nor all thy piety nor all thy wit, can cancel half a line of it.

Omar Khayyam, *Ruba'iyat*

Preface

This is a book about change and transformation. Maajid Nawaz's extraordinary account of his life – from young childhood in Southend through teen years embroiled in street violence and induction into Islamism – makes it relatively easy to understand how political and ideological radicalism occurs. His description of the violent prejudice he experienced in his youth is a salutary lesson in what can happen when institutional racism is allowed to flourish. He makes it very clear how and why he became desensitised to violence and shows how racist aggression created a fertile recruiting ground for Islamist extremism. He writes powerfully about his gradual detachment and inability to feel empathy for others; such was his experience of immersion in radical ideology.

But what is most fascinating to me is the evidence that radical extremists can change; it is possible. Maajid describes his awe at the compassion of ordinary human beings who, after his arrest, unfair trial, ill treatment and imprisonment in Egypt, put aside their own dislike of his politics, stood up for the universality of human rights, and campaigned for his release. Chief among them was Amnesty member John Cornwall. Not only did he prompt Amnesty International to adopt Maajid as a Prisoner of Conscience, he wrote letter after letter of friendship to Maajid himself.

I am moved beyond measure to read of the transformative effects of these letters on Maajid. It reminds me again of why I am proud to work for Amnesty International UK, whose members' actions were so instrumental in enabling Maajid to reconnect with life and humanity. In essence, human rights, compassion and kindness helped to save his humanity. This book is the account of his redemptive journey – through innocence, bigotry, hardline radicalism and beyond – to a passionate advocacy of human rights and all that this can mean.

Kate Allen, Director, Amnesty International UK

Prologue

Southend, 1992

'Slammer': that's my tag when I'm out bombing, plastering the streets with graffiti. I write it without an 'm' – 'Slamer' – because it's quicker that way, and speed counts if you don't want to get caught by the cops. I'm a hip-hop B-boy, into Public Enemy and N.W.A. Tracks like 'Rebel Without a Pause', 'Fear of a Black Planet', 'Fuck tha Police' – their lyrics are deep. I'm in a 'click' suit, baggy corduroys with pin tucks at the bottom, rocking Adidas trainers. My hair's a grade zero up to the top – when not in a red bandana it stands up in a box-cut, with a mad design trimmed up the back. My crew all wear the same clothes, blast the same tunes. Like Erick and Parrish Making Dollars, we look the *Business*.

I'm fifteen years old, and I live in Southend in Essex. This summer, like every summer, the fair is here, in the park across the way from my house. When I was young I used to go to the fair with my folks. Back in those days it was all about the rides: the dodgems, the Egg-Roller, the Carpet Roll. These days I go with my boys, and at night not during the day. Now I don't care about the rides. I go to chill and check out the skins on show, the local female talent.

As Ice Cube once rapped *today was a good day* . . . or at least it had been. The sky is full of blurred lights against the blackness: there's a backdrop of girls' screams and thumping tracks from the rides; that sweet and sour fairground smell of candyfloss and fried onions. We're bowling around, on the prowl, when out of the crowd comes a face I recognise. It's my friend Chill – real name, Tsiluwa. Chill and I are tight. Born in Zimbabwe, he came to Britain a few years ago. He's pelting towards us, criss-crossing through all the people, and I can see straight away that he's relieved he's found us.

'Yo, Chill. Whassup, bro?'

'We've got beef, boys,' he says.

Chill turns round and I follow his gaze to where, and who, he's been running from. Barging through the crowd is a group of white lads in green bomber jackets, and they're stepping to us big time. When they see Chill has friends they stop in their tracks. The crowd between us starts to thin and I can feel my heart racing. The leader, a well-known local thug called Mickey, scopes us as he raises his right hand in a fascist salute. Then his friends are all at it, swearing and giving Nazi salutes, calling us 'Niggers' and 'Pakis' and telling us to 'fuck off back to where we came from'.

It's good to know that in situations like this my boys've got my back. Mickey's threats are clear: I've been here before, but it's not something I'm about to get used to. Especially when it's more than all mouth: I know from experience that they'll be packing knives. If we get caught, we'll get sliced to pieces. The longer our stand-off lasts the more the crowd melts away, and the hustle and bustle of the fair gives way to an ominous ring of space. No one wants to know.

We split. I'm running between the stalls, weaving in and out of people, running so hard I can hear my breath thumping against the screams from the rides. Where's that park-keeper when you need him? I'm glad I know the park well, know where to go. That means I can give these skinheads the slip, and I realise with relief that the shouts of 'Paki!' are drifting further and further away as I make my way to the gate. Then I'm over the road, heading for home. Straight in and up the stairs, up to my room and under the bed where I keep it: my favourite hunting knife. Taking three stairs at a time, *bish-bash-bosh*, I'm down and back out of the door before my parents can ask what's going on. They belong to a generation more tolerant of such trouble, and with a local newsagent's to look after right opposite the park this is definitely not an approach they would approve of. But me and my crew, we think different. Now's not the time to cower and hope the shit blows over. Now's the time to stand with my boys, to back them up. No racist is gonna run us off our own streets.

The group reassembles at one of our prearranged meeting points: the place we head to when we get split up like this. It takes a while but once we're sure it's safe we gather on the corner of Chalkwell Avenue and London Road. We're not looking for trouble, but we sure as hell aren't backing down either. We're not gonna be run down by Mickey and his goons.

Walking back up London Road a white van suddenly pulls up behind us. Back doors open, and out climb a group of proper, nasty-looking skinheads.

Shit, here we go.

I've heard stories of 'Paki-bashing' before. Tales of groups of men driving around in search of unsuspecting victims to stab. But this is the first time I've been the 'Paki' in question. We've been set up. Mickey and his bomber-jacket mates, for

3

all their front, they're just local youth like us. These skinheads are in a different league: big men, built like brick shithouses, in their twenties, tooled-up and ready for action. There's a glint of a blade in the street lights as they climb out of the van. Some are carrying clubs with nails hammered in the ends. If they catch us . . .

My friends all have the same idea as me: we need to move fast. 'My blade!' I think, as I hear them tearing down the street. I've gotta ditch my blade! If they find me with it, they'll think I'm up for a fight. My only chance is if I can prove I'm not strapped, try my luck, see if they'll let me be. I dive into a side alley, duck down, and hide the knife behind a bush. Then I'm out, pelting up the street, in the panic of the moment not sure which way to turn, and – oh *shit* – I'm surrounded. There's five, six of them, around me on all sides. Knives, knuckledusters, clubs. There's the Hitler salute again, pierced by more swearing: *Fucking Paki! Fuck off back to where you came from!*

I can feel my fear rising, my adrenalin pumping. The look on these men's faces can only mean one thing; they know there's no escape for me now, and so do I. This is it, '*that's the way the ball bounces*'. I've had my skins, blasted my tunes, and enjoyed the good times. Now, I guess I'm just gonna get *got* . . .

* * *

Egypt, 2002

Am I being driven to my martyrdom, my *shahadah*? I'm bound and blindfolded with filthy rags, packed between other frightened, hapless creatures, sweltering beneath an unforgiving desert sun. Heat and salt. Heat and salt. It's all I can taste. The sour, putrid smell of fear is thick in the back of the van we are in. It's reeking from the sweat of those I'm trussed up against, and I'm certain I smell the same to them too. Someone to my right is murmuring incomprehensibly: a prayer, a whimper, or just plain confusion. The rest are silent but for the sound of their ragged, laboured breaths, waiting, waiting for what lies ahead.

It seems like four hours since I awoke, maybe five. There's no way to tell. The searing heat could be Cairo, but then again it could be anywhere in Egypt. *Allahu a'lam* – God only knows. Maybe it will be a bullet in the back of my head. The state security, called Aman al-Dawla, has been known to bus people out to deserted areas to do just that. What a mercy that would be. Quick and easy. Just time enough to read my testimony of faith, the *Kalimatain*, before I go. Yes, the Qur'an, I must remember the Qur'an. Chapter *Ya-Seen* will surely calm my nerves. I try recalling the words with all the focus I can muster, but nothing penetrates through the heavy, almost asphyxiating haze.

And then I hear of it, announced with relish as a police conscript, *a shaweesh*, jostles us out of the van and down steps we can't see: al-Gihaz. The Apparatus. Headquarters of Aman al-Dawla, notorious in all Egypt for what has been whispered about its dark, underground cells. Many have come out crazed, unable to speak of what they encountered inside, others have never come out at all.

In here I have lost my name. I am now a number. Forty-two – *itnain wa arba'een* – is what I must remember, and what

I must answer to every time it is called. *Itnain wa arba'een, itnain wa arba'een, itnain wa arba'een.* Everything else is uncertain. I don't know if I will get down these steps without falling, I don't know when I'll be beaten. I have been stripped of defence; my blindfold means I cannot see it coming. Clenching my body in anticipation of the blows is exhausting but it's all I can do. The muscles in my stomach and the back of my neck ache with the effort.

The change in the air tells me I am being shoved below ground. The space becomes constricted; dank, invisible walls start closing in. As I'm shunted through a corridor, the smell hits me like a blow to the gut; the stench of human waste left stewing too long. It cuts through the agony and the fatigue, leaving me gagging for air, begging soundlessly for respite. I feel movement on both sides, the restless stirring of confined bodies. Packed holding cells to my right and left.

With no room to spare, I am made to lie on top of others already lying on the soiled floor of the corridor; we are like human dominoes. I can feel a strange body crushed beneath mine. *Ya akhi* – my brother, forgive me for what my weight must be doing to you. I want to speak but our orders are to maintain absolute silence, or be silenced. Hour after hour, new bodies pile up around me. In the solitary world of the blindfold, I have no way of distinguishing one living corpse from the next.

And so it begins, the long sleepless vigil of al-Gihaz. No rest, no communication, no movement. Shivering and sweltering between carefully orchestrated extremes of temperature, we must be ready at all times to answer the hourly roll call of our assigned numbers. *Itnain wa arba'een, itnain wa arba'een, itnain wa arba'een.* I must not forget. Failing to answer or falling asleep means a vicious boot to my face.

In moments of lucidity I remember that no one, not the wife and child I left behind screaming after me in the middle of the night, or the parents that fretted about my move to Egypt, know where I am. Panic rises like bile in my throat as I struggle to regain control. Allah have mercy. *Hasbi Allah wa ni'mal wakeel* – you are sufficient and the best of protectors. Ever since I dedicated myself to the re-establishment of our Caliphate, I have spent years knowing that this moment would come. Pharaohs have never been defeated without blood and sacrifice, and the victories of the righteous have always extracted a heavy price. But help me through this ordeal, my Lord, as I am scared and alone. *Ya-Seen, wal Qur'an il-Hakim* . . .

Days, nights, I can no longer tell the difference. But I recognise with a shudder when the roll call stops and the 'questioning' begins. A brother somewhere down a corridor nearby – assigned the number one – is yanked to his feet.

Raqam wahid!

Scuffling amid muted cries, he treads his way between the rows of prisoners to a room down the corridor. The door is left open like a warning to the rest of us. Shouts. Thuds. Pleas. And then a noise that turns my stomach. The sharp, unmistakable crackle of electricity, followed by a bloodcurdling scream. *A'uzu billah* – I seek refuge in God! It is hard to imagine the impact of a howl wracked in pain until you actually hear it. A chorus of murmuring engulfs my corridor as all the brothers pray under their breaths. We all know that our own numbers will be called soon enough. Think! I tell myself. Recite the

Qur'an! But my lips are quivering, my throat is dry and my mind is shot with exhaustion and fear.

There are fewer footsteps as the brother is brought back to his place. His limp body is dumped against a wall with a sickening thud of finality. And then:

Raqam itnain!

It's on to number two. With time the threats and shouts of the guard and wailing of the nameless brothers blend into an endless stream of screaming sound. With brutal regularity the numbers are called, growing ever nearer to my own – drawing ever closer.

Itnain wa arba'een, itnain wa arba'een, itnain wa arba'een. I must not forget.

* * *

Texas, 2011

Spring is giving way to summer in Dallas, and I've already decided it's too warm here. My suit collar chafes against my neck as I gaze out of the car that has collected me from my hotel; the neighbourhoods are getting visibly grander as we near our destination. Unsurprising really, given where I am headed.

Dallas has just launched the Presidential Center for Democracy, and the conference I have just spoken at is part of its inaugural proceedings. I was invited to discuss the role of social media in the recent uprisings in the Middle East – mass protests that set the region alight and shook decades of tyranny and repression. Naturally, the rest of the world is paying very close attention. On the panel with me was Oscar Morales, a friend and fellow activist. Oscar is the man credited with organising the largest demonstration against terrorism ever recorded – 12 million people responded to his viral campaign by taking to the streets to protest against the Columbian terrorist group FARC. Together, Oscar and I addressed an audience of global activists on how online platforms can be harnessed to mobilise and feed into traditional media. Surreal. Two years earlier I had not heard of Twitter. Now I was using my account to inform back-to-back television interviews about an uprising in Egypt.

These formalities over, I'm on my way to lunch with the sponsor of the event. I reach a large, imposing house and at the door I am greeted by a butler who tells me that guests are to 'go casual' for this one – in other words, we are to lose our jackets and ties. Uncomfortable with shedding my jacket, I make my way through the patio doors to a huge, immaculately kept lawn, where the other invited guests are mingling and a buffet-style lunch has been laid out.

As enticing as the smell of a Texan barbecue is, even more interesting are the guests at this gathering. I spot former National Security Advisor Stephen Hadley and former Secretary of State Condoleezza Rice chatting in a corner. While standing in the queue for barbecued meat, a man comes over and introduces himself as Michael Meece, Chief of Staff to a former President. He informs me that I have been invited to join our host at his table. Following Meece, I find myself among familiar faces: American activist and campaigner Stephanie Rudat, and various Egyptian and Syrian revolutionary activists. And there, ushering me to an

9

empty seat next to him is the host: former President of the United States, George W. Bush.

So much rushes through my mind as I look into that familiar face, but I keep my own expression neutral. I return the handshake he extends and take my seat. Lunch with Bush: this is something I didn't see coming. Half-remembered memories of television appearances, the public persona, the caricatures, all flash through my mind as I recall his 'War on Terror', his war on me.

A discussion is already under way at the table, and I tune in to catch up on the debate. Bush listens intently to each person, interrupting frequently to ask questions and seek clarification. It's Egypt's future that's being deliberated; the Egyptians are advocating passionately for swift justice for the ousted dictator, Hosni Mubarak. For them, his trial and incarceration will herald a new dawn for Egypt.

But I beg to differ, and feel I must give voice to my concerns. I try to explain why this single-minded focus on 'justice' might be detrimental to Egypt's long-term interests. 'What is needed first and foremost is a constitution, followed by an election process, after which justice against Mubarak can be sought. If Egypt fails to define a constitution for itself at the outset, the first party to win an election will mould it in their own image. Justice cannot be arbitrary; it must be set in law.' I argue this not from detached interest but from a deeply personal place; the suspension of constitutional rights following the assassination of President Sadat in 1981 has impacted my life in a way I cannot begin to explain. I have learnt what Emergency Law and the overriding of individual liberties really means. I have witnessed what Mubarak's regime has been capable of: the paralysing fear, the routine humiliations, the torture . . .

'Stop.' I am interrupted sharply by Bush, who has now turned his full attention to me. 'How do you define torture?'

Has Bush just asked me for my definition of torture? I know immediately his interest isn't merely academic – during his time in office, the question of what did and did not constitute torture was a vital component in the development of the 'War on Terror'. In 2002, Bush's Office of Legal Counsel wrote a notorious memorandum on the subject of 'water-boarding', an interrogation technique involving the simulation of drowning by pouring water over the prisoner's cellophaned face. The memorandum famously, and highly controversially, concluded that water-boarding was not torture but instead an 'enhanced' interrogation technique, thereby making it admissible by US law.

Where do I begin? Should I say how I feel about the overly militarised aspect of the 'War on Terror' and what it has cost the world in terms of human rights violations, reinforcing the terrorist narrative, and widespread damage to countries? Should I bring up Iraq? I've been on record talking about these issues, but how are you meant to respond when the leader of the 'War on Terror' asks you for your opinion over a barbecued lunch in his own backyard.

I decide to deal directly with the question asked. 'How do I define torture? What about electrocution?' I look back at Bush and wait to be asked about water-boarding. Instead, he nods and agrees solemnly 'Yes, that *is* torture', and with a wave of a hand, 'please carry on.'

PART ONE

B-boy

Notice to all passengers, please do not run on the platforms or concourses. Especially if you are carrying a rucksack, wearing a big coat, or look a bit foreign.

Anonymous graffiti in the London Underground, after police killed innocent Brazilian Jean Charles de Menezes at Stockwell station with seven shots to the head, July 22nd 2005

CHAPTER ONE

There is another Gujrat, in Pakistan

I was born in the late seventies, the same time as hip hop was busting its first moves in New York. The B-boys in the Bronx started it all, poppin' and lockin' to the original loops. Afrika Bambaataa, he was there at the beginning. So too were the Sugarhill Gang, sampling Chic and hitting the mainstream with 'Rapper's Delight'. Then there was Grandmaster Flash and the Furious Five; Melle Mel gave voice to their fury in 'The Message'. A dozen years later, I'd find inspiration in this scene, discover my voice in its rhythms. Until then, I'd grow up in isolation on the other side of the Atlantic, fledgling years that mirrored hip hop's own early development.

Even so, my own beginnings could not have been more different from those of hip hop. My birthplace and hometown was Southend, a coastal town in Essex. In Britain in the eighties, Essex was in tune with the times: Thatcher's populist appeal of tax cuts and the right to buy council houses, strident nationalism and an individualist ethos all suited the county. Nobody summed this up more than Norman Tebbit, MP for nearby Chingford and Tory Party Chairman, the minister who told the unemployed to get on their bikes, and whose *Spitting Image* puppet saw him dressed as a skinhead.

The Southend of my childhood was not at all like New York – it wasn't, and still isn't, a place of ethnic diversity. Of its present day population of 160,000, 96 per cent are white. When I was growing up, that percentage was even higher. These days there are Kosovan, Albanian and West Indian communities in the town, but thirty years ago there were no East Europeans, and the main West Indian communities were in nearby Pitsea and Basildon. There were few Asian families in Southend – literally a few hundred people, no more than 0.1 per cent of the population. At that time if you saw a Pakistani, Indian or Bangladeshi face in Southend, you would usually know their parents, where they had been on holiday last year, and the latest domestic scandal that was doing the rounds in their family.

Growing up in such a minority community has to have an effect on you. It was a completely different experience from being brought up in a large Pakistani community, in East Ham or Bradford. It meant that we had no choice but to engage with the wider community, and as a result I grew up feeling far more equipped to deal with cultural differences. The equivalent 'Maajid' in Bradford may not have known where to put himself in an all-white environment. Even today, there are Bangladeshis in Tower Hamlets who have grown up speaking Bangla as their first language, and who despite being raised in the UK made no white friends.

Such communities, in other words, are big enough for people to live their whole lives within them, rather than venture out. The result is that for many people growing up in a place like Bradford or Tower Hamlets the only interaction they have with white kids is when they are facing them in a fight. And the only time they come into contact with white women is when they are chatting them up in the hope of a quick one-night stand. That has a corrosive effect on how each community perceives the other. It's a bad situation, for both sides.

But I'm getting ahead of myself. I need to first explain how my family ended up in Southend in the first place. My family originally hail from Gujrat. This isn't to be confused with Gujarat in India, which gives its name to the more prominent Gujarati community in the UK. There is another Gujrat, in Pakistan. It's a district and a city in the province of the Punjab, in the north west of the country, towards the border with Kashmir. It is near Islamabad, though given the bad roads is still a good two-and-a-half-hour drive away from the capital, and equally far from Lahore. Gujrat lies on the banks of the River Chenab, and my family is said to have settled in the area from the eighth century, coming to the subcontinent with the Arab armies of Muhammad bin Qasim.

Gujrat is a city with a disproportionate influence over Pakistani politics. The Chaudhrys of the area have long held sway within the army, and the city has produced prime ministers and powerful political factions. Gujrat is also fabled for its clan, or *biraadari*-based gangsters and beautiful women. Folklore places the tragic ancient love story of *Sohni Mahiwal* in Gujrat. Sohni, a Punjabi word for beautiful, is said to have

17

drowned in the River Chenab as she tried in desperation to reach her forbidden lover Mahiwal. Infatuated by her beauty, Mahiwal jumped in to save her, and he too drowned alongside his lost love. This story has in turn inspired numerous poems, paintings, songs and even two Bollywood movies. Family legend has it that my *Nana Abu*, my maternal grandfather, spent his childhood during the British Raj in close association with an English doctor, the governor of a hospital in the town of Jalalpur, located in the wider Gujrat district. This Englishman resided in the hospital grounds with his family. Having grown extremely close to *Nana Abu*'s father, the doctor often invited the family round to share meals, festivals and holidays. (Apparently the hospital building still stands, in all its Imperial splendour, in Jalalpur.) As a boy, *Nana Abu*, named Ghulam-Nabi, or servant of the Prophet, developed a deep fascination for this English doctor. Being keenly impressed by his culture, education and generosity *Nana Abu* decided that when he was married and had children of his own, he would raise them all to be doctors, and would run a hospital just like this one. This was to become his guiding dream.

A medical education wasn't immediately available to *Nana Abu*. So with a heavy heart he joined the army of the British Raj in the hope that this would give him the opportunity to follow his ambition. He pursued a vigorous regime of extra-curricular courses alongside his day-to-day routine in the army. He quickly succeeded in qualifying as an accountant, and was appointed to manage the military accounts for food stocks. With all appearing to be on track, and his dream still seeming attainable, *Nana Abu* got married. My *Nani*

Ammi was a beautiful woman from Gujrat named Suraya, the Arabic name for the Pleiades star-cluster. Newly-wed and full of hope, *Nana Abu* took *Nani Ammi* across India to Lucknow for their honeymoon. But that same week something happened that would change the course of history: Partition.

It was 1947 and it had been decided to create two countries: India, which would have a majority of Hindus; and Pakistan – at that time West Pakistan, and East Pakistan (now Bangladesh) – in which the majority would be Muslim. This meant that vast numbers of people had to leave their homes and move across the new border to live: Hindus to India and Muslims to Pakistan. There was chaos and pandemonium. The great human exodus unfolded right before my grandparents' eyes, while on their honeymoon in India. In a panic they rushed to catch a train back to Gujrat, which was suddenly on the Pakistani side of partitioned Punjab. But it was too late. Mob violence and mass murder from all sides accompanying the geo-political divorce were focused on the trains. Bloodthirsty hordes, hell-bent on revenge, were boarding the carriages and indiscriminately killing all Pakistan-bound commuters. Train after train would pull into the station in Pakistan, with all on board dead. These were the ghost trains.

Nana Abu was on one such ghost train. The mob had cut his train in two. The front carriage, where *Nani Ammi* and all the women sat, had been separated and taken off into the distance. The back portion, containing *Nana Abu* and all the men, was held captive to be massacred. By what can only be described as the grace of Allah, somehow *Nana Abu* escaped the massacre that followed. In that chaos, desperately seeking his new bride, and in an era without widespread communications, *Nana Abu* ran from platform to platform, having to avoid rampaging mobs while searching for his wife. He stumbled across her, frantically waiting for him at another station. Together, these traumatised newly-weds fled India, now a foreign country, back into Pakistan, now a new country.

Things changed so rapidly for *Nana Abu* after Partition. Having been raised in a multi-ethnic and multi-faith united India, he lost many of his childhood friends. Those who now belonged to the 'wrong' faith were forced to emigrate to India, others left for England. Disturbed by memories of the massacre he had witnessed on the ghost train, and having been torn from many of his friends, he became restless. Years later in 1965 he decided to make a trip to England in search of his long-lost friends and to rekindle his kinship with British culture. He still had his old dream of building a hospital in Gujrat and planned for his sons to be doctors and help with his dream.

The British education system was seen as something unparalleled and *Nana Abu* wanted his children to have that opportunity. If you had the privilege of visiting his home during those early days, you would often catch him instructing his children, 'Be not as strangers to the goodness and kindness of others. We must adopt as our own, piety, truth, and goodness, wherever it comes from.'

And so he took advantage of his right to live in the UK. Immigration, at that stage, simply wasn't an issue. It was Southend where they – we – ended up: a seaside town with no family links, no halal meat shops, no mosques, and no community. Setting these things up was down to *Nana Abu* and his friends. They created the first mosque in the town and organised space for Muslim burials in the town cemetery. Due to his education, good temperament and thoughtful nature, *Nana Abu* quickly became a leader for his community, maintained relations with his local MP and was widely respected.

Nana Abu was a traditional Muslim, which in those days meant being conservative but in no way extremist or fundamentalist. Expecting his children to accept arranged marriages and wanting them to marry other Muslims were examples of his traditional mindset. Pakistan, like most of South Asian culture, was historically non-dogmatic. That comes from the way in which mysticism became entrenched across the Indian subcontinent. My grandfather was typical of that mindset, being liberal when young, and more religious as he got older. That is – was – a very Pakistani thing to do. I say 'was', because of the rise of extremism among so many young Pakistanis today.

My mother was the third of nine children, and was roughly nine years old when the family moved to Southend. They started off in a rented property for two to three months, then bought their own home. Despite being an accountant back home, *Nana Abu* found that his qualifications weren't easily recognised in England. Undeterred, with dreams of the hospital spurring him on, he supported the family by getting a job as a bus driver, and drilled into his children the need for study, to work hard and make the most of themselves. He typified the stereotype of the hard-working immigrant and was determined to give his children the best chance, and make sure that they grabbed it with both hands.

The result was that his children excelled at school. They started off in some of the worst schools, but ended up going to grammars and on to universities. Every one of that generation in my family is an engineer or a doctor of some kind, apart from those, like my mother, who were married off before they could go to university. *Nana Abu*, for all his forward thinking, still believed in arranging husbands for his daughters. My mother's two younger sisters, Shaba and Shaz, are today married to white men, and these are unions that he may have had extreme difficulty with, had he still been alive.

One day, while jumping up and down on a bed that I wasn't allowed to stand on, my mother walked into the room with tears streaming down her face. I thought she was angry with me for bouncing on the bed.

'Sit down, *beta* – my son, I need to tell you something, but you need to sit before you hear it.'

'What, Ma, why are you crying? What did I do?' I asked.

'No no, listen, you need to listen. Today . . . today your *Nana Abu* passed away, I mean, he died. He's gone to heaven, do you understand what that means?'

Before he could ever build his beloved hospital, *Nana Abu* collapsed and died from a double stroke. He was only fifty-eight years old. I would have been nine at the time, and I still remember how much I cried on that day.

Just as *Nana Abu*'s experiences were unusual, so in a different way were those of my mother and her siblings. Many of them had been born and brought up in the UK. My mother in particular has always been very liberal and progressive in her outlook. Often the Pakistani experience in the UK is for the parents to have been brought up in Pakistan, and then come over. It was unusual, therefore, for me to have a mother who had been brought up in England, speaking in an English accent. It meant that her experience was similar to mine. I was brought up calling her *Baji* – a title for an older sister – and it was easy to relate to her. Until, that is, I became interested in political Islamism: almost immediately, she became representative of everything liberal and Western that I began campaigning against. How such an estrangement could occur is the rest of this story.

One way in which my mother – known endearingly to all as Abi – was determined to bring her children up in an enlightened way was in her attitude to literature. She always encouraged me to read from an early age, and I have many memories of the sort of books that I read at the time. Roald Dahl was a particular favourite: *Charlie and the Chocolate Factory*, *James and the Giant Peach*, *George's Marvellous Medicine* and so on. C.S. Lewis was someone else I read, though I had no idea about the religious connotations of *The Chronicles of Narnia* until much later. I also used to love those Fighting Fantasy books, *The Warlock of Firetop Mountain* and so on, where you'd read a page and be given a choice as to what you wanted to happen next. The idea of being able to create my own story always appealed to me.

All of this was quite different from the old Pakistani tradition of storytelling. Although modern Pakistani literature is currently witnessing an upsurge, the old tradition was oral, and for me that was most obviously represented by my *Tai Ammi*, my dad's brother's wife. When she visited, she would tell us stories, such as *Ali Baba and the Forty Thieves*, but these would be in Urdu, and recounted orally at bedtime. My

23

brother Osman and I would love hearing them because there was something magical in their telling, in the inflection of the story voice and the emotion each line would portray. Rather than putting us to sleep, they would awaken all our senses to imagine a far-away land of flying carpets and genies, or *jinn*. We never told *Tai Ammi* that her stories woke us up rather than helped us sleep. There's a lot of skill within that oral tradition: it's all about telling stories in a way that is intriguing and suspenseful. *Tai Ammi* was very good at that: and this was how a Pakistani mother would bring up her children, and we'd sit on the edge of our seats, wanting to know what happened next.

But as wonderful as this oral storytelling tradition can be, it doesn't necessarily encourage children to read themselves, and even today reading in Pakistan is not as widespread as it should be. How expressive a child could be if parents were to combine these two methods, the old and the new. I believe that it was precisely this combination that contributed to keeping a passion for life within me in the most difficult times.

One book that particularly tested my mother Abi's liberalism and my own changing views as a teenager was Salman Rushdie's *The Satanic Verses*. When this was published in 1988, it caused a huge furore among many Muslims around the world. Its depiction of the Prophet Mohammed, upon whom be peace, was deemed blasphemous and the author was forced into hiding after the Ayatollah Khomeini issued his now infamous fatwa. True to her fiercely independent spirit, Abi bought the book and read it to make up her own mind.

By then, my belief that she was dangerously on the wrong side needed no more confirmation. Abi's response had been a classically liberal one: 'Let him write his book. If you don't like it, go and write your own book against him.' That is Abi through and through.

The other remarkable character in my family is my father, affectionately known to all as Mo. From an early age he grew up with a lot of responsibility. Both his father and elder brother died when he was young, which left him as head of the family before he was married. In the old days in Pakistan, when a man died his wife would often return to her parents' family. The absence of a welfare state left only blood relatives as the safety net. But my father wanted to do things differently. He asked *Tai Ammi*, his brother's widow, to stay with him so that they could bring up his two orphaned nieces Nargis and Farrah as his own daughters. This ensured that *Tai Ammi*, still a *Sohni* of Punjab in her own right, did not have to remarry again merely for convenience. Until this day, over forty years later, *Tai Ammi* remains a widow out of love for her late husband.

My father started out working for Pakistan's navy and trained as an electrical engineer. Unfortunately he contracted tuberculosis and was honourably discharged on medical grounds. To begin with, the navy paid for his treatment and wanted him to return to work. However, he didn't respond to conventional treatment and the navy lost hope. My father then went to see what is called a *hakeem* – a herbalist trained in ancient natural remedies – and he provided a number of powders. Curiously, these worked where modern medicine failed, and I suppose I owe my life to an obscure herbalist who has probably long died somewhere in the Land of the Five Rivers.

My father didn't return to the navy, but resumed life as an electrical engineer: he laid a lot of the electrical foundations in what is now the Pakistani capital, Islamabad. He laid down political foundations too, and it is this proud defiant streak in him that has rubbed off on me. He had been doing some work for the Dawood Group – a powerful industrial group in Pakistan. The company was immensely powerful politically, and unions were prohibited. At this time Pakistani workers, heady with Soviet socialism, became aware of their organising power. And upset with working conditions and knowing that employers would never concede rights unless forced to, my father set up the first trade union in his industry.

Dawood's response was to try to shut them down. My father and his fledgling organisation were taken to court. This was real David and Goliath stuff and my father's eventual victory was a huge coup at the time. Dawood was forced to allow the trade union to operate. Arguably modern unions have morphed into the beast they were fighting, with strikes holding the public, their original constituency, hostage to ever-increasing union demands. However, the original role of unions in improving conditions for workers is undeniable, especially in countries such as Pakistan.

My father then married Abi. It was an arranged marriage, when he was thirty-four and Abi just eighteen. He moved to the UK and used his experience as an engineer to get a job with the Oasis Oil Company in Libya, where he worked until his retirement, and where we were to visit him later on.

By this twist of fate, I had an awareness of Gaddafi's tyranny long before it became common knowledge. My first memory of trouble in Libya harks back to the late eighties. I asked my father why the name of his company had changed from Oasis to *Waha*. My father explained that Colonel Gaddafi had nationalised the company and kicked out all Westerners in revenge for American airstrikes that had killed his daughter. 'But why are you still there, then?' I naively asked. 'Because Libyans like Pakistanis,' he assured me. I didn't understand this. As an ex-pat he was very well paid for the time, and we eventually moved into a large six-bedroom house as a result. Why didn't Gaddafi consider him British? What I wasn't to know then was that in 1974 Gaddafi had gone to Lahore and publicly supported Pakistan's right to pursue nuclear weapons. In turn, Pakistan named Lahore's main sports stadium after Gaddafi. I had no idea how this pursuit of nuclear weapons would go on to affect my own life so profoundly. But again, I'm jumping ahead of myself.

My father went in for the whole oil look. This was the era of the American soap *Dallas* with J.R. and Bobby Ewing. We all loved to watch *Dallas*; in fact I still catch myself sometimes humming its catchy theme tune. Typical of charming, worldly-wise Pakistani men of his day, my father didn't shy away from flaunting his style. He'd wear a Stetson, cowboy boots, a big belt buckle with his name embossed into the leather at the back, and an expensive diamond-encrusted gold watch: these days you'd call that *bling*. Like any child growing up, I didn't rate my father's fashion sense, but I did inherit his love for cultivating an individual style.

The other main effect my father's job had on my upbringing was that it created something of a polarised childhood. My father would alternate between spending a month in Libya, and then having three to four weeks at home. When he was

27

away, Abi would be in charge, and her more liberal outlook would prevail. When my father was back, we lived under stricter, more traditional house rules. This created conflict between my parents – a clash of backgrounds, really, and a generational difference rather than anything more personal. My father was socially liberal but with traditional family values. Abi was a fiercely independent free-spirited beauty, always the first to dance at weddings and the last to sit down.

Work would be the focus of my father's life, but politics would be the way in which he socialised with friends at home. This was a typically Pakistani and typically Muslim way of going about things. His stance towards the pressing questions of his day was essentially a 'plague on both your houses': he was very much anti-colonial, but having lived and worked under Gaddafi, he was also anti-Arab dictators. Importantly, and unlike many of the 'old' European left, he wasn't pro-Arab tyrants just because they stood up to Western imperialism. He was well aware of Gaddafi's record of torture long before it became public knowledge in the West: he knew of the hatred that everyday Libyans bore their leader.

On one occasion we went on a family holiday to Tripoli. This was in the late 1980s after the airstrikes but I didn't have any real sense of what these meant. Life certainly got more awkward for my father, especially after Lockerbie, when Pan Am flight 103 was blown up over the Scottish town. The British government began taking an interest in him – by this point there weren't many people from the UK who were travelling to Libya for work. He was stopped and questioned both to and from the airport. He was even asked to use his position to inform on the Libyans, which he politely declined.

It's hard not to look at *Nana Abu*, Abi and my father without thinking that something from each of them has rubbed off on me. Although they are very different characters, what unites them is the way they have gone against the grain: *Nana Abu* leaving a newly independent Pakistan for Southend to pursue a dream; Abi's liberal views challenging those of her community; my father taking on a leading corporation to set up the company's first trade union. Apart from all the other traits that I may have been lucky enough to inherit from them, it is this instinct to rattle the status quo that strikes me as their most significant influence.

CHAPTER TWO

This game's not for Pakis

I first encountered and became properly aware of racism at around eight years old. I was having lunch at my primary school, Earl's Hall, and as usual I was queuing up with my tray to get my food from the dinner lady. This particular day, it was sausages on the menu. Now, I knew I wasn't meant to have sausages. I wasn't quite sure why, but I was aware that my father didn't want me to eat them. When my brother Osman and I had started at the school, Dad realised that the food served there might be a problem. So to avoid it becoming an issue he'd said to us, 'Eat anything you want, even it is not halal. The main thing is, keep from eating pork. So no sausages.'

The dinner lady put my lunch down on my plate.

'What is this?' I asked.

'Sausages,' she said.

'I'm sorry,' I said politely, handing the plate back. 'I'm not allowed to eat them.' At this stage I was still very much a timid little boy.

'What do you mean, you're not allowed to eat them?' the

dinner lady snapped back.

'I'm . . . I'm not allowed to eat them,' I repeated nervously, but stood my ground. 'My dad told me I wasn't allowed sausages.'

'Why on earth not?'

'I don't know,' I replied quivering. 'All I know is that I'm not allowed to eat them.'

At this point, I remember being very scared, not just as a small child standing up to an adult, but also over why I wasn't allowed to eat the sausages. I didn't really know what they were but my dad had been so insistent on not eating them that I thought I might have some reaction if I ate them. I could feel everyone in the canteen starting to look at me.

'Stop being so *fussy*!' the dinner lady shouted, shoving the plate back at me, so I had to take it. 'This is your lunch, and you're going to eat it.'

The dinner lady followed me round. She came out from behind the counter to where I was sitting, and insisted that I ate them in front of her. Now I was crying. I felt the eyes of everyone staring, as if I was some sort of freak. I was completely conflicted, and didn't really know what to do.

'What a fussy little boy,' she snapped again. 'You *will* eat your sausages.'

With fear literally rising up like a lump inside my throat, caught between parental and school authority, I obeyed the immediate threat, and put a piece of sausage in my mouth. At which point, fear took its revenge and pushed out the offending morsel, along with everything else in my stomach. I vomited all over my plate. As I continued to cry, the dinner lady's stance changed.

'Oh goodness me,' she said. 'You're *allergic* to sausages. That's why you can't eat them.'

I shook my head, tried to tell her otherwise, but she was convinced. 'You should have said,' she continued. 'You should have said you have an allergy.' And she escorted me off to the medical office, where despite my protestations I spent the rest of the afternoon lying down, to make sure I felt OK, until Abi came to pick me up after school.

This whole incident sounds a bit surreal now, which perhaps shows how much things have changed in the last twenty or thirty years. No school in the UK would dare to do this to a child today. I don't think the dinner lady was being deliberately racist: I suspect her attitude was well meaning in an 'eat your greens' way, but there was a lazy cultural ignorance behind it that said much about attitudes of the time. It did not even cross her mind that there might be a religious reason behind my refusal to eat pork.

This wasn't, in fact, the first time I'd come across such attitudes. Originally, my brother and I had gone to the nearest primary school, which was a Catholic one called St Helen's. Here there was no suggestion of respecting our religious difference, no question of us opting out of the morning assembly or the daily singing of hymns. The crunch point came when I asked my father why we all had to eat bits of paper. My father was as confused as I was; until he worked out that the small circles of paper I was talking about were part of taking communion. Again, I don't think this insensitivity was deliberately provocative, but the apparent lack of awareness, especially given the religious setting, is quite shocking. My brother and I moved schools after that.

Earl's Hall was almost universally white: the only other non-white child I remember was a Sikh called Satnam. For the first few years I was there, the sausages incident aside, I was generally very happy. I was very good at art. There was an annual art competition at school, and I won first prize for several years consecutively. I remember in particular a picture I did when I was eleven, which I copied from a photograph of a boy on a drum barrel, writing and sticking his tongue out. My picture was then printed in sepia for a school exhibition, and it made me hugely proud. I acted in the school plays, including one about refugees during the Second World War. I even had a little girlfriend, in a very innocent way called Sarah. The most we ever did was to hold hands, and I think I kissed her once on the cheek. I would go round to her parents' house and her family were always incredibly hospitable. Later on, on our first day of secondary school, I would leave Sarah stating as my reason that 'there are too many new girls here to choose from'. I was eleven. She cried and I felt pangs of guilt, believing her lovely parents would hate me now. But I left her anyway.

Maybe because I had managed to make many friends, I became too 'prominent' for some kids. My mother's attempts to integrate us into British culture all felt quite natural until now. I had joined the Cub Scouts, for example, and really enjoyed it. But when I was about ten or eleven, the atmosphere at Earl's Hall primary school suddenly changed. Almost as if overnight, the colour of my skin defined me to friends who had previously seen only a happy, friendly and sociable boy. When a child sees the world, they don't see their own face, only everything else around them. It's often all too easy for children to imagine that others don't see their face either. The

33

mid-eighties changed this for me, for ever. Concern about AIDS had risen sharply in the public imagination. For all the government education films about the disease, its rise led to all sorts of rumours and accusations in the playground about its origins. One day, a big lad called Tony, who had been a good friend for years, suddenly turned on me.

'AIDS is your fault,' he told me. 'It's people like you that caused the disease.'

At the time, there were stories going around saying how the disease originated in Africa. Not that I was African, but I wasn't white and as far as this boy's knowledge went that was close enough. For the first time since the incident with the dinner lady, I felt like all eyes were on me. The kids had started whispering about me behind my back. Children were scared to touch me.

'You lot have sex with monkeys,' he continued. 'That's how AIDS started.'

The accusations would have been laughable, had it not been for the anger in his eyes.

'That's rubbish,' I said.

'It's true,' the boy sneered. 'My dad told me.'

I tried to reason with him: this was a boy who'd been my friend, who I'd been playing with normally just the day before. But he wasn't having any of it. 'My dad told me I am not allowed to speak to you any more. Now get lost, bugger off, and don't talk to me again.'

Not long after, another friend called Patrick was playing football in the lunch break, and I went over to join in.

'Can I play?' I asked. What usually happened is that you'd turn up wanting to take part, and those already playing would assign you to one or other team, depending on which was short of players. On this occasion I was asking to play and everyone was ignoring me. So I went over to Patrick, who was one of the team captains, and asked him what was going on. He suddenly turned round and punched me hard in the stomach in front of everyone. The unexpected punch completely winded me, and I doubled over in agony, unable to breathe. The inability to draw breath totally petrified me, as I had never experienced such a sensation before.

'This game's not for Pakis!' he shouted. 'Don't ask to play again.' And he wandered off back to his team, leaving me confused and gasping for breath, as I used the railings to support myself from falling to the ground. Once I could catch my breath again, I looked up and saw that I was well and truly standing alone. My friends were all playing football. It was this feeling of being completely alone, rather than the pain, that led to tears welling up in my eyes. As I fought back the tears with all my willpower, I resolved there and then that when I grew up I would never stand alone again.

It was this incident, more than anything else, that destroyed my childhood innocence. Standing in a playground with secret tears rolling down my cheeks, I decided that the world is like an obstacle course, to climb and sit on top of. Any child raised in the UK has experienced the power and allure of Britain's football culture. A child is often judged in the playground by how well they can play, and a social pecking order based on the game quickly arises. After that incident I never took part in football again. The kids at primary school wouldn't let me. By the time I got to secondary school I was embarrassed that I couldn't play, the rejection rang in my ears and I didn't even try to join in. I would have to work doubly hard to climb that obstacle course, without the advantage of playing football.

My parents' response was to turn the other cheek. There was a feeling among previous generations that they did not have a right to fight back, because they were visitors: they were immigrants.

'So what if they call you a Paki?' they'd tell me. 'Just say you are a Paki and you are proud of it, and walk away.' That's confusing advice for a child, of course. Children have a very strong sense of right and wrong at that age: here was something that was manifestly unfair, yet I was being told to accept it. Even though the names and accusations were unacceptable, was I really expected just to take the abuse and walk away?

The fact that my skin colour hadn't been an issue for those early years of schooling says everything about where racism originates: it is a cultural issue, a societal and familial problem that children soak up as they become more aware of the world. But while my generation began by following the same stance that my parents had done, there was one very noticeable difference that separated out those coming of age in the late eighties from earlier times. It was the level of violence that we faced. And violence breeds violence.

What had changed, particularly in places like Southend, was the rise of the skinhead revival culture. Southend had always been a seaside resort associated with the infamous bank holiday clashes between the Mods and Rockers. Fights between gangs of skinheads and Mods together against the Teddy Boys and Rockers were common; as were mesmerising sights of the motorbikes and scooters they all rode. The skinhead culture emerged as an offshoot from the Hard Mods. Interestingly enough, it had originally been quite cross-cultural: for a time there was a love of reggae music and an interest in West Indian culture. But after the split, some skinheads adopted an exclusively white, and aggressively racist line. By the mid-eighties, the violently racist skinheads were the ones that had taken over, and they dominated the football clubs. The evolution of this movement is portrayed very well in Shane Meadows's film *This is England*, which should act as a warning for Britain's new right-wing football-based trend, the English Defence League.

The split in the skinhead movement occurred alongside the rise of the National Front, the NF. This was a far-right political party that advocated an overtly racist policy of repatriation, and was growing in popularity in the same way the far-right British National Party, BNP, would supersede it a couple of decades later. These were bad times; in those days if we saw a Union Jack or the English flag draped in a window we would fear the owner as a member of the BNP or NF. It sounds absurd now, but those flags had almost entirely been hijacked by the far right. By early 1992, Charlie Sergent, later convicted for murder, split off from the BNP and formed an extremely violent neo-Nazi paramilitary organisation called Combat 18, or C18. C18's name comes from the fact that Adolf Hitler's initials are the first and eighth letters of the alphabet. This was one of several groups inextricably linked with the rise of football hooliganism during the period – they would support England vociferously and violently, re-scoring results to remove any goals scored for England by black players. Counting enlisted soldiers among their ranks, and with alliances among loyalist paramilitaries in Northern Ireland, C18 were considered armed and dangerous.

Southend, because of its Mods and Rockers history, was a place where the shin-high Doc Marten boots of the skinheads stomped with some authority. Their green bomber jackets acted as their visible insignia, a uniform for hate. And hate was well and truly on the march. The casual racism of my primary school years had suddenly gained itself a sharper and more sinister edge. As I would later so painfully learn, C18 had formed active cells in Southend. No surprise, then, that those children began to believe that 'football was no game for Pakis'. The compromise choice of earlier generations was no longer available to us: turning the other cheek was no longer an option. It was either time to retreat within the community, to keep off the streets and cower out of sight, or it was time to stand in the path of these thugs, with dignity and honour.

CHAPTER THREE

The doctor who said 'Fuck tha Police'

It was my Uncle Nasir, Abi's brother, of all people, who got me into hip hop. By the early 1990s he was a doctor in Newcastle, working as a general practitioner. Related via us, but not too directly with each other, Nasir had ended up marrying my cousin from my dad's side, Farrah; the daughter of *Tai Ammi,* who told the fascinating bedtime stories. Nasir is a soft-spoken, deeply intelligent and insightful man, and was my favourite uncle. His marriage to Farrah, someone I consider as my sister, made this family my special relatives to visit, and their kids Raheem, Alia and Habiba my closest cousins.

In his mannerisms, dress, career and grammar-school English, Nasir is the opposite of the street culture I eventually got into. But what was so impressive about him is that he had empathy for those who were less fortunate. I remember how he would always go out to the roughest of council estates and speak with the local Geordie street lads, who were otherwise stealing cars and picking fights. I asked him once why he did this, and he replied: 'My surgery's located here; the majority of my patients are from this estate. If I don't speak to them, who will?'

I loved him even more for that, and so did these otherwise quite dangerous Geordie youths. His car never got stolen, and I learnt a valuable lesson.

In the summer of 1989 we went up to Newcastle to visit, and Nasir decided that he would play Osman and me a type of music that we had never heard before. With a glint of mischief in his eyes, he put on a track called 'Fuck tha Police' by N.W.A, Niggaz With Attitude, and pumped up the volume. In 1988, N.W.A had released *Straight Outta Compton*, their debut album, on which Ice Cube, Dr. Dre, Eazy-E, DJ Yella and MC Ren had laid the foundations for what would later become known as 'gangsta rap'. By introducing this one rap track to us, and probably without realising what he had just unleashed, Dr Nasir helped his two young nephews find their voice.

'Fuck tha Police' is a statement as much as it is a record. It gives it to the police for treating black communities like dirt, targeting them and lazily assuming that anyone with a car or a bit of money must be a drug dealer. It slams them for their prejudice and for their violence, and N.W.A promises to mete out its revenge, fantasising about 'takin' out a cop or two'. All of this is delivered by the various MCs with an aggression, a passion that grabs hold of the listener, and a booming drum track as impossible to ignore as the raw seething anger coming from one of LA's roughest ghettos, Compton. Listen to it; it's a history lesson.

The track quite simply blew me away. I was never the same again. It was the attitude and confidence that I took to immediately. This wasn't the sound of someone turning the other cheek: this was the sound of a community finding its voice, and using it to say that they weren't simply going to lie down and take it. There were saying that you treat us like that, and we're going to take the fight straight back to you.

My uncle was of the same generation as my mother, who'd grown up by giving way and stepping back when confrontation arose. This doctor's love for N.W.A and the fact that he was sharing it with me spoke volumes: it must have given vent to all his frustrations growing up. He could turn up 'Fuck tha Police' and even now as a respected GP could find strength in their stand. For me, the N.W.A attitude had more practical connotations: unlike my uncle, whose job had taken him away from having to face such situations, I had my teenage years ahead of me. The experiences of racism at primary school had scarred me, and the thought of having to accept more years of the same was a frightening one. Listening to N.W.A, I realised that I didn't have to. Others were fighting back, and so could I.

The fact that rap lyrics rubbed everyone up the wrong way made me love such groups all the more. People's offence at the expletives helped make the band feel cool. I remember listening to 'Fuck tha Police' in the car, on a cassette player, and my parents being completely shocked. 'What the hell is this?' my dad asked, as Eazy-E rapped about his 'bitches' providing him with sexual favours, while Dad tried to concentrate on the road. New music is often popular for the very fact that earlier generations find it shocking, and that was certainly the case here. And this was 'our' music, misunderstood by others. But in this instance, I spared my father further embarrassment, and turned on the radio instead.

What most people heard was just a load of shouting and swearing: they thought the music appealed because of its shock value. They couldn't have been more wrong. These rappers were bright, street smart and articulate; their rhymes encapsulated the experience of being young, male and black in a way that simply didn't exist elsewhere in the media. This was a time when banana skins were still being thrown at black players at football matches, when Nelson Mandela was still in prison, and when the beating of Rodney King by LAPD officers was about to send shockwaves around the world. The sense of disenfranchisement, that you couldn't rely on the state for help, was very real.

I liked N.W.A for their attitude, and the way they stuck two fingers up to society. When Ice Cube went solo and released *AmeriKKKa's Most Wanted*, I loved that too. There was politics in there – with the Ku Klux Klan referenced in the title, the album starts with a black man on death row being electrocuted – asked whether he has any last words, the death row inmate replies, 'Yeah, I got some last words . . . fuck all y'all!'

The beat then kicks in over the sounds of an electrocution. Powerful, defiant stuff. I took an interest in what we'd call old school hip hop – Grandmaster Flash, Run–D.M.C., Eric B. & Rakim – and although there were great tunes there, like 'The Message', and great stars like the Sugarhill Gang, a lot of it just sounded tinny in its production compared with newer acts like Ice Cube. His was a bigger, fuller sound, with better, more banging beats and fatter bass lines that ripped out of your stereo speakers like nothing else.

The odd thing is that up until that summer Osman and I would bicker like most young siblings, over almost anything. There was only a year and a half between us, and where he was undoubtedly the bigger one, I liked to think I was the sharper one. This dynamic led to a relationship where I would try to use my wit against his power. Many a time this led to clashes and parental intervention. But when Nasir got us both into rap we found a common cause, common purpose. It was like we were suddenly on the same side against the rest. Our bickering stopped and we began sharing music, going out to the same parties and sharing friends. From not being able to tolerate too much of each other's company, we began to feel like a team with a cause. Our cause was rebellion against the status quo.

If it was my uncle who introduced me to N.W.A, it was Osman who first got me into Public Enemy. 'Rebel Without a Pause' was the first record of theirs that I heard, and it still sticks with me now. Here was a group who didn't just have the attitude, but the political insight to go with it. There was always a thought-out philosophy to Chuck D and Professor Griff's rhymes – this was a band sampling Malcolm X and bringing the black nationalist message into teenagers' living rooms. Professor Griff had his security team, the S1Ws – the Saviours of the First World – and an interest in the Nation of Islam. They were fearless.

Public Enemy's first album *Yo! Bum Rush the Show* I didn't like so much because the beats weren't the same quality; much later, when they started adding a heavy metal influence, that didn't do it for me either. But in between, the more I listened to the records, the more the lyrics and influences began to seep into me. I had never really heard of people like Malcolm X before. Now I had a real thirst to find out all about him.

The fact that Professor Griff was an advocate for Islam made an impression, too. Considering myself an agnostic, I had never been a religious person: it hadn't been a big issue growing up. The few times I'd been to the mosque it had been a disaster. The imam didn't speak any English, and got his message across with the use of a stick. I told my parents I wasn't going back because he used to hit children and that was it: they didn't make me go again.

Professor Griff's interest made something I had considered old-fashioned feel vibrant and interesting. He wasn't the only one: in 1993 Brand Nubian used the Muslim call to prayer 'Allahu akbar' as a sample for one of their songs in their second album, *In God We Trust*. I absolutely loved it. I had little understanding at the time that most of these black-nationalist rappers belonged to US-based racist sects of Islam such as the Nation of Islam and the Five Percenters. What mattered was that these sorts of endorsements from young, streetwise rappers made me re-think my identity. The faith I had inherited was no longer some backward village religion to be ashamed of, or apologetic about. It had been re-branded as a form of resistance, as a self-affirming defiant identity. On the back of such acts, the black conversion rate to the religion was going through the roof. Even members of the nascent British hip-hop band Cash Crew ended up converting. All of a sudden, it was cool to be a Muslim.

That September, in 1989, I enrolled at Cecil Jones High School, at precisely the time that hip hop was starting to kick off. If rap was the form, hip hop was the culture. Dr Nasir's little 'Fuck tha Police' intervention couldn't have been better timed. I had left primary school intent on never letting anyone pick on me again. Here, at Cecil Jones, I changed my dress style, wearing a baggy uniform with my sweater tied round my waist; and changed my hair, closely clipping it to a 'grade one' on the sides while leaving it long on top, and I got my left ear pierced. The rules of Essex back then dictated that piercing the right one was 'for gays'.

On my first day at school, age eleven, I remember consciously talking myself up to people as someone you didn't want to mess with. In fact, I got so carried away that someone even tried to call my bluff and I nearly got whacked again. A very crude ranking system operates in school playgrounds, the 'hardest' kids are known, and a pecking order is quickly but firmly established as kids jockey for position in the first few weeks of term. I soon realised that merely talking myself up would not be sufficient. I needed the right friends, the right 'crew', and I ruthlessly began to seek them out.

The fact that I was one of the first kids from my year to get into hip hop made my task of building a crew easier than I had expected. White kids were queuing up to talk to me, not just about rap music but the whole hip-hop scene. Hip hop was something that could more than compensate for my absence from the football pitch. My skin colour was suddenly something that kids wanted to be associated with. Very quickly, Aron and Martyn, respectively the first and second toughest kids in our school year, had become my closest friends, and I was to be their very own trendsetter teaching them the ways of the B-boy, or someone living a hip-hop lifestyle.

It instantly bonded me with all the popular kids in the older classes too. In my school year there were no black kids, and only two other Pakistanis, one being my cousin Faisal. But in the year above was a boy called Michael; we all called him Moe. He was Kenyan British, and had a group of friends in his year, including Faisal's older brother Yasser. A year up again, and there was a kid called Mark, who was West Indian and equally respected, and friends with Osman. In those early days, we were a small community and hip hop was our way of life. We had a certain style of dress, spoke in a specific slang, and we clipped our hair very short on the sides, sometimes carving patterns into it, and then left it standing long on top. We believed that we had discovered 'cool' where all others had failed, and we quickly bonded with each other over the music.

Word went around that we were connected with the scene in London. If you messed with us, we could make a few calls and bring down heavy B-boys from the big city. We saw the benefits of this sort of hype, but back then it was all about survival. These London connections, knowing the hardknocks two school years above me, and having my own crew meant that in Cecil Jones no one dared mess with me again. Gone for ever was the boy who cried alone in a school playground because he wasn't allowed to play football.

It was almost like having bodyguards. Aron and Martyn looked up to me for my knowledge of the hip-hop scene, its dress, style and sounds. As a result they developed a loyalty to me, especially the bigger of them, Martyn, who we called Sav. If anyone said so much as a rude word to me Sav would stand ready to defend me. But I never forgot what it was like to be victimised, which pushed me on a number of occasions to stop my best mates from getting too rough with other kids. But I didn't always step in. Sometimes, in my twelve-year-old mind I felt that kids 'deserved' it, for example if they had said something racist. In such circumstances I would not intervene, believing my playground sense of justice vindicated such behaviour.

I became very close to Sav in particular. He used to live right opposite the school with his nan, and I would often stay the night at his place. He and I would just chill together, listening to mellow hip hop in his room till the early hours of the morning. In fact, it was while staying at Sav's one night, at the age of fourteen, that I was greeted with the most amazing news. My dad had called and Sav's nan told me to come down to answer the phone. Unsure why my dad was calling so early in the morning, I came down rather worried.

'Congratulations, *beta*, you have a baby sister!'

Whooping with joy, I rushed out of the house, loyal Sav joining me on the bus, and together we travelled down to Southend General Hospital to meet Sorraiya the second, a constellation of stars and a pure bundle of joy.

I've never been one to do things by halves, and once I got into hip hop, I bought into the scene big time: not just the music but also the look, the clothes, everything. I'd wear what we called 'Click' or 'Extreme' suits: named after the brands. These were a pair of matching jackets and trousers, the trousers being as baggy as you can imagine: almost Aladdin genie type, and we would fold them in at the bottom with what we called 'pin-tucks'. The top would be baggy too, and come complete with a hood. The trainers would be Adidas, big and fat to match. Wearing the right labels was everything, and we'd travel up to London to buy the gear, from specialist shops in Brixton and Camden.

At primary school, I'd won prizes for my artwork. Now I used my talents to write graffiti. I chose 'Slamer' as my tag. With my friends I would go round 'tagging' and 'bombing' – tagging is where you write your name, and 'bombing' – in those early years – is where you'd completely plaster a wall with your tags. I'd use 'Polka' Pens, which were these big, fat permanent markers with nibs as thick as your thumb. You would have to give the marker a shake to keep the ink fresh, and whenever we got the chance, we'd tag up any wall with them. Alongside my tag, I'd write different words and captions – 'fight the power', things like that. I'd draw bode, too: these were little characters, strange-looking duck figures who'd stand by the side of your work. I'd also sketch 'pieces', which were basically pencil sketches of graffiti on pieces of paper, which you'd then use as a stencil for a larger, sprayed picture. But I never really got into the spraying side of things and only tried that a couple of times.

There was an area in Southend that the police left specifically for graffiti called 'The Yard'. It was a derelict area left alone in the hope that by being allowed to tag there, we wouldn't graffiti elsewhere. A lot of kids hung about there taking drugs, and that's where I went to begin with. Pretty soon, I graduated to the streets, because that was where you'd get your work seen. I'd always have my pen with me, and if

I saw a wall I liked, and the coast was clear, I would tag it. When we went bombing, it was a bit more planned: a group of us would target somewhere and blast the whole area in a specific raid. The whole cat and mouse thing with the police just added to the buzz I got from doing it. I was chased a number of times by the police, but always gave them the slip. I was smart enough to never get caught, and smart enough not to get into the spray-painting side of things. That was a far bigger process: to spray-paint a high street wall involved covering an area five times the size; to do that, and do it properly, you could be sitting there for an hour or so. The chances of getting caught, therefore, were that much higher, and if they did catch you, they'd really throw the book at you.

Graffiti is a culture where if you're shit, everyone is quick to tell you. The mark of respect for a graffiti artist is how long your 'piece' and tag stay up on a wall. Out of raw respect, other artists will not paint over something they think is good, and anyone who does paint over it better be prepared for a beat down. However, if your stuff is no good, or if you are seen as an amateur, you'll quickly find the word 'lame' written over your work. The offending person would then leave their own tag at the side as a direct challenge. The only way to get even was to be good.

Once again, in the days before the mainstreaming of hip-hop culture and the appreciation of artists like Banksy, this was classic counterculture stuff. No one, apart from my friends and I, knew who 'Slamer' was, yet here was this guy with his name scrawled all over Southend. It was two fingers to the police and law and order: we were challenging their authority, and there was nothing they could do about it. That gave us the edge, credibility among those in the know, and we felt we had a way to fight back.

As well as graffiti, I also got into dancing to the tracks and live rapping, called MC-ing, at nightclubs. Back then British hip hop was in its early days. Acts such as London Posse, Silva Bullet, Gunshot, Blade, Hijack and Hardnoise would go on to lay the foundations for British rap superstars, with many subgenres such as Grime emerging from this scene. I preferred rapping to British hip hop beats, which were faster and rougher. We'd go to these under-eighteen nights in clubs that were open down by the seafront, or 'The Front' as we called it. We would jump around to the sounds of Onyx, and House of Pain, then we'd get up on stage for a lyrical excursion over an instrumental. My MC name was 'Black Magic'. The white kids, they didn't know what to do, and despite trying hard couldn't really move to these strange new beats, and so they looked to us for direction.

Once, I won a dance-off in one of these clubs. My prize was a Sega Mega Drive, which had just come out at the time, the latest in game technology. If I now tried those dance moves, I'd probably break my back! I used to jump up high in the air, and land straight on my knees on what was a wooden dance floor: madness. From that position I'd throw a few flips, and bounce back up. I wasn't as good at the dancing and MC-ing as the graffiti, but it helped that few others knew what to do.

Our B-boy sub-community just kept growing; we would meet kids on the streets and just bond because they were into the same scene. It's like we instantly knew how to relate to each other. That's how I met people like Marc, and Chill, or Tsiluwa. Marc was a white kid, and a great rapper. Once of his extraordinary abilities was to be able to freestyle on the spot, and his skills made him the right friends. Chill had recently moved from Zimbabwe, and was walking in the wrong direction on a night of a particularly violent racist incident, an attack involving a hammer to the head of a friend – this was a preferred style of attack by Essex-based racists. I saw Chill walking in the direction we were running from, told him what had happened and asked him to stick with us if he wanted to be safe. This kicked off an instant brotherhood between us, and together we got up to a great deal of mischief.

On one occasion Chill and I, both being fifteen, decided to see if we could get into an over-eighteens nightclub. If anyone looked at us, at our builds and lack of facial hair, it was obvious that we were much younger. To get in we cut off some hair from our heads, and glued it with Pritt Stick to our chins. We laughed and laughed at how ridiculous we looked – Chill, who had Afro hair, looked like he had a pad of Velcro stuck to his chin – but we put our blazers on, queued up, and got away with it. We went straight to the bathroom and washed it all off. After that, because we'd been in before, the bouncers would let us in every time.

All of this – the music, the clothes, the hairstyles, the graffiti, the dancing, the clubbing, the MC-ing, the lifestyle that was hip hop – meant that none of us had any problems with girls. They were almost like groupies, white middle-class girls who'd got into hip hop and wanted to be a part of it. This was a time when the idea of mixed relationships became extremely fashionable, especially on the female side: there was a whole group of girls, many from nice girls only schools, who

51

wanted to be in mixed relationships. They'd talk to us about how mixed-race babies looked so cute. Such talk would make us laugh, and we thrived on the attention, making various female connections in different towns across Essex. We were just out to have a good time, and were buzzing on a sound, an identity, that we could finally claim as our own.

CHAPTER FOUR

Matt, the stranger who was stabbed for me

While life in school was improving a great deal, the situation outside was escalating into something far more serious. Although my generation was being exposed to and becoming interested in music emanating from black culture, older generations remained unmoved by hip hop and threatened by its associated culture. This was a generation who still had the mindset of the father of the boy at primary school, who had filled his son with all that rubbish about AIDS. It was these older, violently aggressive groups of white youths we had to be wary of.

The result was that when we went out, we made sure that we never walked anywhere alone. If we were out in the town, we'd be in groups of five, six or seven to be on the safe side. We were an overwhelmingly non-white group of B-boys, and as we got deeper into the hip hop culture a lot of our white friends began peeling away from us. This was either from fear of attack or through feeling out of place. But Sav, the biggest lad in my school, always remained loyal to me, and was prepared to stand by my side till the end. I'd seen him take blows from iron bars to his head, yet still get back up, brush off his clothes and walk on. A tougher man than Sav is hard to find. In fact, he still DJs at hip-hop events, and has a vinyl collection that would make most envious. But the rest of our circle eventually narrowed to either West Indians or Pakistanis. As I mentioned we were united by the threat we all faced when Combat 18 came into being in the early 1990s. And the guy with connections to Combat 18 was Mickey. Whenever and wherever Mickey or his crew saw us, they would draw their knives and hunt us down like animals.

How could we stand up to these men who were so much older than us, and dangerously tooled-up! It got to the point that from the age of fourteen I began carrying a knife every time I went out. This went on for several years. I bought it in the Lake District, where I went on a trip with school – one of those adventure holidays where you go abseiling, canoeing, that sort of thing. In those days, you could buy a knife as a kid without any questions asked. Crazy really. It was a big hunting knife; six-inch steel blade and grip handle with a holder that you could strap to your back. That was very effective in concealing it – I once spent time in a police cell without them ever knowing what was hidden under my shirt. What I particularly liked about this knife was that within the design of the main blade, there was a second, hidden knife. I'd attach this one to a string round my wrist, so if the bigger knife ever slipped from my hand I'd still have the second one ready as a backup.

I bought the knife for protection, pure and simple, not to look for trouble. I'd practise getting it out, make sure I was up to speed, could unclip it and whip it out at a second's notice – the sort of moment where a fumbling could make the difference between getting stabbed and your attacker backing away. I'd sharpen it constantly, make sure the blade was in perfect nick, and learnt how best to hold it in a fight. I was fully prepared to use it, but, thankfully, and due to pure luck rather than my judgement, I never had to. In those days I trusted that thing more than God, and so we formed a kind of perverse bond. I would look over it from time to time, running my finger along its blade, and wonder whether it would in fact save me, or get me killed. I still keep it in a drawer next to my bed to remind me of those difficult times. I'm still not sure whether I love the thing or hate it.

When saying earlier how my situation differed from that of my parents, this is what I mean. Back then, if you got threatened it was all about fistfights, maybe the odd kick – it wasn't nice, but there wasn't the same level of threat of serious injury. That all changed with the skinheads and the arrival of Combat 18: from being the exception, knives suddenly became the norm. Their favoured form of attack was with hammers or screwdrivers but they also carried clubs and butchers' knives. That started a bit of a localised arms race, with everyone tooling up in response to everyone else. Suddenly, everyone in Essex was carrying, in a way that the hardknocks hadn't been, fifteen years before. Good friends of mine got badly hurt – Moe, for example, had his head smashed with a hammer and was lucky to survive. That was the climate non-whites faced in Southend, and that was why we carried knives. We were being hunted down in our own streets by C18 for sport; they even had a name for it: Paki-bashing. Friends were being randomly stabbed, hammered and clubbed, just because of the colour of their skin. I defy anyone to convince a teenager that he has no right to defend himself in such circumstances. If tooling up could deter such attacks, then for all the risks involved we believed it was bloody well worth doing.

It is time to complete that story of the scene at the fair in the park, when Chill ran to us for help and I had ended up surrounded by skinheads. If you recall, uselessly outnumbered, I had dumped my own knife in a desperate attempt to convince the skinheads that I was no enemy. Who was I fooling? For C18 my skin colour alone was a sufficient crime! Finally surrounded by them, their mouths frothing with frenzy, their eyes glazed with bloodlust, I knew that my time was up. These men had come from hell, in their white van, to Paki-bash this fifteen-year-old *kidult*. To submit to death is a strange sensation; it can only be fully understood by people who have no choice but to find hopelessness attractive. The mind searches for ways to console the heart, telling it: 'It's OK, when you're dead you'll feel no more pain.'

And that's all I wanted really, for it to be done without much pain. But I didn't die. In fact, the strangest thing happened. It was, and remains rather surreal. A passer-by, a respectable-looking studious type of white guy, saw my plight and entered the fray between the skinheads and me. Despite the panic of the situation, I think he managed to tell me his name was Matt. I cannot be certain about this, but I feel an urge to humanise him, and so I'll call him Matt anyway.

'Don't worry,' Matt said, 'I'm with you.'

I remember thinking, 'What the heck? Who are you?' Instead, though, I cautiously thanked him.

Matt didn't look like a fighter at all. Perhaps he was one of them, undercover, trying to lull me into a false sense of security. Perhaps he was secretly tooled up, and ready to scare them all off. 'Maybe I won't die here after all?' I began to think. Maybe this guy is some sort of Bruce Lee, he'll be able to take them all on, and extract us both from this mob. Why else would he jump into the middle of a knife-fight like this?

Remembering what happened next still brings tears to my eyes. Matt turned to the skinheads. 'Guys! Guys!' he said, causing them to look round in surprise. Being white and having managed to get close enough to the circle of violence surrounding me, they had assumed he was with them. For who would be crazy enough to put themselves in the path of hammers, clubs and knives for an unknown fifteen-year-old Paki?

'Come on, leave it out, yeah?' he said trying to pacify the situation. 'Leave this kid alone.'

The skinheads looked round at Matt. His intervention seemed to infuriate them even more.

'He's a fuckin' Paki,' one snarled at him, 'and you're a fuckin' Paki lover!'

'Guys,' Matt said, slightly more nervous this time, yet trying to mediate again. 'Come on, let's not do anything stupid here. He's just a kid, yeah?'

Perhaps it was the fact that he wasn't part of our world that made him feel he could talk the situation down. Perhaps where he came from, a well-meant request and a bit of gentle reasoning was enough to resolve any situation. This, though, was my world not his. As they came charging forward, from all sides, I knew they would ignore him and stab me anyway. 'Thanks, Matt,' I thought, 'at least you tried, mate.' An honourable thing to do, for someone you don't know. And so I prepared to meet my end.

What happened next will haunt me till my dying day. In sudden horror, mixed with a perverse relief, I watched as the skinheads swivelled their attention to Matt instead. Like famished hyenas they descended upon him, plunging their knives deep into his torso, beating on his head with their clubs and knuckledusters.

'You fucking Paki lover!' they screamed.

All while the Paki was left by their side untouched. Matt's arms were up, flaying, shielding his head with all the strength he could muster. And he was collapsing under the sheer brutality of their vicious assault.

With penetrating, all-pervading shame I instantly realised that Matt was no Bruce Lee. Matt had no weapon. Matt had no plan. He was just doing for me what I was now failing to do for him. He stood up for me, and he was being beaten to a pulp for doing so while I was forced to watch. And I knew that if I joined him I would probably die. My sense of honour urged me to fight. This was my fight goddamnit, not his! But my common sense scolded me in return, I would have no effect, I was an unarmed boy! All that would be achieved by me joining in would be both our murders. So, for what seemed like an eternity in shame, I watched, frozen, as the C18 thugs clubbed him, stabbed him and kicked at his head while he lay on the floor. And not one punch, and not one kick was turned my way. In the distance, police sirens were ringing out. Thank God someone was finally coming! Come, save us! The C18 thugs heard the sirens too, and gleefully appraising the damage they had inflicted, ran off without so much as looking at me again. It was as if I didn't exist. And as I looked at Matt, all bones and blood on the floor, I felt like I didn't deserve to exist. C18 had left me totally untouched while a white stranger lay bleeding profusely on the floor having taken *my* beating.

As the police and ambulance approached, Matt miraculously staggered up off the floor, walking in the direction of C18 and defiantly shouting back at them. As if to say, 'Here I am, I'm still standing. You did not defeat me!'

I learnt later that as well as the multiple stab wounds, they'd punctured his lung. Somehow, though, he had still found the resolve to wave his fist and shout after them until the effort was too much, and then he collapsed again. The paramedics, who had by now arrived, surrounded him instantly in a fierce effort to save his life.

The police, meanwhile, were at their worst. They looked at the white guy lying in a heap of blood on the floor, heard shouts coming from the C18 lynch mob standing off at a distance, and decided that it was the fifteen-year-old Pakistani B-boy in full hip-hop gear who needed to be questioned. I was still locked in my place, my feet refusing to move, when the police radioed in my identity code. For a moment, my mind tangentially wondered how it was they always managed to classify me as an IC 2.3, the police code that profiled me as mixed white-Mediterranean and Afro-Caribbean.

'No, you're speaking to the wrong guy . . .' I tried to explain.

'I'm not going to ask you again,' the officer insisted. 'I want you to tell me what your gang was doing to that man.'

I snapped out of my dazed state and quickly turned nasty on the policeman, shouting and swearing at him at the top of my voice.

'What're you asking *me* questions for, you fucking pig? They're right over there, the guys who stabbed him up! You can *hear* them laughing, you can *see* them, why aren't you going over to arrest them before they leg it?'

'I'll arrest you if you don't calm down,' was the police officer's response.

So I checked myself. My main concern was to convince them to arrest the guys who had done this to Matt. I suffered the interrogation in the hope that it would speed up their work. It didn't. The officer eventually saw that I was innocent, but by that time the skinheads were long gone in their white van, and the ambulance was carrying Matt to the hospital.

Confused, exposed, alone and angry, they left me standing right there in the street. Looking back and forth, I wondered if an angel had just descended to save my life. Was Matt real or had he been sent by God to shield me from murder? I half expected the skinheads to come back and finish the job. After failing to fight alongside Matt, I now believed that I deserved it. I had been unarmed, but so was he. Yes, as a fifteen-year-old, I was outsized, but Matt was outnumbered. It didn't stop him. Since that first day at Cecil Jones, I had always thought myself brave, now I was just full of shame. I found myself wandering back, unconsciously, to recover my knife so foolishly hidden. If I hadn't dumped it, maybe I could have helped him.

I never got the chance to thank Matt for intervening. I knew he hadn't died, because it would have been all over the local papers, but I didn't know his surname or how to get hold of him. He'd just walked into my life, taken a stabbing for me, and then disappeared again. The guilt I felt drove me further away from my white friends, and I became even more anti-establishment due to the bungled police reaction.

This police response was pretty normal for the time. We had zero trust in them. 'Fuck 'em', as N.W.A had taught us. Our suspicion of them was matched only by their apparent hatred of us. I'd often have 'Paki!' shouted at me by passing white vans of another kind, police vans – we called them meatwagons. These years ran in tandem with the short life of a promising young black man called Stephen Lawrence. In 1993, a year after this attack on Matt, Stephen Lawrence was brutally stabbed to death on a South London street by a similar racist lynch mob. It took another lifetime, eighteen years, and the courage of his friend and eyewitness Duwayne Brooks, to finally bring his killers to justice. I remember watching reports of Stephen Lawrence's murder with deep sadness. I was Duwayne Brooks. The kid that got away. And that could so easily have been me, dead on the streets of Essex just a year earlier. It crossed my mind whether it was the same crew, Gary Dobson, David Norris, who had stabbed Matt. One thing I knew for sure, we didn't need the Macpherson Report, the official inquiry into the miscarriage of justice around Stephen Lawrence's murder, to tell us that the police were 'institutionally racist'. We suffered such racism daily.

By this point, our posse of B-boys was almost exclusively an ethnic group, and now included those in a similar situation from other places in Essex such as Pitsea and Basildon. Because there was only one and a half years between us, Osman and I began merging our two groups of friends. From my lot, the younger crew, there was Chill, Moe and Andre from Southend, Ricky, Paul, Ade and Yusuf from Pitsea. Ricky's older brother Rowan headed the older lot. Rowan rolled with Will and Aaron, and Osman would join them when he could. Rowan was renowned throughout Essex. He was dangerous, and people knew his name. Our bonds of friendship were particularly close, forged through a common love of hip hop, through mad times at parties, and by standing up for each other in bloody armed confrontations against racists. The younger ones, my crew, felt like my true brothers, and we believed nothing could ever divide us. Most of the wider posse was Afro-Caribbean, but Osman and I had introduced a couple of other South Asians, like our cousin Yasser and our Bangladeshi friend Ronnie.

I was out late one evening with Osman and Ronnie, playing pool. Earlier that day, like many sixteen-year-old boys, Osman had been messing around with a plastic pellet gun; we called it a BB gun. Playing in open view, he hadn't thought to conceal what he was doing. Keep in mind that in those days terrorism was mainly associated with the Troubles in Northern Ireland. But someone, somewhere, saw what Osman was doing, and unknown to him had called the police, convinced that he was going to commit an armed robbery. The police took this accusation seriously, and mounted an all-day surveillance operation. So by the time I joined Osman and Ron later on, we were already being secretly staked out by a host of armed officers. We finished playing pool about two in the morning, and got into Ron's car to drive home. Our stereo was, as usual, testing the frame of Ron's old car with the heavy bass line of rap tracks.

'That's weird, man,' I quipped from my back seat. 'I guess pigs can fly after all!' I was referring to the police helicopters hovering above us.

'Someone must be in deep shit, man,' Ron laughed. 'I guess they're lookin' for some real heavyweights.'

'Yeah, man, someone's not gonna get much sleep tonight,' I laughed back.

'Look! It's goin' down,' Osman interjected, as police cars sped past us at top speed with their sirens on.

But were we in for a surprise!

Suddenly the police cars up ahead skidded to a halt, horizontally blocking the road in front of us. More cars had appeared from behind, blocking our escape. Ron slammed the brakes on.

'What the ffff . . .?' he muttered in disbelief as armed officers carrying sub-machine guns appeared from nowhere on either side of the car. 'Stop the car!'

'Do not move your hands, do not move your hands!'

'Stay absolutely still! Do not move!'

We sat deathly still in absolutely silence. None of us found this even slightly funny any more. As the helicopter spotlight lit us up, the armed officers rushed to the car doors and pulled Ron and Osman out of their seats, through their still-attached seatbelts, and slammed them on the ground then held them in locked positions. As I watched armed police putting a gun to my brother's head, my mind again became obsessed with tangential details. The car was rolling forward slightly. That's strange, why was it doing that?

'The handbrake!' I thought to myself. 'Well done, Ron, you haven't pulled your handbrake up!'

Just then a hand grabbed my collar and lifted me out of my seat and down onto the ground with a violent thud and another gun greeted me. Of course, it was to Ron's credit that he didn't reach down for the handbrake; they would have thought he was reaching for a gun, and he would probably have been shot dead.

None of this was making any sense to me. I hadn't been with Osman in the daytime and didn't know he had been playing with his plastic BB gun. But there was no time for thought, and certainly no time for questions.

'You,' the officer shouted in my ear, 'are under arrest for suspicion of armed robbery.'

'Huh, wha . . .?' It wasn't registering in my brain.

'In other words, you're nicked, mate. Get 'im in the car.'

I was fifteen years old. I had no criminal record. They threw us all in the cells for the night while they inspected the 'evidence'. Because I was under sixteen they had to wake Abi up at 3 a.m., and tell her on the phone that both her sons had been arrested on suspicion of armed robbery. Crazy. In the morning, after all that, they handed Osman back his pellet gun in a plastic bag and let us go. On the way out, furious at being profiled, I decided to ask one last question, 'Is there anything, anything at all that we did wrong?'

'No, you did nothing wrong. It was a misunderstanding. Sorry about that.' And that was it.

This mixture of police incompetence and ignorance made us hate them, while simultaneously fearing their powers. The one time I did attempt to take things further with the police it blew back in my face. I went in to positively identify a suspect who had stabbed a friend of mine. I pointed out the right guy, but they had to let him go, apparently because of a 'procedural error'. Worse, I was now exposed as the person who had made the positive identification. I have lost count of the number of knife attacks we were subjected to by racists, many of my friends had been stabbed, but the police rarely managed to make any arrests, and hardly ever pressed charges. The racist gangs would always boast about 'contacts' in the police. I have no idea if this was true, but the bottom line is we were not protected. And in the absence of any incentive to change our mantra, we kept singing it loud, 'Fuck tha Police'.

Not trusting the police to protect us meant that we had to rely on our own protection, which we found among our crew and through fighting back. As our numbers increased, and our confidence grew, the levels of violence we faced got worse. We'd be set upon suddenly, like once down on the seafront when snooker balls were flying past heads like cannonballs, or when another white friend, Dan, was knifed, or that time at Southend Central Bus Station when Aaron got stabbed in the side, and Rowan fought off two men armed with kebab knives, using nothing but a crutch he'd 'borrowed' from an old pensioner waiting for her bus. Once the men had stabbed Aaron and run away, Rowan politely handed the crutch back to the startled old pensioner. One of us once resorted to using a metal-tipped umbrella as a weapon, spearing a skinhead Millwall fan who had come down from London and decided to march up and down our high street shouting 'We hate Pakis!' He ended up on the floor in agony with a fractured skull. There was the time Ricky, Paul, Chill and I had been hounded out of Ockendon by a white mob chanting about not wanting niggers in their area stealing their women. Our entire crew returned in three cars the next week to 'bum rush' the house of their ringleader. We were learning how to fight back, and the message was spreading.

One day, I happened to come across none other than Patrick. This was the same Patrick who at eleven had punched me hard in the stomach because I dared to ask to play football. With that one act he had changed the little boy that I was, he made me see in colour when before I saw only human beings. It felt like an age since my days at Earl's Hall.

I was walking down the high street in my full B-boy gear: a red bandana, my Redskins baseball cap – because they used Red Indians as their logo – my 'Click' suit and big trainers, the lot. And there, I saw him. That punch was something I had never forgotten. The moment he saw me coming he turned the other way. From his reaction, I could see that he also remembered what he'd done. This sparked the residues of anger within me, and I headed straight for him. I wasn't with my crew on this occasion; I'd left them somewhere nearby. Yes, it was just Patrick and me again. I had my knife on my back as usual. Patrick, for all his cocky confidence back at primary school, was not a street kid in the way I'd become. He saw me, he saw the look in my eyes, and he began to cower.

'Please don't hit me. Maajid, please don't hit me.'

I hadn't even said anything, and the kid was begging me not to do anything.

'I'm sorry,' he continued, starting to cry. 'I'm sorry, just don't . . .' the strangest sight – as if he was shrivelling up in front of me.

Patrick's comments he'd made all those years ago were not ones he'd repeat now. Largely due to the reputation of us B-boys, it was no longer acceptable to be racist in the way it had been, even just a few years earlier. Seeing me that afternoon, it was clear Patrick knew that. The ball had bounced back, and the power dynamic had shifted. I saw that, he saw that, and strangely that was enough for me. Despite all the violence I'd been involved in, I had always had a justification for it in my teenage mind; it was all a form of escalating self-defence. I'd never bullied or picked a fight with a defenceless, unarmed person, and I wasn't about to start now.

'You're a chump!' I shouted at him. 'Get the fuck out of my sight.'

Patrick looked at me in surprise, having heard of our reputation. He turned and skulked away. I didn't need to attack him: it was enough to see his reaction when he saw me. I felt good about myself, pleased that I'd not become as bad as them, the racists. But there was something more there, too: a sense of satisfaction and vindication. I was on the right path. The incident that had begun the spiral of abuse I'd received had finally ended. I had won.

CHAPTER FIVE

The green rucksack with no bomb

If you haven't felt the fear and helplessness that violent, organised racism makes you feel, it's difficult to understand. Your entire body, due to the colour of your skin, is a moving target. And you cannot leave your skin behind, or pretend it doesn't exist. At any moment hammer-wielding hooligans could use you for target practice. In such extreme circumstances, self-defence must be a sacred right; the 'turn the other cheek' philosophy would have got our skulls crushed. The sad reality is, however, that self-defence usually ends up increasing the cycle of violence.

When I saw my uncle in Newcastle that time, introducing me to 'Fuck tha Police' by N.W.A, it showed me that resentment and anger doesn't just go away – it stays, simmering under the surface. Long term, it's no way for society to function, for different ethnic groups to rub along with each other. I'm not saying that my *kidult* way of dealing with the situation was the answer, but it was *an* answer. At the time, it felt like the only option open to us. Without support from the police or society at large, it felt as though it was the best way to respond – to stand up and take the fight to the racists, in the hope that they'd leave us alone. There's a sort of brutal logic to that position, but once again it's one that doesn't go to the crux of the problem. It's a kind of 'Cold War' thinking, where an uneasy peace is created from the knowledge of what damage the other side could mete out.

Two factors have altered this landscape since then. The first of these is the way society's attitude to racism has changed: within my lifetime, it has gone from being accepted to becoming taboo. Racist stereotypes on TV, people appearing with black painted faces, the sort of things I remember growing up have now significantly reduced. The 'Golliwog' on Robertson's jam jars is another good example. It's a small thing that many people would never think twice about. This pitch-black doll may well have had less sinister intent when created in the late-nineteenth century, but by the time we were teenagers the name had been shortened to the pejorative 'wog' and Enid Blyton's popular depiction in *Noddy* of Golliwogs as mischievous car thieves was the impression that stuck. That logo was taken off Robertson's at the turn of the century. It says how much society has moved on that it would now be incongruous for the emblem to return.

Stephen Lawrence's murder and the subsequent Macpherson Report into the policing of the Met was also a milestone. I mentioned Lawrence's murder earlier in the context of the climate I was growing up in. The violence leading to his death could have happened to any number of us. Aaron at the bus station, Moe attacked with a hammer, Dan slashed in the arm as he shielded his face, Matt – it still amazes me that during my kidulthood none of the incidents I was involved in ended up with someone being murdered.

As shocking as the Lawrence murder was, it was the police's *un*response that really wound us all up. The fact that no one was convicted sent a strong signal to minority communities. It felt as though the police weren't bothered, or incompetent, or both. That was why the Macpherson Report remains such a culturally significant moment. Those two words – 'institutional racism' – probably had more impact on relations in this country than any of the countless books on the subject. It wasn't just a few rotten apples or a rogue officer here or there; there was something more endemic about the general culture that needed to change.

To be fair, the police force did change. It wasn't an overnight thing – cultural shifts don't work like that – but the general attitudes of the police have undoubtedly improved from where they were twenty years ago. Of course more can still be done, as the shooting by the police of innocent Jean Charles de Menezes on the Tube highlighted, but police are no longer shouting out 'Paki' from their meatwagons. This is partly because the police force is no longer exclusively white. Even one of my old family friends from a Pakistani background, Atif, is now a policeman with Essex Police. It's funny, I remember playing the popular childhood game 'knockdown ginger' with Atif and his little sister Saima. We would simply ring people's doorbells and run away. I also think that the eventual conviction of two of Lawrence's murderers in 2012 is significant. To stick at it, to find new evidence and to finally jail Norris and Dobson for the murder indicates a changed attitude.

But there is still a huge amount of work to be done. And for all this progress on race issues, another form of identity politics was lurking in the shadows, eventually to emerge as an even more intransigent challenge. Most young Britons of the Muslim faith were of South Asian origin, born and raised in crowded single-ethnicity British ghettos. Places like Tower Hamlets for Bangladeshis and Bradford for Mirpuri Pakistanis. Though tensions with non-Muslim communities did occur in these areas, part of the problem was a lack of contact with 'the other'. As race began to take a back seat, and Afro-Caribbean communities began to enter the mainstream through popular music and culture, into these ghettos came war-torn Muslim North Africans, Arabs and Somalis. A new generation of youth born in the ashes of conflict quickly found that they had one identity shared among them all: Islam.

Many British-born Muslims simply did not consider themselves part of the mainstream race debate. The Rushdie affair helped this shift along somewhat. The communities adopted a more isolationist stance, a policy of self-exclusion. For many, the nature of how they identified themselves was changing. So instead of calling themselves British Asians as my parents had done, this generation now defined themselves as almost exclusively Muslim. They believed that their allegiance to the global Islamic community, the *ummah*, hindered them from defining themselves as being part of the country they were born in.

To see how this self-segregation took hold, you only need to look at how weddings changed. When I was growing up the

Asian weddings we went to were mixed, both ethnically and in terms of religion. They were also mixed gender-wise and dancing was the norm. Slowly, weddings involving Muslim couples went from being a celebration to being more akin to a sombre religious ceremony, with no gender mixing and certainly no dancing. Segregated with a curtain and often manned by frustrated men dividing whole families along gender lines, this shift symbolises how the culture changed.

What had caused this shift was a mixture of mutual discrimination and suspicion at home, and a growing awareness of events overseas. Bosnia was particularly crucial in bringing about a shift in identity among Britain's Muslims, as was the Salman Rushdie affair. In Bosnia, white, blond-haired, blue-eyed indigenous European Muslims were being massacred just because they were Muslim. The effect was to bring about the exact opposite. In reaction to these atrocities, Muslims in Europe began reasserting their religious identities even more. It was a natural defence mechanism. But it also exacerbated self-segregation and increased the shift in our self-identification as *politically* Muslim.

Into this fray jumped groups advocating politicised Islam, the Islamists. No other phenomenon has contributed to the rise of Muslim identity politics as much as these. Emerging in a postcolonial Middle East and South Asia, these groups quickly realised that far more potent than Arab socialism would be an ideology that utilised rather than undermined the Islamic emotions of the people. Islamist groups quickly spread and multiplied, arriving in Europe along with Arab asylum seekers and South Asian immigrants.

For the middle years of my life story, this approach to

politics is precisely what I passionately believed in. But that's not till later on. Essentially, what is important for now is to know that the rise of Islamist groups was a key factor in shifting Muslims away from their national identities towards a more exclusively Muslim one. It has taken me a while to resolve many of these pressing challenges posed by identity questions in our globalised world. Initially, retreating into group identities can be a useful tool for lobbying to overcome legal and institutional discrimination. However, beyond the legal, there comes a point when solving class, economic and cultural divisions can only be achieved by increasing mutual integration and participation among all in society. Instead of mutual integration, however, we witnessed a shift from ethnic communalism, where only a brown person is assumed able to represent brown people and so on, to religious communalism, where only a Muslim is assumed to be able to represent other Muslims. Such entrenched communalism and its advocates, who have abused the original intentions of multiculturalism, have brought nothing but division and the balkanisation of Western, and other, societies. This is where I am now on these issues. But there's a long way to go before I reach this conclusion. First, I need to explain how I became an Islamist in the first place.

I was back in the same park with the usual posse. Osman was with me, as was a friend called Nas. Nas's original name was Christian Nathaniel – he was Greek, and from a Greek Orthodox background. He was into the same music as us, and the fact that his skin was of a Mediterranean complexion was enough for the skinheads to consider him a Paki – if their prejudice wasn't so threatening, their worldview would have been pathetically comic. Under the influence of the times, Nas had converted to Islam and had changed his first name from Christian to Nasir.

Once again we were spotted by Mickey and his crew; there were about half a dozen of them. They were carrying baseball bats, and no doubt were strapping knives. They caught us by total surprise, so we split in different directions. Eventually, once we'd properly tooled up at my house, we re-emerged looking for the rest of the posse, and headed back to our recognised rendezvous point on the street corner opposite my house. Osman, Nas and I were the only ones who made it back; the others must have gone their separate ways.

Then, and I don't know if this was luck or learning, we saw Mickey and his entire crew heading our way. We were completely outnumbered. There were some bollards on the side of the road, and they began banging their baseball bats against them, like some sort of war cry as they headed our way. But by now we were battle-hardened. This time, despite being grossly outnumbered, we stood our ground. This was right outside our home; we could see our front door, if we didn't have a right to walk here, then where on God's earth could we walk? I had my knife strapped to my back as usual. Osman had a green rucksack on his.

The stand-off continued, and despite outnumbering us Mickey began to look nervous. We were only three, yet we were refusing to stand down and this made him doubt himself. Next, to our surprise, Mickey stepped forward and asked to parley. For a moment, Osman and I exchanged confused glances. Mickey had never before uttered a single word to us. The irrationality that was his hatred suddenly began to utter rational sentences. It took us a moment to get used to seeing Mickey as anything other than a knife-wielding demon from hell that only knew the word 'Paki!' Once we composed ourselves, Osman indicated to Mickey that he should go over the road, while he too crossed over and waited for Mickey to join him. The war cry of baseball bats dimmed, and a worried-looking Mickey walked over to join my brother. What followed was a tense few minutes. My brother and Mickey were deep in conversation. Nas and I were switching between watching them, and watching Mickey's mates; Mickey's mates were staring the two of us down. Everyone was poised, hands wrapped around baseball bats or fingers ready to unhook knives, in case it all kicked off.

After about ten minutes, we noticed that the talking had stopped. Mickey and my brother were making their way back across the road. They crossed over, halfway between the two groups and shook hands. This was nuts. I watched in disbelief as Mickey returned to his friends and told them to stand down.

'That's enough, lads,' he told them. 'No more trouble here.'

'Eh?' I asked Osman. 'What did you say to him?'

Osman looked at me with a level of confidence in his eyes, 'I told him we're Muslims and we don't fear death. We're like those Palestinian terrorists he sees on the television blowing up planes. We're suicide bombers. We've been taught how to make bombs and I've got one in my rucksack. If you even try to make a move, I'll set mine off. Trust me, I don't give a shit. If we have to take ourselves out to take you out, then that's what we will do.'

'Damn, man! What did Mickey say?' I asked.

'He believed me when I told him he was messing with the wrong guys.'

Osman's bluff played on Mickey's racism, no question about it. Mickey may or may not have watched the news, but he knew his Combat 18 literature. This depicted Muslims as terrorists, and suggested that we were all murderers given half the chance. So when Osman said he had a bomb in his rucksack, and that we had links to suicide bombers, it confirmed every prejudice that Mickey came to believe about us.

'If we feared death,' Osman had told Mickey, 'we'd be running away from you. Why would we be standing here when we're completely outnumbered? It's because we have the power to call backup and fight you to the death.'

Calling for backup was the sort of language Mickey understood. It's what he'd done previously and so he figured that this must have been something that we were capable of as well. If he'd even bothered to question the racist propaganda he'd swallowed, Mickey might have seen through this. But this was someone who considered Greek Nas a 'Paki'. In his warped worldview, such statements made sense.

The discussion between Osman and Mickey was the end of our trouble with Mickey's racists. Mickey had decided that we were too dangerous, too connected to take on, and had made his peace with us instead. While Mickey was explaining his climbdown to his crew, there was still one question that played on my mind. Just as I had done that time at the police station, I decided I needed to ask him something, to understand.

'Hey, can I ask you a question?' I asked.

'All right,' Mickey replied. I saw a different look in his eyes for the first time. The venom had vanished. Now there was wariness, a sliver of fear in his gaze.

'I want to know why you started all this in the first place,' I said. 'Back in the park that day when you hounded Chill. You seemed to know his name. What happened?'

Mickey paused, for once a little unsure of himself. But his reply was pathetic, 'We're tired of all you lot taking our women. We saw your mate Chill pulling all these white girls, and we'd had enough.'

It was, frankly, ridiculous. The driving force behind that original attack was as simple as old-fashioned jealousy, with a racist twang. Mickey had seen the way that hip hop had interested the girls, and how they all wanted to get in on the scene.

Osman's successful bluff affected me more profoundly than any other event till now. I realised for the first time the futility of relying on men. For all the security that knowing people like Rowan had brought, there was only so far this could go. Rowan was a rock, and I owed him much, but there was no way he could always be around. And while packing knives offered limited protection, it just escalated matters without addressing the root problem.

That problem, put simply, was respect. What I realised was that when I asked Mickey why they started on us, he looked at me and talked to me in a different way. He was no longer looking down on me. He was in fact scared. And that came from the assertive new identity Osman had adopted. Islamism. It had done what years of knife-fights could not. It had won the psychological war, and defeated our enemy. For the first time, I caught a glimpse of its power, and how it was capable of transforming my standing at a stroke. Osman, who by this point had become a committed Islamist, had been banging on about this for a year, but I'd never really taken him seriously. I was still a B-boy: that was my culture, and my rule book for climbing that obstacle course called life.

The violence I'd been subjected to, the police discrimination, a greater awareness of foreign conflicts such as Bosnia, all this undoubtedly made me highly receptive to the Islamist message. I was desperately looking for answers. But while all that was essential background, it was that afternoon in the park, and the fear in Mickey's eyes, that triggered my decision to take things further.

Now, here, with a defeated and retreating enemy, I finally understood what my brother had been talking about. Islamism, I realised, could give me the respect that I'd craved since primary school. Hip hop had helped us a great deal; it created new friends, but it hadn't been enough to defeat our enemies. It hadn't been enough to provide me with the courage to help Matt. Yet here, today, grossly outnumbered I stood my ground with Osman, and we won because we invoked Allah. Islamism, in one conversation, did what hip hop couldn't do. It was alive, beating in the hearts of men, and it was prepared to sacrifice everything to regain lost dignity. It wasn't interested in singing 'Fuck tha Police'. Islamism was shouting from the tops of mountains 'Fuck all y'all!' And I wanted a dose of that courage.

CHAPTER SIX

When Babri Mosque fell in India

Important to grasp is how Islamism differs from Islam. Islam is a religion, and its *Shari'ah* can be compared to Talmudic or Canon law. As a religion, Islam contains all the usual creedal, methodological, juristic and devotional schisms of any other faith. In creedal matters, there exist ancient disputes, from which we have the two major denominations of Sunni and Shia, each giving rise to numerous sects within their ranks. From methodological disputes, legal theorists and traditionalists debated whether scripture was best approached through systemised reasoning or oral tradition. From juristic differences, major schools of law emerged. And from a devotional angle, lapsed, traditional, fundamentalist and extremist Muslims have always existed. Superseding all these religious disagreements, and influencing many of them politically, is the ideology of Islamism. Simply defined, Islamism is the desire to impose any given interpretation of

Islam over society as law. Understood in this way, Islamism is not another religious schism, but an ideological thought that seeks to develop a coherent political system that can house all these schisms, without necessarily doing away with them. Whereas disputes within Islam deal with a person's approach to religion, Islamism seeks to deal with a person's approach to society.

As a political project, Islamism was inspired by the rise of European fascism. Like its European ideological counterparts, Islamism was not safe from its own schisms. Some groups wanted to bring about the 'Islamic System' by working alongside the status quo; these were political Islamists, like the Muslim Brotherhood. Others were more revolutionary, wishing to upturn the status quo.

To the untrained eye, such Islamist groups seem 'moderate' because they rise above sectarian disputes and tend not to be fundamentalist in devotional matters, focusing more on politics. But when understood as above, one can see that though religious extremism and fundamentalism may pose social challenges, it is Islamism that seeks real power. Like Mussolini's fascists, who were also socially progressive, it is the totalitarian aspect of Islamism that gives rise to major concern. Much later on, Islamism would influence religious fundamentalists too. This gave rise to a militant strand, Jihadism, and the emergence of groups like al-Qaeda. Jihadism then is the merger of literalist religion with Islamist politics.

My own journey into Islamism resulted in me joining a revolutionary group, known as Hizb al-Tahrir (HT). Sitting between political Islamists and the militants, HT aims to unify all Muslim-majority countries under an 'Islamic state', appropriating for it the term Caliphate, or *Khilafah* in Arabic. They hope to attain power by means of a military coup and seek to impose one version of Islam over society. This journey started in 1992 with Osman walking down the high street in Southend and being handed a leaflet. Because Southend was so white, it was normal for us to stop and talk to any brown face we saw. The pamphleteer was a man called Nasim Ghani, a British Bangladeshi Muslim who, like us, had grown up in Southend and was now studying medicine at Barts in London. He was someone that we could relate to easily: he was articulate and smart. It felt impressive to us, as fifteen or sixteen-year-olds, that he was studying medicine. You had to be bright and committed to be doing that.

The leaflet that Nasim handed Osman was about the Babri Mosque in the northern Indian town of Ayodhya. Built by the first Moghul emperor Babar, the mosque had been there since 1528, and had long been a flashpoint between Hindus and Muslims. Hindus believed that the site was the birthplace of the Hindu deity Lord Ram. Religious violence at the mosque was first reported in the 1850s, and in 1984 Hindus began a campaign to 'liberate' the site, replacing the mosque with a temple for Lord Ram. When a court order ruled that the mosque be protected, Hindu supporters decided to take matters into their own hands. A crowd of 200,000 broke through the cordon around the mosque and tore it down, using a mixture of hammers and their bare hands. Eyewitnesses reported that the extra police who had been sent to protect the mosque stood back, rather than intervening.

81

The episode was the trigger for the some of the worst violence India had seen for decades: over 2,000 people died in the riots that followed.

'Hideous Hindus Massacre Muslims' was the rather offensive title of the leaflet. I still remember that title. That one leaflet has changed the course of my life in ways probably unthinkable for its anonymous author. It laid bare the behaviour of the Hindu extremists in what was a shocking and deeply inflammatory episode. At this point in his life, Osman, spurred on by the likes of Public Enemy's Professor Griff, had taken an interest in politics. He followed the 'Intifada' that had been going on against the Israeli occupation of Gaza and the West Bank, and the role of Yasser Arafat's PLO. This struggle for Palestinian liberation, and the crushing Israeli response, complete with tacit American support, had long been a running sore in international relations. In the context of my story and so many others, it was undoubtedly a factor that justified the Islamist narrative of victimhood. The conflict, and the accompanying Western insouciance, came across as manifestly wrong. Identifying with the resistance movement was an easy thing to do. It reinforced what we were experiencing on the streets of Southend: it was Muslims who were on the receiving end of things, and the state didn't care. It was another element in pushing my identity away from being British or Pakistani, and toward defining myself as exclusively *politically* Muslim.

The Intifada had been going on since 1987, so by the early 1990s it wasn't anything new. Like the regular racist attacks, the stories on the news from Gaza and the West Bank were just part of the status quo: this was how it was. The reason it caught Osman's attention was the first Gulf War in 1991, when Saddam Hussein invaded Kuwait, and combined United Nations forces removed him. Saddam Hussein, albeit a brutal tyrant, was a champion of the Palestinian cause and his provocation of Israel (including the launching of Scud missiles at Israeli towns) kept the issue in the news, and grabbed Osman's attention.

But the Babri Mosque incident in India was something different. The direct assault on and destruction of an ancient Muslim place of worship felt particularly shocking. The number of people killed in the subsequent violence was horrific. It strongly reinforced the message that Nasim with his leaflet and Hizb al-Tahrir in general were pushing. Southend, Gaza, Bosnia, Iraq, India: wherever you went in the world, the story was the same – Muslims were unprotected and under attack, and now was the time to do something about it. After all, we didn't believe in turning the other cheek.

Nasim was everything the mosque imam in Southend was not. Here was someone who was young, slick, articulate and successful, and he didn't have a beard. He was studying and living in London, which for us surviving on the edge of Essex felt like a glamorous, exciting lifestyle. When he handed Osman that leaflet, he was exactly the right person, in the right place, at the right time. Osman was receptive to such a message, and when Nasim suggested he came to a talk, to discuss the idea further, Osman agreed.

It is worth mentioning here that Nasim would turn out to be not just any pamphleteer. He was, in fact, on the path to becoming the leader of HT in the UK, and the founder of the organisation in Bangladesh. As someone who has gone on to co-found movements myself and has met numerous political leaders of all stripes, I can tell you that Nasim is one of the most committed recruiters I have come across. He is not especially handsome, uniquely intelligent, particularly well dressed, deeply devout, or exceptionally articulate, yet he combines just that right level of all these traits to give him a sort of safe, friendly, dependable-leader quality. I have rarely encountered anyone with such a skill to say the right thing at the right time, in order to convince a person to follow him. He's not someone who leads through sheer force of his personality, or authoritarianism. He is pragmatic, rather than dogmatic. An ordinary guy, but extraordinarily good at being so, if that makes sense.

Nasim would go on to play a huge part in my life. In the years that followed, as he rose up the ranks, I became a kind of protégé. It seems, looking back, a remarkable coincidence that he came from the same background as me. Perhaps that's partly why we connected. If Nasim hadn't been on a break from university and decided to leaflet Southend, then perhaps my life might have turned out differently. But he stopped Osman, got talking, and the first link in the next stage of my life was in place.

Osman started going with Nasim to his talks and study circles, and pretty soon became a changed person. Everything we'd been doing together – going to clubs, chasing women – was now anathema to him. To begin with, I thought he was crazy. 'What's wrong with you, man?' I'd ask. I'd mock him and laugh at him, but to my surprise he'd just take it. He stopped going out with our group of friends, told women to stop calling for him at our house. Generally he just retreated.

As much as Osman's change surprised me, it pleased my dad. For many years at home, it had felt as though my brother and I had sided more with our mother – taken advantage of her more liberal views. For the first time, one of my father's sons had taken a serious interest in Islam. At this point, my father didn't understand what Islamism really meant. What he saw was his son taking an interest in religion and behaving more like the traditional Muslim he had always wanted us to become. He approved of that and encouraged it, and that led, inevitably, to a change of mood in the household: the balance of power, as it were, had started to shift. You could see it in Abi's reaction. She didn't know how to react or respond to Osman's criticisms of her behaviour. Later on, when I joined him, she would become even more isolated.

At this point, my impression of *practising* Islam was still based on my early teenage experience of visiting the mosque. Osman's conversion felt not only as if it had come out of nowhere, it also felt like a retrograde step. To go back to that, to spurn all the girls and partying just didn't make any sense.

Osman, though, was nothing if not persistent, in trying to get me to go along with him. During that year he worked on those friends he thought would be most receptive, Moe, Nas and myself. We all eventually converted. Although I would dismiss what he said at first, there was no denying the inner confidence or self-belief when he spoke. As he continued to talk to me I realised one of the fundamental points about Islamism that so many people fail to understand. The way Osman was speaking wasn't in the orthodox, religious way of the imam with a stick; he was talking about politics, and about events that were happening now. That's crucial to understanding what Islamism is all about: it isn't a religious movement with political consequences, it is a political movement with religious consequences.

Osman had learnt well what the study circles had taught him. There's no doubt that in Nasim he had an excellent teacher. Nasim was able to expound his theories into a simple, coherent narrative that Osman soaked up. As part of Hizb al-Tahrir training, he had the answers and counter-arguments at his fingertips, so any questions I had he could throw straight back and respond to. The mixture of this and his inner belief was impressive.

Nasim knew that Osman and I were already quite anti-establishment. He knew that what he needed to do was channel our energies from hip hop and race issues to something more serious, more global. And he had just the thing to achieve this, the Islamist narrative. This was a powerful toxin. As is often the case with convincing arguments, it resonated with some truth. Nasim argued that the suffering we had experienced in Southend, the attacks by Combat 18 and the discrimination we felt from the police, these were not isolated incidents but part of a bigger picture. It was wider than just Southend, far beyond Ockendon and the rest of Essex. And we were deluded if we thought that it was just a race thing. Yes, race was a factor, but even if we solved that, Western society would never be satisfied with us. How much whiter could you get than the Muslims of Bosnia, and just look at what was going on there while the rest of Europe stood by and watched. And he continued, look at our brothers in Palestine, at Kashmir, or at the Muslims killed for defending the honour of the Babri Mosque in India. Why is it that every conflict and war today involves the killing of Muslims? Are you that blinded to believe this is a coincidence? Are you as shallow as the racists to believe it's merely about skin colour? The truth is that there is an international effort to keep Muslims down. They intervene in Kuwait for oil, yet stand by and watch as Muslims get murdered in Bosnia because, truly, they cannot tolerate a Muslim power in the heart of Europe. And if they cannot tolerate white Bosnians, what makes you think they'll ever accept you? We have gone from being the world superpower, the Islamic *Khilafah*, to being the downtrodden minority who get stabbed in the streets of Essex, and we've sunk so low we don't even know how to identify the problem.

The first time Nasim mentioned the concept of 'the *Khilafah*', I hadn't even heard of it. That, though, just served his argument. 'Why do you think you have never heard of it?' he asked. 'Because it is the West that has written the history books, and decided what they want to teach in schools, even in Muslim lands after they left us their colonial ways. In the "official" version of events, the last bastion of the *Khilafah* was called the "Ottoman Empire"; they don't call it by its real name. This *Khilafah* sided with the Germans against the British in the First World War, which is why they don't want to tell you its history. They tell you it was the Turkish Empire that was disbanded because that is what they want you to believe – they don't want you to know what the *Khilafah* really was. Do you think the Ottoman *Khilafah* would ever have stood by and allowed Bosnian Muslims to get slaughtered? Muslims stood united and protected under this entity before 1924. The West doesn't want this to happen again, which is why they are working so hard to the stop the reunification of Muslims.'

This logic led to the somewhat curious position of Hizb al-Tahrir endorsing Saddam Hussein's invasion of Kuwait during the first Gulf War. They supported it, because it fitted in with their narrative of Muslims uniting under a single entity. It also explained the American intervention – not because they wanted to uphold the principle of national sovereignty, but because they wanted to stop such an entity beginning to form. It wasn't that HT were fans of Saddam Hussein: far from it, the first martyr of HT was killed by Saddam in 1964 because they fiercely opposed the idea of Arab socialism – Ba'athism. But if Saddam was in charge of two countries, then that was one less tyrant the group needed to overthrow.

The Western response to repel Saddam and reinforce Kuwait's territorial integrity was nothing more, Nasim argued, than a reinforcement of their imperialist past. The British and French had carved up the Middle East in anticipation of the collapse of the Ottoman Caliphate: these were countries with borders drawn quite literally with a ruler at the Sykes–Picot summit in 1916. Look at the right angle that separates Egypt and Sudan: is that a natural, historical boundary? These are the anachronisms of Empire, still visible on the maps of today. Kuwait and Iraq were artificial entities. The West intervening to uphold these boundaries was the reinforcement of its own set of colonial rules, not ours.

Everything about the modern Middle East, according to HT, was a product of this colonialism. Even the government of Saudi Arabia, on the face of it a deeply conservative Muslim regime, was an imperialist puppet regime – allowing the Americans to base their troops there, and selling them their oil. Saudi Arabia was in fact created as a reward to the House of Saud for their rebellion against 'the *Khilafah*'. Throughout the region, there were agents of the West in charge, torturing the true Muslims to keep them from power: rulers like Mubarak in Egypt; the Shah of Iran before his fall in 1979; even Saddam Hussein had been the beneficiary of Western support for many years. The West talked of democracy, and yet pumped millions into propping up these brutal dictators to keep the real force from coming to power, Islam. For HT, none of these regimes had legitimacy: their political authority was based on that of their current, neocolonial masters.

I was sixteen at the time I started hearing all this. When you're that age, already angry and disenfranchised, you're very susceptible to absolutes. This globalisation of our grievance was what many would later come to know as the powerful Islamist narrative. It would go on to stir the hearts of thousands of young Muslims around the world, leading to the creation of groups who would commit many atrocities in its name. At that time, before al-Qaeda was ever conceived, all this sounded highly credible to me. I didn't have the political knowledge to come back and challenge what I was being told and I didn't trust the typical authorities to tell me the truth. I could see the passion with which Osman would lay out his new position, hear Nasim's carefully crafted narratives coming through in what he was saying. I could sense the way it chimed with my own experiences: could smell the atmosphere on the streets. And considering everything my young mind could see around me, it sounded credible.

To begin with, I stuck with what I knew: with hip hop and the counter-culture messages the lyrics contained. Even here, though, things were changing. Within Public Enemy, there had always been two competing voices on the mic. The group was first and foremost Chuck D's band – his strident belief in black power, in ensuring the work of Martin Luther King and Malcolm X was brought up to date for a new generation gave PE's message an untainted authority. But equally important for the band's message was Professor Griff. Griff was a member of the Nation of Islam: he didn't drink, didn't smoke and had his S1Ws, his Soldiers of the First World, dressed up in military gear, carrying imitation machine guns on stage. Griff's politics were more radical, and more controversial. He had given an interview to the *Washington Post* in which he claimed that 'Jews are wicked . . . [and responsible for] the majority of wickedness that goes on across the globe.' He asked if it was 'a coincidence that the Jews run the jewellery business and it's named Jewellery?' The group's response was to fire Griff for anti-Semitism. For a PE fan like myself, the split was shocking. Public Enemy had politicised me: now there were schisms emanating from the camp. So where hip hop had once given me strength and identity, its impact was dulled a little from this confusion. I was now facing a split along similar lines at home, between Osman and me, and was desperately trying to work out which way to go.

The culmination, though, was that final meeting with Mickey. The show of strength that I had been part of in Ockendon suddenly felt quite a parochial event. The strength that my brother's conviction and politics brought with it seemed immensely powerful. I'd caught a glimpse of what it could do in Mickey's reaction. I could only begin to imagine its impact if this was replicated on a global scale. The fact that my brother succeeded with a green rucksack where all my knife-fights and shows of strengths had failed, made me think.

I remember something else too. Whereas, before, his dependable green rucksack had PLO graffitied over it, now he had struck out PLO and started to write the name of a group unknown to me: Hamas.

'What's that mean?' I naively asked.

'Forget the PLO sell-outs,' he said, 'they're not Islamic. This is Hamas, the *Islamic* Resistance Movement. The future belongs to Hamas.'

Oh cool, I thought, Professor Griff would like them, then. And I agreed to go to study circles with him, to see what Hizb al-Tahrir were about.

CHAPTER SEVEN

A land where foetuses are cut from wombs

Hizb al-Tahrir study circles took place in people's houses. There would be five to six of us, sat round in a circle with the speaker at the centre. Nasim or another speaker would talk to a set theme for about an hour and then take questions afterwards. The content would be more political than theological, with occasional reference to Islam to back up the point. There was a methodology to these discussions, the framework of which I've continued to use effectively to this day: always destroy before you build. HT was very good at taking apart existing deeply held prejudices, stripping them down to their bare bones and then rebuilding a new set of reference points. Often it was said, if you try to build on top of existing corrupt concepts, one day your ideas will fall like a stack of cards. In keeping with this, the circles first focused on a thorough critique of ideas such as freedom, human rights, and democracy. Every critique addressed an intellectual, political and scriptural angle. These discussions were like a thorough deep cleansing. Such was Nasim's contempt for Western society, that it was clear his country of birth was no part of his identity. Indeed, he defined himself directly against this.

There was no link between these study groups and the local mosque. In fact, the separation between the two was more than that: the study groups were critical of the religious classes. This disdain was based on piecemeal history, with an element of truth that had been embellished out of all proportion. During the British Raj, there was a theory among some Muslims that the best way to further themselves was to appease their colonial rulers. The Hindus were in the majority, and it was said that if they ruled India they would use their power to oppress the Muslim community. The best way, therefore, to protect Muslims was to keep the British in power – a trade-off between being allowed to pray, fast, and practise rituals, and having to subjugate themselves to foreign rule.

Islamists used this position, which some religious clerics took in India, as evidence against all religious clerics. They had lost their way and turned Islam into Christianity, a meek, spiritual creed that has no effect on life and no control over society. Again, there is some truth to this narrative. Muslim religious leaders had indeed let modernity overtake them, had become politically complacent and were grossly out of touch. These were the types sending mosque imams to teach us in Britain, who could not speak English. Rather than admiring the piety of Muslims who quietly went about practising their faith, Islamists disparaged them for not challenging the neocolonial state they were living in, or the 'Westernisation' it brought with it. Secular Islamic heritage, historically strong among traditional Muslims, was taking an Islamist battering. It didn't help that some of the staunchest advocates for this secularism were not democrats but Arab despots. It followed therefore that it was Islamists who were going to liberate the lands and minds of Muslims by teaching them the impact Islam demands to have on life, society and governance, by overthrowing these despots, rejecting the West and reclaiming their identity, and by establishing the true system for Muslims, 'the *Khilafah*'. Secular Muslim heritage, caught completely unawares and half asleep, caved in.

The meetings were therefore primarily political rather than theological in emphasis. Of primary importance was the overall narrative of Islamism: historical facts and theological points were chosen to support this, rather than beginning with the information and postulating a theory from it. So the information and stories chosen were never lies or untruths, but seldom were they the whole truth. The element that supported the story was mentioned: the part that complicated the issue was ignored. That was true of both history and theology: where a reference to Allah was relevant, it would be dropped in.

But there was never a session on how to pray. There was never a session on how to fast. There was never a session on how to read the Qur'an. We learnt how to pray alone, and prayed because it was considered important to keep up the ritual, and because it was part of the ideology as a whole. But it was very much only part of the overall scheme: Islamism is a total theory that encompasses politics, economics, societal affairs and personal spiritual ones. For Islamists, the faith element was something of a given – it was the politics and other issues that were the focus of attention.

The speaker brought to each meeting what was called that session's leaflet, usually a single sheet of A4, divided into two columns with a heading at the top. This would be the subject of that day's discussion, a single, straightforward idea that they wanted the group to adopt.

At one of the first study circles I went to, the leaflet was entitled 'Born to be Brown'. The basic idea was that skin colour is irrelevant, and what mattered were ideas and narratives. Just because someone is brown doesn't make them your brother: the person of the same skin colour as you can just as easily be your enemy. What matters is whether or not you were a Muslim: by Muslim, they meant an Islamist, which is what they considered to be a 'proper' Muslim. The dividing line did not fall between ethnicity or nationality: it was about Islam versus everyone else. That involved a recalibration of one's identity, to start defining yourself as Muslim against the rest of the world.

This particular leaflet stuck in my mind because it challenged the bricks and mortar with which I'd built up my teenage identity. My group of friends were almost uniformly drawn from the minority communities of Southend. We'd joined together because of the threats we had faced, and through a shared interest in hip hop and black culture. Now, what I'd previously found strength in, I was told was irrelevant. That was quite a lot to take in; after all, the racism I'd experienced was part of the pathway for wanting to join HT. To stop thinking in terms of racial lines and start thinking in terms of Muslims versus the rest was quite a shift.

I had very few Pakistani friends. Most of my friends growing up had been white English non-Muslims and then, when the racism kicked in, we became part of a West Indian group. I didn't really feel affiliated to Pakistan or to Britain: and I knew I was not West Indian. So there was a real vacuum as to who I was, which was the ideal place for someone to be before recruitment to an Islamist organisation. So they were able to offer me an identity that had previously been absent.

The study circles were supplemented by videos, and most strikingly, those of the conflict in Yugoslavia and the appalling treatment of the Bosnian Muslims by the Serb forces. Again, I think it is important to remember that this was taking place prior to the Internet taking hold: the technology was not yet up to the sort of dissemination of videos we are familiar with today. Back then, it was all about VHS cassettes: copies would be made and meetings would be arranged to watch these tapes. This was footage that wasn't shown on mainstream media, it was shocking, appalling stuff, especially to a raw sixteen-year-old.

The footage reached us because people from the UK had gone to fight in Bosnia. British Muslims went as civilians, trained in camps funded by the Saudis, fought in Bosnia and had come back again to recruit more soldiers. This was at a time when, amazingly, going abroad to fight in a war was unlikely to get you stopped and questioned, as long as you were not fighting against your own troops. In some ways, Bosnia was no different from the situation then in Afghanistan: in both cases, there were Saudi funds available to train and fight. There were training camps all over Bosnia, and a huge growth of Saudi-built mosques that were clearly aimed at funding a religious revival in the country. The major difference with Afghanistan was the proximity. This was a war taking place on the European mainland, a conflict that was less than a three-hour flight away. When these fighters returned to the UK, they were treated like heroes: with their big beards and talk about Islam, they felt like our very own Che Guevaras.

The videos featured disturbing, sick content. Trays of what appeared to be genitals cut off from Bosnian men by Serbs. Footage of pregnant women with their bellies cut open and their babies ripped out alive. You'd see the dead woman on the floor with the baby lying next to her, the umbilical cord still attached, and the gash down the front of her stomach. There would then be combat footage as well, of trained Muslim fighters defending themselves against the Serbs. The footage was well put together considering the limits of technology. Some scenes were a little grainy but they'd been edited professionally to get a powerful message across. I hesitate to use the word 'propaganda', because that has negative implications, but that is essentially what they were. There was a genocide going on, and the appalling crimes committed were being used to further an Islamist recruitment drive across Europe. And it worked.

What these videos showed me were two things in particular. Firstly, it reinforced the narrative that Nasim had taught me in the 'Born to be Brown' discussion. These were individuals whose death was nothing to do with the colour of their skin. The fact that they were Muslims was the salient issue, as shown by the fact that all the individuals were white. Second, the fact that Britain and other Western governments were doing nothing about it reinforced their 'blind eye' approach to world politics. When it was Muslims who were under attack, and there was no oil to defend, the West wasn't interested in getting involved. And why should they? These were our people not theirs, which is why we needed 'the *Khilafah*'.

The terrible, unfolding events served as the perfect recruitment ground for Islamism. These people were being killed simply for being Muslims. Worse, because they are not Muslims with the 'proper' understanding, they don't even understand why it is happening to them. But Islamism offered a powerful explanation, which is why this shift in identity politics began to occur both in Bosnia and across Europe. In some ways, you could argue that just as Pakistan's troubles with violent Islamism – Jihadism – were born through Afghanistan, European Jihadism was born through Bosnia.

The first time I saw the videos, it was a shocking, traumatic experience. I was so angered by what I saw that my immediate response was a desire to go and fight in Bosnia myself. I wanted to take up arms and defend the Bosnians. I remember Nasim having to take me aside to give me a long talk to calm me down. He told me to stop being emotional, to think about the rational point here instead. No matter what you do, no matter how many people go out there, it's not going to change the long-term game. This is not just happening in Bosnia, it's everywhere. There are fires being lit all over the place. You can get a bucket and try to put one out, or you can step back and look at the root cause of all this. If we had 'the *Khilafah*', our armies could stop such atrocities happening. This was the Hizb al-Tahrir message: what we needed was to work efficiently to control the mindset of the military top brass in

Muslim-majority countries in order to eventually establish a state. Simply joining the fight would mean one more soldier lost for the cause. It may save one or two people there, but wouldn't change anything in the long run.

For HT, those videos were undoubtedly a powerful recruiting weapon. We would organise viewings for people, and while they sat there stunned by what they saw, we would tell them they were wasting their lives while all this mayhem unfolded. What are you doing with your life? we asked. How can you be happy with yourselves, going out for a laugh and a kebab on a Friday or Saturday night when all this is happening on your doorstep? The video and the following speech would always have the same, radicalising effect. Half would want to join HT there and then: but there were others like me who would want to take direct action.

The challenge for us, like Nasim had done with me, was to talk these people down. It didn't always work. Omar Sheikh, for example, was a student at the London School of Economics, who attended a HT-backed conference at his university about the situation in Bosnia. The leader of HT at the time, Omar Bakri Fostok – who used Mohammad as his surname – was a keynote speaker at this conference. Omar Sheikh's diaries tell of how the conference galvanised him, but that it didn't go far enough. HT offered him a coruscating analysis of the situation, but didn't provide any solution. The answer for him was Jihadism. Sheikh went abroad, and at the time of writing is still imprisoned in Pakistan accused of the murder of American journalist Daniel Pearl.

In terms of the growth of Islamism the war in Bosnia was crucial to its spread across Europe. From that it can be seen how Islamism spread in the Middle East and Asia. European Muslims being radicalised by events in Bosnia, Egyptians being radicalised by events in Palestine, Pakistanis being radicalised by events in Afghanistan, it's a similar theme all over: grievances, identity crises, charismatic recruiters and compelling narratives. It's not a huge leap of imagination to picture yourself in the same position.

For me, the procrastination of Western governments over Bosnia resonated strongly with my own experiences in Essex, and the inaction I saw from the police. This was how it was, I reasoned. It was down to Muslims to defend their own community. These days, looking back from a post-9/11 world where Western intervention has been so frequent, we forget that in the early 1990s the world was a different place. This was an international landscape still adjusting to the end of the Cold War, where every decision was worked out with regard to what the Soviet response might be. The early 1990s asked new questions about whether interventions within a state for humanitarian reasons were justifiable – Rwanda and Somalia were some other examples. The Bosnian situation asked all sorts of awkward questions for the West: how would the Russians respond to their involvement? Was this an internal conflict within Yugoslavia? Were Bosnia's attempts to leave Yugoslavia any different from Chechnya trying to do the same from the Russian Federation?

The upshot of all this was that the Western response to Bosnia was paralysis. The United States, under Bill Clinton, did not want to get involved and saw it as a European issue. The British response, with John Major and Foreign Secretary Douglas Hurd, was vacillation. If the West had been more proactive, if they had intervened earlier and harder as when Tony Blair and NATO did so over Kosovo, the situation would have been different, not just for Bosnia, but perhaps also for the spread of Islamism and for HT.

In Bosnia itself, it was left to the new government to sort out the rising Islamist penetration. The new president knew his country's own culture and history. He knew their Muslim heritage hailed from Turkic Ottoman Sufi roots, and not Saudi-Salafist, or literalist, roots. The Bosnian government began to root out the jihadists who had come to fight there. They recognised the threat from within, and the potential for another Afghanistan situation if they did not act. But while Bosnia was successful in doing this, the influence of its fight lingered on far longer.

What did Hizb al-Tahrir see as the answer to all this injustice meted out to the Muslim populations of the world? The answer was the creation of 'the *Khilafah*', a Muslim superstate that would sweep across all current national boundaries. Within 'the *Khilafah*', HT's version of Islam would be the ruling philosophy. Apostates, adulterers and minorities considered abhorrent, like homosexuals, would suffer the death sentence. Criminality would be met with tough justice, thieves would have their hands cut off. Rights such as free speech would be curtailed, because 'God's law' must trump all.

Surprising for some people is how easy it felt to switch my mindset to this new political viewpoint. I'd felt I'd found my connection with hip-hop culture, but it fell away with little argument. Why was this? Part of it was down to my particular set of circumstances and upbringing. The message of Islamism was almost tailor-made for someone like me: intellectually curious and brought up in a Western environment. I didn't have the family or religious background to counterbalance what Nasim was telling me. The HT way of analysing things was, ironically enough, a modern, European, socio-political interpretation of religion. That was the way I'd been educated at school, so I understood the reasoning from the start.

Secondly, there was Nasim himself, an intellectually charismatic guy. The authority and confidence with which he spoke on any number of subjects made a huge impression on me, at an age when I was easily influenced. And the subjects he talked about related directly to my life, something my father or the imam were unable to do. He knew about politics, philosophy, theology, all the issues that bands like Public Enemy had raised, but which he was able to take further and expand. The way he tied these different issues up felt nothing short of intellectually intoxicating. It felt revolutionary, and that's exactly what it was: advocating a revolution.

Thirdly, the political element of hip hop was starting to peel away. What had originally excited me was politics that bands like PE and N.W.A had brought to the table. PE had carried on without Professor Griff (and their next record, *Fear of a Black Planet*, continued to take no prisoners) but the whole anti-Semitic episode had dented their popularity, and their best days were behind them. The vanguard of hip hop was increasingly becoming gangsta rap: the new stars were people like Cypress Hill, and the underlying messages were less about anti-authority anthems, and more to do with boasting about drugs, violence and women. Chuck D famously describes an early gig where a PE fan had seen a flyer with Malcolm X on it, and asked who this 'Malcolm the Tenth' character was. The new generation of hip-hop fans were asking the same sort of questions.

The way hip hop was changing reinforced what Nasim was telling me in the study circles. You related to their music, I was told, because you have been through similar experiences of racism and discrimination. 'But Chuck D is not a Muslim. Flavor Flav is not a Muslim. Ice Cube is not a Muslim. They do not know the solution to the problems they rap about because the message has simply not reached them'. That is where Hizb al-Tahrir and Islamism came in. So it seemed perfectly natural for hip hop to go one way, and my thinking to go another. I stopped listening to the music and started listening to HT instead.

PART TWO

Islamist

To live is to war with trolls in heart and soul.
To write is to sit in judgment on oneself.

Henrik Ibsen, *Peer Gynt*

CHAPTER EIGHT

An Islamist takeover

At sixteen, recruited to HT's cause and now full of the zeal of the converted, I wanted to move to London to be where the action was. Having finished my GCSEs, I told my parents that I wished to attend Barking College in East London to do a specialist graphic design course. I managed to convince them that this course wasn't available in any Southend college, which my parents accepted. At this point they were unaware of the nature of my Islamist beliefs. My father, in particular, saw a son who had calmed down from the B-boy excesses of his earlier teens, and appeared to be settling into the life of a traditional, hard-working Muslim. And so it was that I moved out of the family home to study.

Of course the graphic design course was just a front. HT was far bigger in the capital than Southend, and I desperately wanted to be part of it. By this time Nasim was in charge of HT's activities in East London, and with his help I got a room in a flat with some other activists at 69 Chesterford Road, in the Manor Park area of East London. This was known as the *da'wah* – or mission – house, a flat dedicated to planning HT and occupied solely by supporters. By now I was an HT *daris* – student – the stage before membership. This meant that I was committed to attending HT events and partaking in official activities. My flatmates, all HT *dariseen* were recruited at university.

They included a student called Saleem, a former body-builder and all-round friendly guy. There was Sohail, a student from Milton Keynes in his second year at Guildhall University. He was a good laugh. Another was Yaseen, an intelligent man who went on to leave HT and became a teacher. Then there was Ali, who would pop in to stay occasionally, and who at the time we revered because he was already a member. Another was Nas, the Greek friend from Southend; he had converted, moved to London with me and was an HT supporter.

Ours was a proper student house, with all the mess that entailed, but it was fantastic to be in the thick of the action, surrounded by 'brothers'. I loved it. From the get-go, the house was used for HT activities. We'd go fly-posting, putting up stickers and posters, handing out pamphlets and leaflets, and advertising talks. We would spend all night doing this: cutting up boxes to create our boards, sticking posters onto the cardboard, punching holes and running the string through them, ready to be tied up. Then we'd load the cargo into someone's car and blitz the local area, tying our posters to lamp posts everywhere. People would drop in to the flat from all over London. From the typical town atmosphere of Southend, and the feeling of being part of a fractional minority, I now felt plugged in to a far larger community, a thriving London network buzzing with ideas.

This set-up accelerated my commitment to HT. Before, I'd been going to study groups once a week. Now I was living with other activists, and talking about the cause every day. For the first time, I had a real sense of how the movement was a national and global phenomenon. All the major universities had recruitment drives: Oxford and Cambridge, Exeter, Durham, everywhere. We were fast taking over. The 1990s in London was the decade of Islamism. As many women as men were joining the movement, and somewhere we were told was probably our future partner waiting to meet us. All this created an all-enveloping sensation – this movement would shape how my life unfolded.

There was also the fact that I was living in London for the first time. East Ham might not have been that far from Southend, but it felt like a different world. The diverse community of East Ham made racism less of an issue. And the rising strength of Islamism and Jihadism meant for the first time that you didn't mess with Muslims. With that knowledge, I could walk the streets with confidence.

When I arrived, Nasim appointed one of his protégés, Ed Husain, to help me settle in. Ed, a passionate HT *daris*, was studying at Newham College. We quickly became very close. Before term started Ed asked me which college I was enrolled in. Barking College, I told him.

'You don't want to be in Barking *ya akhi*, my brother, all the action's at Newham College. I'm at Newham's East Ham campus. That's where all the Muslims are, and that's where we could really kick things off together.'

I went along with him to the East Ham campus and was blown away by the number of Muslims there. So I switched from Barking to Newham and from the graphic design course to doing A levels. I didn't tell my parents straightaway – if they discovered I was just doing A levels, they would see no reason why I couldn't be doing them in Southend like Osman. By the time they found out it was too late to change. They weren't completely happy, but they accepted my reasons – or at least, the reasons I gave them. As long as you're studying, they told me, that is the important thing. I assured them that I was.

The truth was that I was at Newham for an HT takeover. Rather than studying, I was campaigning and recruiting, and regularly skipping lessons to do so. As soon as I set foot in Newham, the recruitment potential of the place was clear. Newham was a big college with two campuses – one at East Ham, one at West Ham – with thousands of students and many Muslims.

Ed Husain, who was in his final year, needed to hand over his HT drive to someone else and I was the perfect replacement. Ed was a studious type; at seventeen years of age he wore a blazer and shirt to lessons. He was a good public speaker and more devout than I had been, or ever would become. I liked his religious devotion, it helped to calm my wilder side and we developed a deep, lasting friendship. I went to his house, got to know his parents and remember spending Ramadan breaking my fasts with his family. It soon became apparent that Ed and I could work together as a strong team. We led a group of four core HT supporters: Sarfraz, and Mustafa, two big guys who were dependable types; Shehzad, a sociable guy who knew a lot of people; and Rehan, lovingly called 'Mr Bean' by our adversaries due to his physical stature and his propensity to intellectually fall over himself. We were able to call upon support from neighbouring colleges. One such college was Redbridge College. There, a diminutive yet fiery young HT *daris* called Abdur Rahman was replicating what we were doing at Newham. We would regularly share ideas and pool resources.

When the opportunity to become president of the Student Union (SU) arose, Ed suggested that I should run for the post, and that our HT group should stand on a single slate. The campaign to become SU president is instructive for a number of reasons. First, there was our reason for wanting to run in the first place, and that was our desire to become the dominant Muslim group in the college. When I joined, the Islamic Society (ISoc) at Newham was dominated by the Saudi-Salafists, or literalists. In those days, before the merger between some Salafists and Islamism, the Salafists hated HT and everything we stood for. In the UK, a group called JIMAS coordinated all Salafist activities. JIMAS were known rivals. They loathed us more than non-Muslims, for what they saw as our twisting of the Islamic message. The Salafist philosophy was far more religious than the HT message: there was no political element to their thinking. They dismissed our views for not being religious enough and we in turn dismissed them for providing religious cover for the Saudi king and other absolute rulers.

The Salafists controlled the college ISoc and this meant they had control of Friday prayers. Because of their control of Friday prayers, they were able to bring in big crowds to their events, and this helped to perpetuate their control.

Before I had gone to Newham, HT had never really been in a position to challenge this hegemony. Now, though, we felt confident enough to give it a go. If I could become president of the Student Union, then I would be in charge of funding for organisations such as the ISoc. I could then reduce ISoc's money, and their influence, at a stroke. I could even find a way to divert the money towards HT and our own aims.

We put up candidates for all the various posts on the Student Union executive. The Salafists were completely wrong-footed by our tactics, and soon found themselves adrift in the campaign. We were more people-savvy and culturally aware. I had my B-boy background: by contrast the Salafists were wearing traditional Arab robes and strained to be pious. We would be listening to music and wearing jeans, and they did not know how to handle that: they could see it made us popular, but thought it was irreligious. For the Salafists, the emphasis of their message was purity. Their manifesto was about sitting in the prayer room, talking about how to fast, and the benefits of leaving the world behind. Their starting point was the scriptures, whereas ours was the real world. We would talk about Afghanistan and Bosnia in a way that made our message sound relevant, whereas theirs just felt out of touch.

The female Muslim vote, in particular, came across to our side, partly because we were seen as trendy young guys, and partly because of the Salafist attitude to women. Salafists would criticise women for not wearing headscarves, to which we'd say, 'Do you think the Bosnian Muslim woman was wearing a headscarf when she was raped? How does that make her any less your sister?' We had a female HT supporter who stood for the role of women's officer, and who didn't wear a headscarf; we conveniently tolerated that if it could win us the elections. We secured the female votes, hands down.

On a more basic level, we were more aggressive in argument. Nasim had taught us to come back at our opponents. I'd learnt the answers to their questions and would fire back a response to whatever accusations they made. That's a powerful thing to do when you're in front of a crowd, having a debate. It makes you strong and your ideas coherent. The Salafists didn't really have a response: their only resort was to their religious purity, which didn't have the same resonance with most people's lives. A few years later, of course, this would change: Salafism and Islamism would fuse to form Jihadism, most famously seen in the rise of al-Qaeda. That, though, was in the future.

The election was a runaway success. I didn't only become student president: all the other HT candidates won as well. Overnight we had completely outmanoeuvred the Salafists of JIMAS and the ISoc. We were now the most senior students on campus, with authority to override the ISoc, to represent students in front of management, and to control student funds. At the same time, we set up the Debating Society to arrange events and bring in external speakers. On the forms, we claimed to have been inspired by Gladstone and Disraeli, and by parliamentary debates. We managed to hoodwink the management into letting us set up an HT front group. Such takeovers were happening across UK campuses; Islamism was firmly on the rise.

CHAPTER NINE

12,000 Muslims screaming '*Khilafah*' at Wembley Arena

The ISoc Salafists were not the only ones incapable of dealing with us. The same was true of the college authorities, who had been caught completely off guard.

The student-affairs manager was a chap called Dave Gomer. He was the point of contact between the college authorities and students. A friendly, affable, well-meaning guy, his politics were forged in an earlier era, a time when student protests were about sit-ins and strikes and occupying the Student Union. To someone of Dave's generation, student protest was 'kids being kids' and a healthy part of someone's political education. As you can imagine we ran circles around that man.

Unlike the student protests in the 1960s, by using religion and multiculturalism as a cover, we brought an entirely foreign lexicon to the table. We knowingly presented political demands disguised as religion and multiculturalism, and deliberately labelled any objection to our demands as racism and bigotry. Even worse, we did this to the very generation who had been socialist sympathisers in their youth, people sympathetic to charges of racism, who were now in middle-career management posts; people like Dave Gomer. It is no wonder then that the authorities were unprepared to deal with politicised religion as ideological agitation, and felt racist if they tried to stop us.

The nearest comparison to our plans was, in a curious way, that of communism. The Cold War had not just been a battle between two military superpowers and their satellite states, but between two competing ideological systems. The West understood that communism was a direct threat to its way of doing business – the Soviet Union was both a physical and existential threat. This was why there was so much concern about 'reds under the bed' and the McCarthy witch-hunt in the 1950s. The campaign against communism continued right until the end of the Cold War, Ronald Reagan dubbing the USSR the 'evil empire' in the *Star Wars* parlance of the age.

Islamism demanded no less of a root-and-branch overhaul of society. But because it was cloaked in religious garb, no one quite knew what to do with it, and people were desperate not to offend. There was confusion over whether to define our activism as a cultural identity, an ideology or a faith. To top it off, Islamism went through a decade of being embraced by both the left and right wings. The default left-leaning liberal position was to embrace the movement as part of multicultural sensitivity: to tell people to stop practising their faith was imperialism in nineties clothing, a colonial hangover bordering on racism. Instead, we were embraced as a new generation of anti-colonial politicised youth. Curiously, the default position on the right was to embrace us too, because it had been the Afghan Mujahideen, backed by the CIA, who fought the Soviet Union. Lest we forget, this was when Hollywood films such as Stallone's *Rambo 3* portrayed the Afghan Mujahideen as heroes.

In fact, the only groups who were speaking out against HT at this stage were people like Jeremy Newmark – now of the Jewish Leadership Council – and gay-rights campaigner Peter Tatchell. This was fantastic propaganda for the Islamist narrative: the opposition of pro-Israeli and pro-gay-rights voices only reinforced the message we were trying to get across to Muslims. Back then Tatchell was something of a lone voice on HT, no one was listening to him, but credit is due to the man. 'The most dangerous of the Islamic fundamentalists is Hizb al-Tahrir', he wrote at the time. 'Hizb al-Tahrir is especially active on college campuses in London and Manchester . . . there is a hardcore of fundamentalists who are fanatics . . . Many [. . .] believe that all Muslims will go to Heaven if they kill for Allah.' His views and warnings were ignored, and we were left laughing at people's ignorance. In fact, as president of Newham Student Union, I remember an occasion when Ed and I received a press pack from the Union of Jewish Students, warning all unions about HT activities on campus. They had arranged a training and awareness day. As Newham College's Student Union, we decided to attend. That day we learnt all they intended to do to thwart us, and we simply returned to Newham to use it against them.

The authorities should have taken a different approach.

Imagine if it had been the far-right British National Party (BNP) growing on campus. Suppose that it was racism, instead of Islamism, spreading throughout the student population and the BNP had decided to stand in Student Union elections. If that had happened, and the BNP had taken over, the college would have acted immediately. They certainly would have seen the need for a solution, if only for their own reputation and the impact on admissions. They would have cited the college constitution about how hate speech was not allowed, how the BNP was an external political group attempting to hijack the college, and probably stopped them. But because of the religious element in our message, and the desire of the authorities not to offend our religious sensitivities, we were left alone.

Our success in winning the student elections felt as though it was part of a bigger picture. A few months before, HT had held a global *'Khilafah* Conference' at Wembley Arena and it was packed. I was one of 12,000 people attending from across the world. This was an astonishing sight and a huge boost to my belief in the cause. I still remember the roar of the crowd as it reached fever pitch, all 12,000 chanting *Allahu akbar*, God is Great! I recall how the thunder of their stomping feet shook the arena, and the world's media finally paid attention. It was hard not to come away without thinking that the momentum of historical change was behind us.

Becoming Student Union president felt like an extension of this momentum. Newham was the first college where HT had succeeded in gaining control of the union, which meant that the HT leadership noticed us. So I persuaded the then UK leader, Omar Bakri Muhammad, to come down to speak at the college, and this became another feather in my cap.

Omar Bakri Muhammad was a Syrian in the UK on political asylum; in those days he was a rather charismatic figure. Under Omar Bakri's leadership HT swept across the UK. This would not have been possible without his group of influential, rhetorically gifted lieutenants. The most outstanding of these was Farid Kasim, a former socialist, who converted back to Islam when he joined HT. Extremely articulate and intellectual, Kasim led the drive to recruit the student population into HT and used his former socialist tactics to do so. There was also Dr Abdul Wajid, Burhan Hanif and the three Khan brothers. Under Omar Bakri's leadership, these people successfully targeted universities, and got the organisation to the point where they could gather 12,000 supporters for the international conference at Wembley.

However, as well as growing in numbers, the UK section of HT was also growing in notoriety, which alarmed the *qiyadah* (HT's global leadership). Founded in Jerusalem in 1953, HT had chapters in almost every country in the world. Their sole purpose was to use their global presence to re-establish 'the *Khilafah*' in a Muslim-majority country. HT in the UK, however, was directly pitching the group's struggle against British society. Under Omar Bakri's leadership, they wrote pamphlets describing how they would conquer the political establishment, and would have the Islamic flag flying over Downing Street. Other pamphlets were overtly anti-Semitic. These tactics were provocative, and began to get the group noticed. The *qiyadah* didn't like that: it wanted to use the UK as a base for fundraising, for recruitment, media and diplomatic cover. It didn't want the British wing of the organisation to rock this carefully balanced, money-providing boat.

In Newham, rather than keeping a low profile, we continued to ratchet things up. As well as having control of the Student Union and its finances, we also had strength on the streets. There was a well-known local Pakistani gang in East Ham. Everyone in the area knew about these lads, and that they weren't to be messed with. To our delight, one of their former main guys decided to join HT. This gave us respect on the rough streets of London's East End, and we could enter any youth club or gathering, safe in the knowledge that we were protected.

In college, our campaigns became increasingly provocative and difficult to ignore. We put up a series of posters with a picture of a Muslim woman wearing a face veil, an AK-47 by her side. The image was a picture of a female Iranian revolutionary guard. Not that we were fans of Shi'ite Iran, but the picture was great for the point we wanted to make. The title of the poster, advertising a talk we were hosting, was 'Women of the West – Cover Up or Shut Up', and we put it up everywhere. As you can imagine, that drew a response from both students and staff. It was the first time that people started complaining about the Student Union, and we got called in to see Dave Gomer. We were completely unrepentant, and I justified our stance to the end.

'All I'm asking for is for people to leave us alone,' I argued somewhat disingenuously. 'This is how we believe women should dress: if you don't want to dress like this, that's your decision, but don't criticise our women for doing so, *i.e.: shut up!'*

Into this atmosphere, we arranged for Omar Bakri Muhammad to come and address the students. We wanted to make a good impression on the leadership and spent the week before creating a buzz about his visit. On the day of his talk, the hall was rammed full: everyone wanted to see him and hear what he had to say, including the Salafists. They turned up in the hope of heckling him, but Omar Bakri rebutted them with his usual flair. Here was someone who did have a beard, who spoke Arabic, and who had the theological authority from having studied *shari'ah* (Islamic jurisprudence) at Damascus University. By demonstrating that we could argue not just in terms of politics but also religion, we began to overshadow the Salafists, and this talk became a hugely successful coup for us.

Omar Bakri's appearance came amidst rising tension within the college. The conflict between HT and the Salafists was only one of the battles raging across campus. More serious, in some ways, were the racial tensions that had built up between Pakistani students and African students. For a long time the African students had been the dominant, threatening force within the college. They would intimidate the Pakistani students, and were also responsible for a wave of muggings. They demanded that students hand over their money, and got into fights over women. They did all this in the knowledge that the Pakistani students were unlikely to fight back.

I saw myself in these Pakistani students, the younger me who'd been punched and kicked in the stomach. Already battle-hardened, I understood instinctively that what these students needed was a cause. If they had a reason to stand up to these bullies, the tables would turn. The African group in college wasn't as large as the Pakistani one, but the active element of the former was bigger.

So I took it upon myself to change this, and to coordinate the Pakistani students into a force to be reckoned with. Being non-Muslim Africans, our opponents lacked my secret weapon – Islam. I immediately knew what would inspire the Pakistanis; I needed to recreate that rucksack moment between Osman and Mickey right here in the college. I had to inject them with the fever of Muslim jingoism. And so, unannounced, we walked into the student canteen, stood on the tables and just addressed all the students in full view. We blatantly challenged the non-Muslim Africans in front of everyone. And dared them to step up to the power of Islam, and warned them of Allah's wrath if they messed with Muslims. We were grossly outnumbered during these outbursts; there were usually only two or three of us. Yet we faced them unflinchingly, with a fire raging in our chests and the sort of conviction that animates one's expression. The African students didn't know what to do. Our brazen confidence threw them, and they just stood there gaping, watching us humiliate them orally. Ours was a calculated conflation of the HT message and self-defence: galvanising the students with the HT narrative, and getting them interested in the group's activities at the same time.

We'd inspire the students with tales of jihad, assure them of backup through our networks, but most of all we led by example. In the middle of such confrontations, which would often spill out into the college courtyard, we would suddenly drop into coordinated prayers, right there in the open in front of our adversaries. And after our prayers, we'd stand back up and shout *Allahu akbar* at the tops of our voices in unison, like a war cry. The African students all had knives; some of them were carrying machetes. But after everything I'd been through in Southend, that sort of weaponry didn't faze me. By this point, I'd been going around with my knife strapped to my back for years. It was second nature to me. I was so desensitised to the threat of violence that I could stand up to the African students without thinking twice. Imbued by my Islamist beliefs and the confidence of my election victory, I stoked the acrid atmosphere still further. Our display of fearless religious zeal did the trick, it galvanised the Pakistani youth, and it made them stand as Muslims. But it was only a matter of time before someone got badly hurt.

CHAPTER TEN

Servant of the Compeller

Hizb al-Tahrir's view on violence was that, while it condemned its members attacking others, it was reasonable to defend oneself. This policy wasn't universally agreed among the group's members; some from the more intellectual contingent thought it better not to carry weapons. They argued that it made the group look bad, and made it possible for people to conclude that we were terrorists. By not carrying any form of weapon, they argued, the distinction between HT and jihadists would be more clearly defined. For those of us facing groups like the African students, this all seemed somewhat theoretical. In practical terms, we needed to be able to defend ourselves, so I encouraged the Pakistani students in college to get more aggressively 'defensive'. The Africans quickly realised that something different was happening here – for the first time, they understood that things weren't going their way but they remained unsure of what to do.

One day, while all this was unfolding, a student who I didn't know approached me.

'Brother Maajid,' he said, 'there is someone on campus asking for you. He is going round trying to find out where you are.'

'What does he look like?'

'Tall,' the student said. 'A really tall black guy.'

My alarm bells immediately started ringing. This guy must be a friend of the Africans I thought. They must have called for backup to put me in my place. This is it, I thought, it's time. Everything I'd learnt back in Essex taught me to face such danger head on, so I walked around the college looking for this guy. I wanted it to be me who found him, rather than the other way round. And find him I did. It was hard to miss him, he was exactly as the student had said: a lanky twenty-something black guy, an entire head and shoulders taller than me. Adrenalin pumping, I walked straight up to the guy, fully expecting trouble. 'You're looking for me?'

'*Assalaamu alaykum, akhi*, are you brother Maajid?' he turned and said with a huge smile and a warm embrace. He smelled of the traditional scented oils, called attar, favoured by our Prophet '*alayhi salam* (upon whom be peace) and sold in contemporary Islamic bookshops.

It turned out that the lanky outsider was a jihadist Muslim from South London called Sa'eed Nur. Sa'eed had come to offer his 'support' to the now notorious 'HT brothers' in Newham College.

'Brother Maajid' – he always addressed me so respectfully – 'I heard of the great work you brothers are doing here and I'm here to offer you my support. No one can mess with you while I'm around, that's my promise *insha' Allah* – God willing.'

Sa'eed Nur hailed from a nascent jihadist scene that was

developing in Brixton, then one of London's roughest areas. He embodied the merger between religious literalism and Islamism I mentioned earlier. And though I wasn't a jihadist myself, I was relieved to have found his support: I felt confident in my ability to convert him to our cause over time. Sa'eed became, in effect, my bodyguard: he talked of bringing down 'fifty gunmen' from Brixton if we needed them, though he wasn't short of weaponry himself. At that first meeting, he reached into his leather jacket and pulled out a sword.

'This', he said, 'is Abdul Jabbar.'

In Islamic tradition, *Jabbar* is one of the ninety-nine names of Allah: it translates as the Compeller. Putting Abdul in front of it rendered the meaning: Servant of the Compeller. That was the name Sa'eed had chosen to give his sword.

'I've heard you're having some trouble with some nasty *kuffar* – infidels, here in the college. They're pestering our sisters?' Sa'eed asked, looking sincerely disturbed at this thought.

'So any time you need help,' he continued, sliding the sword back away, 'just give me a call, *akhi*. I'll come down *fee sabeelillah* – in the path of Allah – and sort it out for you.' He then handed me his home phone number written on a piece of paper, and with another embrace sought my leave, ironically with the words '*assalaamu alaykum* – Peace be upon you'.

The first time he turned up, Sa'eed Nur felt like a gift from Allah. Here was someone who appeared, as if out of nowhere, to offer us unconditional physical support. The *seerah* – life of our Prophet *'alayhi salam* – seemed to affirm such divine providence. Islamic tradition relates how the Prophet was granted similar *nussra* (support) by the conversion of his warrior uncle Hamza to Islam. By drawing analogies between Sa'eed's appearance and Hamza, we reinforced our belief that ours was the righteous path. The fact that Sa'eed was black was perfect: it reinforced the point I'd been making to the Pakistanis that this wasn't a racial issue. The dividing line was between Muslims and the rest of the world. Whether it was the white Muslims in Bosnia, black Muslims like Sa'eed or Pakistani Muslims, it was our *deen* (religion) that gave us our identity and united us.

The next time Sa'eed came to campus, with steely determination he asked to see the Africans. I pointed them out to him and he strode over to speak to their crew. If my standing up to the gang had surprised them, seeing this lanky black man taking our side shook them even more. I'd already warned Sa'eed that they'd be packing knives, but with Abdul Jabbar hidden inside his jacket, and Allah on his side, that didn't worry him much at all. He walked right into the centre of their group, in front of a packed and gawping student common room, and offered to take them all on, at the top of his voice, in one clean sweep.

'You dirty *kuffar*! You think you're bad men? I'll have fifty gunmen up in here in no time!' he growled.

'We love death more than you love life. Come, all of you, come and taste death if you dare!'

And not yet satisfied with the level of physical intimidation he had just wrought, he went round, one by one, asking each of them who felt confident enough to challenge him. None of them stood up to him.

'Right,' Sa'eed said, 'if you're not man enough to take me on, you stay away from my brothers!'

And there it was – the Muslims of Newham College had just found their rucksack moment. This wasn't a private confrontation. Everyone saw it, and word quickly got around. You could almost see it ripple through the student body. They knew now that they had Sa'eed to back them up if things kicked off. Likewise, they saw that, though I didn't quite have Sa'eed's menacing presence, I had challenged the Africans and had come away unscathed.

These events took place over a couple of months, during which the whole atmosphere in the college changed. Sa'eed would come down regularly, and wander around the campus with impunity. Security, it has to be said, was fairly lax. The authorities never challenged the fact that a man in his mid-twenties was hanging about, and there were no metal detectors to pick up that he carried a sword. Buoyed by his support, we were running campaigns like the 'Cover Up or Shut Up' posters. We were inviting Omar Bakri and other high-profiles leaders to speak, confident of the reception we'd get. And the Pakistani students were making their presence felt for the first time. Our vision of Islamicising the college was going to plan.

The Africans, however, were still adjusting to this shift in power. After the initial shock of being challenged, and watching the Muslim students assert themselves, the hardcore elements of the gang began to regroup. One day, there was a stand-off in the common room. This would all have been fairly typical stuff, were it not for one of the African crew, Ayotunde Obanubi, pulling out a penknife and slashing at a Muslim student. No one was hurt, but everyone split, and word of what had happened got around pretty quickly.

I was outraged. The following morning, I organised a show of strength. I got as many Muslim students to gather in the courtyard as I could, to take part in a spontaneous rally. As the African students stood there aghast, we chanted '*Allahu akbar!*' marching round the square declaring our presence. Again, we prayed right there on the street in front of the courtyard, supremely confident that the Africans would not dare attack us while we prayed. For us, prayer had become a propaganda tool and a means of intimidation, not the calming spiritual experience it was meant to be. And then he arrived. I'm not sure who had called Sa'eed, he'd offered his number to everyone, but he was aware of the incident in the common room and his eyes were bloodshot red. If I had known better, or cared to know, I would have recognised the look on his face for the bloodlust that it was.

The atmosphere was suddenly speed and adrenalin. Ayotunde was there with his gang. He watched with contempt as we marched and chanted. He'd come prepared. He was ready for trouble. Then suddenly Sa'eed approached him. Words were being exchanged. I decided I must get closer. Ayotunde had already pulled out a pair of butcher's knives: two big, ugly, nasty blades. He was waving them at Sa'eed. He was shouting at Sa'eed. He was attacking Sa'eed. I am behind Sa'eed. Ayotunde is slashing with his butcher's knives at Sa'eed's leather jacket. He is trying to stab Sa'eed. What to do? How to react? I reach for my blade. I unclip my blade. What to do?

But my world slowed down again as soon as Sa'eed's voice resonated across the courtyard. There was an air of absolute calm in him. He was in an uncanny, almost hypnotic, control of his emotions. If he felt threatened he certainly didn't show it. Instead, he looked at Ayotunde and in a measured matter-of-fact tone, said: 'If you don't put them away right now, I will have to kill you.'

That sentence has haunted my soul to this day. Ayotunde didn't heed Sa'eed's warning but continued slashing at his leather jacket with the knives. By this point, I was certain that Ayotunde was going to get hurt. I told myself this was self-defence. We Muslims are a just people, I thought, but we're not pacifists. We don't transgress, but if someone wants to pick a fight, they'd better be prepared to fight to the death. Sa'eed opened his leather jacket and pulled out Abdul Jabbar.

Then, from the corner of my eye, with my hand still on my blade, I noticed Dave Gomer, the student-liaison officer. He was standing right behind Ayotunde. He had come rushing out of the building after all the commotion. I saw him take in the situation, size up Ayotunde brandishing his butcher's knives, Sa'eed with his sword, and me standing behind Sa'eed. Gomer didn't recognise Sa'eed, wasn't particularly aware of who Ayotunde was, but knew me all right. He looked at me, straight in the eye; it was the most arresting glance, one of extreme disappointment, rather than anger. The look was of someone feeling so badly let down. I trusted you, I could see him thinking. I trusted you to keep all this under control. Gomer couldn't have known that I had unsheathed my knife, not from where he was standing, because it was still hidden behind my back and beneath my clothes. But I was there, and for him that was enough.

It was one of those moments where my life could have gone one of two ways. Sometimes the smallest of decisions can have the largest consequences. But Dave Gomer's look cut through me. His cold disappointment at what I was doing sliced through the white heat of my adrenalin. It pulled me up sharp, and for a crucial split second I had a flash of realisation about what I might be about to do. I slid my knife back into its sheath, clicked it back in place and pulled back, completely back. No one knew what I'd done, no one knew how close I had been. Till this day Dave Gomer has absolutely no idea of the effect his look had on me. He probably thinks he failed at that college. But without his presence, my life would have taken an entirely different turn. And for that, I will be forever grateful to him.

The sad truth is that while I was fortunate enough to have Dave Gomer there to check my behaviour, there was no one around to check Sa'eed's. No sooner had I slipped my knife back into its sheath, than he was doing precisely the opposite with his sword. In one swift, calm, almost mechanical movement, Sa'eed plunged his monstrous blade, Abdul Jabbar, the Servant of the Compeller, deep into Ayotunde's chest.

That was the signal. As soon as Sa'eed knifed Ayotunde, from all sides young Pakistani kids came piling in: some had weapons like hammers and knives, others were just kicking and punching. It was a vicious, frenzied assault way beyond my control at this stage. Ayotunde, I knew immediately, had no chance.

Dave Gomer was sensible enough not to do anything either. If he'd intervened he could have ended up like the headmaster Philip Lawrence, who was killed trying to break up another London knife-fight. As it became clear that Ayotunde wasn't getting up, everyone involved ran. There was pandemonium. There were people screaming, onlookers wanting to get out of the way, those with weapons wanting to disappear before the police appeared and there was blood all over the floor. As the emergency services arrived some sort of order was slowly restored. The paramedics went straight to Ayotunde, and desperately tried to revive him as his body convulsed in its final death throes. I stood there and watched Ayotunde Obanubi die.

CHAPTER ELEVEN

The womb that bore me

The college courtyard was now a murder scene, and the police were soon asking questions. I hadn't been involved in the actual attack and felt that I had no reason to run. I wanted to give the police our side of the story, to explain what had been going on. Ayotunde had attacked first; he'd brought knives to a sword fight, and lost. Sa'eed Nur had responded in self-defence. That sounds brutal, I know, but at the time it's what I believed.

Though I was never arrested myself – having *just* avoided being directly involved – the police wanted to see if I could be a prosecution witness. I was introduced to a young lawyer, who was an up-and-coming HT *daris* at the time. His name was Anjem Choudary. Having run the events of the day past Anjem, he assured me that there was nothing prejudicial to the defence in what I said. And as we sat together discussing this in a fast food restaurant I remember Anjem commenting on how 'sharp' I was for a seventeen-year-old.

'This one will make a great *da'i* – activist – one day,' he said, turning to his colleague.

Anjem Choudary would later go on to lead one of Britain's most notorious, and eventually banned, Salafi-Jihadist organisations, known as al-Muhajiroun. (More recently, Anjem had completely forgotten our meetings, until I gave him a rude awakening during our now infamous debate hosted by Jeremy Paxman on BBC *Newsnight*. It's worth catching online for entertainment value alone. Back at Newham College, full of a sense of injustice, I recalled my story to the police. I said that Ayotunde had been armed with two knives and had attacked first. I explained how the African students had a long history of bullying the Muslim students, and this incident was the culmination of that. My opinions were so strident that when Sa'eed Nur was arrested and charged with the murder, my views never made it to court. Nor was I called as a witness by the prosecution because my memories did not suit the conviction. I wasn't called by the defence because it would have looked as though Sa'eed was part of an organised Islamist conspiracy, and that wouldn't have helped his defence. I had to find out for myself afterwards that Sa'eed had been put away for life. One of the students, sixteen-year-old Umran Qadir, was also convicted for participating in the murder. Though charges were eventually dropped against another student, Kazi Nurur Rahman, he would go on to be arrested in a 2005 police sting, buying three Uzi sub-machine guns and beginning negotiations to purchase Sam-7 missiles and rocket-propelled grenades.

As the crowds began to disperse, Ayotunde's friends passed me and whispered harsh calls for revenge. My instincts kicked in. I knew that to avoid retaliation these guys would need to witness just how doggedly we were prepared to defend ourselves. The initiative had to be seized by us, and speed was everything. That night I was picked up by some of the former Pakistani gang members; they had managed to find out where a few of the African students lived. We reached their address and parked up outside, keeping the car running with its lights on. Our aim was to be seen, and so we waited until someone came to the window and saw us. Immediately, the curtains were drawn in what was probably fear. We wanted to scare them and send a message – if you haven't had enough yet, we're still here and have more to offer. Once they'd seen us, we drove away, job done.

I'm not proud of what I did. And behaving like this certainly wasn't something endorsed by HT. What we did that night, a calculated move to instil terror in the hearts of men just after their friend had been murdered, is probably the lowest I've ever stooped in my life. Despite all that has happened since, I hesitated including this detail in my story. Sa'eed Nur's hypnotically calm, chilling warning *If you don't put them away right now, I will have to kill you* still chills my blood over seventeen years later. But ultimately, I want people to gain a true glimpse of what it was like during the heyday of *Londonistan* and how we got there. It is difficult to argue now that going to their house that night was self-defence, but that's what we did. My seventeen-year-old reasoning was that the African students had started it. They'd come tooled up and had lashed out at Sa'eed Nur. We needed to petrify them enough that they backed off. On a crude level, it worked: they stopped.

My deepest condolences go to Ayotunde's family. Such a cold-blooded response to the murder of another individual was part and parcel of the person that I'd become. There was a total desensitisation from the violence I'd grown up around. My reaction, too, was inextricably bound together with my membership of HT. And everything I am today, and all the work I'm doing to push back against Islamism, would not be possible if I had not joined HT and then left all the wiser.

It is very difficult to separate who I am now from everything I have been through. I remain cognisant – as brought out so starkly in William Golding's *Lord of the Flies* – that given the right circumstances most ordinary people are capable of descending to despicable depths. I might now actively campaign against the views that HT espouse, but my skills in being able to argue and to organise, to rally and inspire, all undoubtedly come from my training in the organisation. To ask if I regretted joining HT then is a difficult question to answer. It would mean I regretted who I am now; that I regretted my current work, myself, and I don't think that can be the case. Some people may not like that answer, but it's the only honest one I have. Sometimes the truth can be like that: harder and harsher, more bitter than people would ever care to admit. And that's why my truth keeps hurting me every day.

The murder incident redoubled my commitment to HT. Dave Gomer's intervention seemed to square with the views of the HT leadership, that direct action was not the way. Once you went down that route, you were exposing yourself to the consequences. The more I thought about it, the more I realised that I shouldn't have driven round with some of the former gang members that evening. That was an aberration. The HT philosophy was to challenge and to stir things up, but take things no further. The murder reinforced for me that the HT line was the right one to follow.

That was despite the response of the HT leadership to events. It was Ed Husain and I who were responsible for HT at the college. Ed had been nowhere near the incident: he was studying hard when the murder took place. As I was the one who had been there in the thick of it, I went to see Omar Bakri to explain what had happened. I was smart enough not to mention the former gang members, but told him everything else. As far as I was concerned, I had been following the edict of the group to the letter. I was whipping the place into fervour as per his instructions. Omar Bakri, after all, had visited the college himself the week before, and had offered no criticism of our conduct. Indeed, he'd seemed delighted with what we'd achieved.

Omar Bakri, however, was under pressure from the *qiyadah*. As I mentioned earlier, he was criticised for the way the British wing was bringing heat on the whole organisation. On top of this, there were voices within the UK organisation that were critical of his tactics: these included the physicist Fouad Abu Mohammed. On two fronts, then, his provocative leadership was under attack. Now that a murder had taken place, the dissenting voices rose to fever pitch.

Even so, I still expected his support for what happened. Omar Bakri sat and listened to everything I said, and then ignored it. He went out and gave media interviews where he denied any HT role in the incident, said the organisation had never campaigned on the campus and condemned Sa'eed Nur for the attack. I was deeply saddened by this. Though it was true that HT had no direct role in the murder itself, condemning Sa'eed Nur without condemning ourselves was a step too far for me. Sa'eed had come to the college to help us; we were the ones, under Omar Bakri's guidance, who had whipped up the tension. Now this brother was being sold down the river for the sake of political expediency. My support for HT didn't waver, but my belief in Omar Bakri never really recovered from that. Whereas before I would have unconditionally followed whatever instructions he gave me, I now felt myself doubting his sincerity.

As it turned out, one of the outcomes of the murder was that it saved me from following Omar Bakri. His attempts to shore up his position by distancing the group from the murder were not enough, and his leadership deteriorated to the point that, just a few months afterwards, he was suspended by the *qiyadah*. Seeking a new niche, Bakri reincarnated himself as even more extreme. He became a Salafi-Jihadist and went on to form the now banned group, al-Muhajiroun, which eventually became the banned Islam4UK. Anjem Choudary, the diminutive but passionate Abdur Rahman from Redbridge College and some other prominent HT activists followed Omar Bakri in this folly. About a dozen or so of al-Muhajiroun's members have since been convicted for terrorism-related offences in the UK alone. This new group continued the same aggressive tactics Omar Bakri had employed while leader of HT, most notoriously protesting in Luton when the bodies of soldiers are returned from Afghanistan. That protest led to the creation, in response, of the now infamous far-right anti-Islam group called the English Defence League (EDL) headed by Tommy Robinson, real name Stephen Lennon. It's deeply ironic that Islamist and anti-Islam extremist groups have a symbiotic relationship with each other, feeding off each other's paranoia and propaganda: far-right extremism, Islamism, more far-right extremism, more Islamism and so on.

If Omar Bakri hadn't given those press interviews, he may have had my continued support. When he founded his new organisation, like many HT members I could have followed him. But having lost that emotional pull towards him, it was easier for me to stay with HT proper, and their new policy of drawing back from aggression. For example, it was decided that showing the videos of the atrocities in Bosnia was pumping up emotions to a fervour that was difficult to control: the line between Islamism and Jihadism was in danger of becoming blurred. The new leadership wanted to distance itself from any suggestion of violence: an order went out that the carrying of knives or other weapons for self-defence was no longer allowed.

In terms of my passion, I was closer to the position of Omar Bakri than this new leadership. But Omar Bakri hadn't backed me up, whereas those that remained had done so. And so I gave them a chance. Nasim was crucial here. He was rising through HT ranks rapidly, and was insistent that I stayed in the group. Importantly, he believed my version of what had happened at Newham. That meant a lot, and in return I fell in behind the group's new direction. I stopped carrying my knife around for the first time in years. I'd got so used to having it strapped behind my back that to begin with it felt strange not having it there, that something was missing. I could have thrown the knife away I guess, but instead I decided to keep it. It remains in my desk drawer till today, to remind me of where I've come from.

Omar Bakri wasn't the only person to leave HT: in completely different circumstances, and for different reasons, Ed Husain also decided to leave. Unlike me, he hadn't had to grow up around such violence. The murder brought him up sharp. He wanted no part of it or the organisation after that. Importantly, he had just met Faye, another student at the college and his future wife. Faye had managed to show Ed a different way, that he didn't need to be so angry, and Ed followed Faye to a softer form of Islamism, before moving away from it completely. I tried hard to change Ed's mind about leaving, went to his house on a number of occasions to try to dissuade him, but without success. We talked at cross-purposes: I was trying to have an intellectual discussion, to reason with him to stay, whereas Ed's decision to leave was an emotional one. Ed's departure from the group was a painful moment: we had become very close friends over the previous months and I knew our relationship would simply not be the same again.

The final change was over my education. Having let the situation escalate, Newham College now made up for lost time. Determined to root out the problem, the school expelled the entire Student Union committee with immediate effect. 'Your presence', the letter read, 'is not conducive to a safe and secure environment in the college.' As you can imagine, my parents hit the roof. Again, my saving grace was that my expulsion was not for the murder. I had not been arrested or charged for that, and so I could say to my mother that they were overreacting – they were banning me because of my political activism.

Nevertheless, Abi and I had a huge argument about what I should do next. I wanted to start again at another London college: to carry on as before, continuing my HT activities. Abi, though, wanted me back in Southend where she could keep a closer eye on me.

'Why don't you go to the local grammar school?' she argued.

Grammar schools are selective schools, and still around in counties like Essex, where only those students who gain high grades are admitted so they can be taught in an accelerated environment, away from the comprehensive school system.

'You've got the grades and could do well there.'

I was only thinking about HT, and insisted on returning to London. Back and forth this discussion went on through the night. Abi said that she wouldn't fund me going back to live in London. I responded that I was going, and I would find the money so I could do so.

That was too much for her. Even though I hadn't been expelled for the murder, and even though she didn't really understand it, my mother sensed that something had happened at the college to get me expelled. She could tell that there was something about the crowd I was involved with that she wanted to keep me away from. The argument got more and more heated, until at about four o'clock in the morning, exhausted, she lost hope; but she didn't stop. Totally exasperated by her errant, stubborn son who would not come home, Abi started to weep and began beating her womb.

'I curse you!' she sobbed between the blows against her stomach. 'I curse the womb that gave me such a son: a son who will not listen to his own mother!'

As I watched her in horror, I felt every blow she inflicted on herself. 'Stop it!' I implored, forcing down her hands, and I began to cry. I couldn't watch her do that; it was too much for me, what had I reduced my mother to? So I stopped arguing, and agreed that I would come home, and try to get into the grammar school. It was the best decision I had made in a while.

Soon after I went for an interview at Westcliff High School for Boys, with the then headmaster Mr Baker. My immersion in the culture of hip hop at secondary school level meant that I didn't pay much attention to my GCSE grades, which just about qualified me for admission but were nowhere near the grades that all the other students there had gained. However, I was able to talk Mr Baker into letting me in.

'I am a lot more mature from my time out,' I explained. 'I want to study and really believe I could do well.'

I didn't tell Mr Baker that I had been expelled from Newham College. Instead I said that I'd decided to take a year out. Before everything was computerised such manoeuvres were so much easier to pull off. In fact, it was not until many years later, when Mr Baker invited me back to the school to address the student assembly, that I revealed during the course of my talk how I had talked him into letting me in without telling him about the murder and the expulsion. The students all burst out in approving, roaring laughter, while poor Mr Baker flushed every shade of red until I thought the man would have a heart attack.

If nothing else, my HT training had taught me how to argue. To Mr Baker, my seventeen-year-old self must have come across as an articulate and confident young man. To Abi's relief, I impressed him, and he offered me an unconditional place. Abi's desperate intervention to force me to stay in

Southend saved my academic career. I certainly would not have ended up at university if on that night, in the early hours of the morning, Abi hadn't beaten the womb that bore me.

CHAPTER TWELVE

A show of hands to harden the heart

Westcliff High School for Boys could not have been more different to Newham College. I'd gone from a secondary school, where I could count the number of black and Asian people in my year on one hand, to a London campus where Muslim students were the largest bloc. Now I was back at a boys-only Southend school, where again almost everyone else was white.

I stood out from the start, and not just because of my skin colour. I was unique in my year for having taken a 'year out'. I was a year older than them and more experienced. I also had my own car: a Vauxhall Astra SRI and I had a formidable reputation in the town from my pre-HT days. When I turned up, many of the kids knew who I was. 'You're Maajid? *The* Maajid?' 'Yes, I am, and I'm back,' I said.

A combination of that and the fact it was a grammar school meant, for the first time in my career, I was not under threat. The other students were intelligent and studious, a little sheltered but well meaning. By contrast, I probably seemed exciting and dangerous. In the time since I'd joined HT and been away in London, the whole problem of racism in Southend had died down substantially. A younger generation of B-boys, Moe's younger brother, Chill's younger brother and others had taken over and Southend would never be the same again. During those two years I spent studying for my A levels, I experienced almost no racism whatsoever.

This peacefulness allowed me the time and space needed to really develop intellectually. I'd always been reasonably capable, but had never bothered to apply myself before – I used to rely on 'winging it' to get by, without making much effort. Now, feeling settled, I got into my studies. I discovered what I could achieve if I really put my mind to it. This excited and inspired me.

Even now, the teachers that I had there still stick in my mind. My history teacher was Dr White – he had a PhD in his subject, and really knew his stuff. A number of the students were scared of him because he was strict, but intellectually he was amazing. The combination of discipline and knowledge meant that he had a huge amount of respect in the school. Mr Moth and Mr Skelly, who took my economics class, were also fantastic teachers. I appreciated the fact that my teachers genuinely seemed to like me, and that I could talk to them one on one.

Mr Moth was a lovely guy. He was gay, and quite relaxed about it, but because my 'gaydar' was so terrible I failed to pick up on this. Once, some students and I had managed to get on to the topic of homosexuality. I found myself openly making homophobic jokes while waiting for our economics class to begin. Behind the jokes was the fact that in HT we prescribed death for homosexuals in our '*Khilafah*'. Mr Moth entered as my jokes were in full swing, and I continued, totally oblivious to the hurt I could have caused him. A kind soul, he went along with my childish jokes by hiding under the table and pretending to shake as the class roared with laughter. It was only afterwards, to my utter embarrassment, that everyone said to me 'You do know he is gay, right?'

Despite this Mr Moth continued to treat me not just with respect, but also with encouragement. I can credit him as the teacher who made me see for the first time what I might be able to achieve academically. I'd been thinking about doing a law degree, which before the A-star grade was introduced required three Bs at A level for entry. When the time came to apply to university, Mr Moth shocked me by setting my official predicted grade as an 'A' in economics – that meant I could get in to study Arabic and law, which required these higher grades to apply. I remember asking him in disbelief, 'Are you sure?' But he responded with certainty that I could do it.

'I predict that you'll go very far in life, Maajid. You'll become something like an ambassador, or take on a similarly important role.'

To myself I thought, 'I'd rather be the Caliph's ambassador to Britain.'

But still, I was grateful that Mr Moth held me in such high esteem. This was a moment akin to when Dave Gomer gave me that look just before the murder. I had this overwhelming feeling that I didn't want to let Mr Moth down. Predicting an 'A' to a former B-boy from a comprehensive school background was a risk for Mr Moth, but as a kind and dedicated mentor he had shown faith in me, and so I worked harder for him.

However well I got on at Westcliff High School I still couldn't quite shake the sense of feeling different. Part of the history syllabus was British Imperial history, and so we studied British India. We looked in detail at the Raj. We studied events like the Indian 'Mutiny', where even the name of the event is significant. In the Indian subcontinent the event is referred to as a 'The First War of Independence', rather than a mutiny implying false rebellion. During one lesson, as we were discussing India and the Raj, the teacher asked the class, 'How many of you here are proud of our Empire and its achievements?' Everyone put a hand up, except for me. 'Is there anyone who isn't?' All looked round as I put mine up. This moment stuck fast in my mind. I sat there in class and pondered for a while that 'No matter how well I get along with these people, no matter how much I hide my beliefs, they will always see me as belonging to a race they *civilised*.' It was just enough to override the individual kindness Mr Moth had shown me, and for me to interpret his behaviour as an exception to this norm.

On the whole, although I was studying economics, politics and history, the subject matter did not contradict the knowledge I'd gleaned from being in HT. The Ottoman Empire and Muslim history weren't on the syllabus, so those issues never came up. In economics, we looked at different theories like those of Keynes and the classicists; in politics it was about studying different systems and how they worked;

all of which merely reinforced what I'd been taught by HT. Even when we were discussing topics, like India, where there was a natural difference of opinion between the other students and me, that was OK. Part of the way that history was taught in the school (as, indeed with my other subjects) was to look at the pros and cons of any particular argument. So the fact that I considered the Indian Mutiny an uprising was fine – the important thing was to be able to look at both sides, before coming up with a conclusion.

I remember having one discussion with my politics teacher Mr Bergen about democracy and its flaws. I argued that the British system created a situation where, under the first past the post system, a party could win a minority of the vote yet gain the majority of seats in Parliament. Mr Bergen's response was to paraphrase Winston Churchill, that democracy was the worst possible system of government, with the exception of all the other ones. I took this as a victory. I thought, you only think that because you do not know about the alternative, 'the *Khilafah*'. But I didn't take the opportunity to come back at him with my HT beliefs: I wasn't there to push my case or try to recruit, I was there to learn. I wanted to get to university, and be in a position to begin recruiting again. Instead, I continued to test and hone my arguments.

Although I had left Newham behind, and the London flat and all the regular discussions with other HT activists, my game plan was still very much focused around the group. When Omar Bakri left, he took with him not only the more aggressive tactics, but also the more thuggish elements of HT. What remained was the more thoughtful, more serious side of the organisation. The emphasis now was on activists focusing on their studies – HT didn't want people getting expelled or ruining their education. They wanted to produce pillars of society who believed in our ideology and who would be of real use in Muslim majority countries. In an echo of my grandfather moving to Britain to make the most of its schooling for his children, HT stressed how respected the British education system was abroad. To gain qualifications in the UK and then travel to work in places like Egypt, Pakistan and Jordan would give the activists access to the best jobs. That suited HT's cause: they wanted to control the intellectual life of a nation, to be in such a position of influence that they could hijack the army and instigate a coup. The fact that recruitment was on the rise in British universities gave them an opportunity to do this.

Nasim continued to look out for me, and while still studying for my A levels, I was fast-tracked into an elite group of five activists they wanted to make members as soon as possible. One evening a week, I would drive up to London for my *halaqah* (private study circle). The calibre of the people was high – once again, I was the youngest in our group, and the intensity of the sessions helped my education. For example, amongst the material we studied was Marxism and the concept of dialectical materialism. The detail we went into was far more advanced than what I was learning in my politics A level, so when I went back to class I had a knowledge and intellectual rigour that in many respects was way ahead of the other students. Constructed ignorance, I now call the state of my HT thoughts back then, a sort of pseudo-intellectualism that is just enough to make a teenager feel highly intelligent.

As well as the week-night study sessions, I also gave my weekends to recruiting. Despite the way things had turned out at Newham, the leadership remained impressed with how I'd brought interest and activists to the cause. I was selected as part of a team seeking to create an HT cell at Cambridge University. I'd go up on a Saturday morning and spend most of the weekend there. Among the team were Amjad Izmeth, a British-Sri Lankan medical student from Barts Medical College and Reza Pankhurst, a British-Persian computer science student from King's College.

We would go to the prayer hall and the mosque, and get talking to the students. We'd befriend them, take them out for food and engage with them in discussions about Islam and, ultimately, Islamism. There was a student called Arshad, who was reading Arabic at Cambridge and had already expressed an interest in HT. It was up to us to firm this up, and make him properly committed to the cause. During this time, as well as going to Cambridge, I also recruited a cell back in Southend. The Muslim community there were pleasantly surprised at my and Osman's conversion, and many held me up as an example to their sons, which I took full advantage of. We played on that notoriety and named ourselves the 'Essex Islamic Forum'. Among those I recruited was Sajid Verda. Sajid was an actor, and a successful one: he'd gained a role in the television adaptation of *Adrian Mole* and was destined for bigger things, until we recruited him. We told him to give up his acting and focus on his activism, which he did. Such immature advice probably ruined his career. I also recruited students from the other local grammar school, Southend High for Boys. Although there were Muslims at Westcliff, I made the decision not to recruit there. I couldn't risk being expelled again, and left them alone, to the point of not even speaking to them.

At the same time, I was thinking about my university choice. I had wanted to study Arabic, and my father wanted me to study law. There was one university that offered a combination of both, and that was SOAS: the School of Oriental and African Studies in London. To my delight, I got the very grades my teachers had predicted, and I was offered a place at SOAS. This pleased my parents enormously: more importantly for me, it also pleased HT. Out of our elite group I was the first one selected to become a full member of the group, a *hizbi*. It wasn't a big ceremony: just one on one with Nasim, who by now was one of the leaders of the national group. I swore an oath of allegiance to God, the Qur'an and to obey and follow the instructions of the group's leader, or *amir*. I promised to represent the ideology at all costs, and to be prepared to make sacrifices for the cause. Convinced of the injustice of non-Islam, or *kufr*, I meant every word I uttered with the chilling sincerity of a true believer.

CHAPTER THIRTEEN

The romanticism of struggle

If I had thought becoming a full member of Hizb al-Tahrir was going to lead me into an inner sanctum of understanding, I was in for a shock. Within a couple of days of taking my oath, I was instead introduced to a world of internecine fighting and ideological division. That's the polite version: what was almost as accurate a comparison was Monty Python's film *Life of Brian*, with the Judean People's Front arguing it out with the People's Front of Judea. This, though, wasn't comedy, but a real life episode with a vicious sting in the tail.

It wasn't just the UK division of HT where disagreements over policy erupted: the same was true of the global leadership as well. The leadership had been in the hands of Abdul Qadeem Zalloom; he was from Palestine, where the group had its origins and had huge support there and among Palestinian Jordanians. However, some of the more dogmatic and puritanical elements of the group were unhappy at the way he ran things. One of the many disputes, and it was here where things entered *Life of Brian* territory, was over the introduction of colour into publications. HT's books had traditionally been white, with a red font on the cover: under Zalloom's leadership, a variety of colours had been introduced into the group's publications. For the purists, this was anathema: they felt the look of the books had always been different, and were easily recognisable in bookshops. Now they just looked the same as everyone else's: symbolic, to them, of the way that under Zalloom's leadership the group was losing its distinctive message.

A new grouping was led by Abu Rami, who had previously been a member of the leadership committee. Rami's stance found favour in Europe and in the Far East, whereas Zalloom's support was in the Middle East. The UK was one of the countries unsure which grouping to support. Some of its senior members, like Farid Kasim, instinctively decided to side with Abu Rami. He had been Nasim's mentor in the same way that Nasim was mine.

All this was happening as I became a member. Within a matter of days of taking my oath we were receiving delegates from the Middle East, pitching to HT in Britain to take their side. There was a cloak and dagger element in all of this. No one was ever quite sure where the global leadership was – they kept their locations hidden for security reasons. Also no one was completely sure which side a delegate was from. Was he from the original leadership or from Abu Rami? Was he pretending to be from the other side in order to check our reaction? It was typical of the way the organisation was run that no one was completely sure.

In a member's house in South London about thirty or so UK members gathered to be told it was down to our own consciences who we decided to back. I may have been the youngest in the room, but I felt compelled to speak.

'How dare you come here and tell us to choose!' I snapped. 'You know that the means to acquire the leadership is done through the electoral college of the *qiyadah*. What you should be saying is that Abu Rami is a *nakith*, an oath breaker, and a *baghi*, a usurper. You have no choice but to consider him and anyone who associates with him as usurpers.'

The delegate was taken aback by the ferocity of my argument.

'Brother Maajid,' he asked. 'How long have you been a member of HT?'

'Two days.'

'Well,' he said, somewhat patronisingly, 'I've been a member for fifteen years.'

'I don't care,' I came back, now even more riled at his attitude. 'The *haq* – truth, isn't judged by how long you have been a member. What is right is right, and that's the end of it.'

By this point, although he hadn't said so, I was certain he was touting for us to join Abu Rami's group.

A couple of days later a second delegate arrived from the Middle East. He was Algerian, and was there to argue the case for Abdul Qadeem Zalloom's leadership. For the majority of us this man felt like the real deal, and we were inclined to trust him. Together with another *hizbi*, Irfan, I took the Algerian back to the hotel where he was staying and returned to my student halls of residence feeling more relaxed about the situation.

The following morning, however, when Irfan went to pick him up, there was no reply from his room. After knocking repeatedly and getting no answer, Irfan persuaded the hotel staff to let him in. He discovered the Algerian delegate lying dead on the bathroom floor, his trousers round his ankles. There were no signs of trauma or bullet wounds on his body.

He hadn't struck me, when we'd dropped him off the night before, as someone who was about to die. At the same time, there were no shortage of enemies who might have wanted him dead, and the techniques were available to do so. The Israelis, for example, were known for using non-traceable poisons. We knew that because we were attempting the overthrow of certain regimes, it was likely that their intelligence agents were operating against us. And it could have been an internal affair: Algeria was locked in a vicious civil war between its military leaders and the Islamist and jihadist rebels. Then there were rumours that the split in HT had been caused by Jordanian intelligence infiltrating our ranks, there were suggestions that Abu Rami was acting on behalf of Jordanian intelligence, and it was they who had killed the delegate for his support of Zalloom. We never got to the truth, and probably never will.

Then Abu Rami also died. Again, trying to discover exactly what happened was impossible. Prior to Rami's death Zalloom had confidently written to all HT chapters around the world, offering an amnesty to any members who had left – they could come back into the fold within a certain time limit. Rami had died just around that time limit. Zalloom then wrote another letter, slamming Rami and his followers: anyone who hadn't rejoined before his death would never be allowed to return.

Even so, my life was moving forwards. I was at SOAS, doing a course I wanted to do. I was a full member of HT. I was seen as one of the most effective recruiters in the organisation.

I was given the responsibility for coordinating activities across Central and South London. Two of my *dariseen* at that time were Adam Mohamed and Imad Shoubaki, a Palestinian whose brother had been martyred in the Bosnia jihad. Both these two would later go on to be arrested in 2007 under UK terrorism law after seeking urgent flying lessons, allegedly paid for in cash, and being linked to BA pilot Samir Jamaluddin, whose brother Yakoob was also associated with HT. Adam, Imad and pilot Samir were eventually acquitted, but Samir lost his BA job and Adam and Imad probably returned to the Islamist subculture.

During these years I once bumped into my old friend Ed Husain from Newham by the steps of SOAS. By now Ed was a history student at the University of North London, and had joined the Labour Party. We greeted each other warmly, and soon moved on to discussing New Labour. Ed had become a huge, huge fan of Tony Blair.

'How can you admire that infidel, that *kafir*?' I asked.

'What's wrong with him?' came Ed's slightly frustrated reply.

'He's an enemy of Allah.'

'Maajid, I must tell you, anyone who calls Tony Blair an enemy of Allah, is my enemy.'

I was taken aback; this was my one-time best friend, whom I'd loved dearly.

'Even me, *akhi*?' I asked rather disturbed. 'Because I cannot say otherwise, Tony Blair is my enemy.'

'Then we can no longer be friends.' And with that Ed Husain walked right off out of my life, cutting all ties. 'Rather extreme of you', I thought without a hint of irony.

At this stage I felt that something was missing in my life. That something was a meaningful relationship. I'd already had my share of romantic liaisons, starting way back with Sarah – the girl I'd left on my first day at secondary school because there were 'too many girls here'. At Cecil Jones girls were a big part of the B-boy scene, and I loved it. Once I joined HT, however, all this changed. The group frowned on such behaviour, and wanted its followers to behave less promiscuously and to focus on their studies. HT wanted you to do things properly. If you were interested in a girl, it had to be serious and then you could approach her family with a view to marriage. If the family agreed, then you would become engaged. You would be allowed to see and speak to each other, but you were not allowed to be intimate. You would have to be patient, wait for the marriage arrangements to be made.

Before my expulsion from Newham, there was a tall, beautiful Pakistani girl who attended some of my talks, at the time not in a headscarf. I did things properly, and got my friend Ed Husain to talk to her on my behalf. The girl was flattered, expressed an interest and even donned the headscarf soon after. We made approaches to both sets of parents, to tell them that we were interested in a betrothal with a view to eventual marriage once we had finished our studies. Our parents met to discuss the matter, but much to my disappointment her parents opposed our relationship.

It transpired that her father had already fixed her betrothal, against her will, in Pakistan. Just before I started university she went with her parents to Pakistan, on the assumption they were going there to visit family. While there she was married to her cousin – an arranged, pressured marriage. The girl I had waited two years for was suddenly taken from me without warning. I was angry, and the girl was heartbroken. She called my number and said that she was prepared to run away to be with me. Abi, delighted at the idea that a girl could potentially calm the wave of anger she could see rising in her son, offered to take her in and protect her.

Ever the ideologue, ever trying to be righteous, I failed her miserably. I didn't want to do anything that went against the teachings of HT, or bring the group into disrepute. So I played it by the book and told her that I didn't want to break up anyone's family. I said that the issue was now a religious one, and that she needed to see a religious cleric, a *shaikh*. This *shaikh*, I told her, would be able to rule on the legitimacy of her marriage in Pakistan. They would be able to say whether or not the marriage was void because it had taken place under duress. If a *shaikh* ruled the marriage illegitimate, then we would be free to pursue our relationship.

The *shaikh* the girl chose to go to was a Salafist. In her innocence, she wasn't in tune with the whole debate: as far she was concerned, a Muslim was a Muslim. As soon as I heard who she had gone to I felt my stomach turn. I knew already what the Salafist answer would be. Unlike her, the Salafist *shaikh* was very in tune with the debate. He knew exactly who I was, and when the girl explained the situation, he quickly backed up her parents. Yes, he told her, your marriage is quite legal. You must forget all thoughts of a relationship with Maajid. So, I thought, the Salafists finally got their revenge. I had won the crowd at Newham but they made sure that I lost my heart. And so, full of delusions of piety and sacrifice, I said goodbye to my college sweetheart, failing to offer her the support she so clearly needed. In my heart, I would be hard pressed to say that romanticism was dead. Though it was more like the romanticism of a cause, of a struggle that had won a decisive battle against the romanticism of love.

Eventually, recognising my situation and by this time studying at Queen Mary and Westfield University, Osman told me that he'd met a young Pakistani woman he thought might be suitable for me. I met her in public places like cafes, and I quickly realised she was everything my brother had promised, and perhaps most importantly of all she was a leader for the HT sisters on her campus. Her name was Rabia, a name popularised after the Muslim Sufi saint Rabia al-Basriyya; it literally meant 'the fourth'. True to her name, fourth of seven sisters, Rabia was a biology student raised between Karachi and London. She had a homely feel to her, a serene pretty face, a quiet, high voice, and she was an all-round sensible and loyal person.

Once again, I went through the process of approaching parents about the possibility of marriage to their daughter. This time, my reception was different. The father had been a senior banker with Pakistan's Habib Bank, and all seven of his daughters supported HT, and had pressured him to become a follower as well. His response was to become increasingly devout, to the point where he left his job a year before he was due a golden handshake from his bank. He'd come to the conclusion that bank interest was to be classified as usury, prohibited by Islam. He quit his job, didn't take his retirement package and instead set up an Islamic bookshop in Shepherd's Bush. That is where my discussions with him about his daughter took place.

This time round, the father approved of my proposal to his daughter. He saw a smart young man, a law student, promising to take care of his daughter in the Islamic way. To my delight, Rabia Ahmed and I got engaged.

I took the second year out from university to get married, which we did full of idealism during the month of Ramadan in 1999. I was twenty-one years old. We moved into a two-bedroom flat in Stepney Green, East London, that Osman had previously been living in. It was not a great start to married life – within a week of moving in, the landlord reclaimed the flat and kicked us out. We ended up in a filthy bedsit in Whitechapel, one of the scummiest places I have ever lived in. There I contracted a permanent dust allergy, and my nose has never been the same since.

We weren't to stay in the flat for long. We found another one, a nice flat in Wembley that we were just about to take when once again my HT activities took over. Rabia was about to face for herself the true extent of my attraction to the romanticism of struggle. A communiqué had been issued from the *qiyadah* asking for British Pakistani members to go to Pakistan and help found the group there, with immediate effect. With dreams of a coup fit for a caliph, I told Rabia that I wanted to answer the call.

CHAPTER FOURTEEN

Dreams of a nuclear Caliphate

In 1999, Pakistan successfully tested its first atomic bomb. It was now a member of that small group of countries that could boast nuclear weapons capability. For Hizb al-Tahrir, this meant that if it could infiltrate the Pakistani military and successfully instigate a coup, then 'the *Khilafah*' they dreamed of could start its life as a global heavyweight. Overnight, our dream of a Muslim superstate felt that much closer.

The difficulty was that HT had virtually no representatives in the country. It had never invested time there because of the view that 'the *Khilafah*' should emerge from an Arabic-speaking nation. The second problem was that the few HT members who were already there had been abysmally unsuccessful in drumming up recruitment.

Initially the response to my idea to go was negative. Nasim was extremely reluctant for me to travel and felt I would be better off continuing my studies. As part of my course, I was already due to spend a year in Egypt studying Arabic, and could be of better use there. My parents, too, were doubtful. I told them that I wanted to go on a one-year study course to reconnect with my Pakistani roots. Remembering a much more tolerant, diverse and spiritual Pakistan as a child, Abi thought this trip could do my Islamist fervour some good. My father, though, smelled a rat. I will support you through your degree, he said, but if you go to Pakistan I'm afraid I can no longer support you.

By now, he had a far clearer idea of my politics, and wanted no part of it.

I listened to Nasim's advice, and initially agreed to stay on my course. But then a second communiqué from the *qiyadah* came through, more insistent than the first. It implored members to drop everything, and move to Pakistan with immediate effect. That second letter decided the matter for me. I told Nasim that I really wanted to do this, and this time he didn't try to stop me. A little later the permission came through for me to go.

As I was preparing to leave, I came across Reza Pankhurst again, one of the students who had led the recruitment drive with me at Cambridge University. By this time he had relocated to Egypt and was back in London tying up some loose ends. I told him what I was doing and he became fascinated with the idea of moving to Pakistan as well.

Rabia and I packed our things. Rabia, as a member of HT, could understand why I wanted to go, and offered me encouragement. My father was true to his word. Dismayed by what his son had become and by now very critical of HT, he refused to offer me any financial help. He told me not to tell Abi what I was really up to, so as to protect her feelings. So I didn't, and because I enrolled in Punjab University for a year Abi was happy to let me study and experience Pakistan. I also told her that I wanted Rabia to meet our family, which sounded plausible enough. Because of this, Abi sent out money behind my father's back and keenly kept in touch. This help from a desperate mother trying to heal her son turned out to be invaluable, as there was no money coming from HT. They paid for our flights to Pakistan, but after that we were considered to be on our own.

One evening, before leaving, my gut was telling me that I needed to settle something. I thought I would never be coming back, and wanted to make amends with my old friend Ed Husain before I left. We had parted ways that day on the SOAS steps rather angrily, but now I just wanted to hug my friend goodbye before I left. So I jumped into my car, at this time a beige Nissan Micra, and whizzed over to the Forest Gate area late one night and knocked on his front door.

'Who is it?' came the weary question from behind the closed door.

'I, er, *assalaamu alaykum*, this is Maajid, I'm here to see Ed. Is he in?'

'I'm sorry, but I'm afraid he's not.'

And with that, I headed to Heathrow for Pakistan. I remember Osman dropping me off at the airport and how he cried as he hugged me goodbye. He knew the truth about why I was going. Please look after yourself, he said.

In 1999, full of Islamist zeal, and at twenty-two years of age, I arrived in Lahore determined to help foment a military coup in Pakistan. Although I had visited the country before, it had been when I was a small child, and it took me a while to adjust to our new surroundings. Because the pound was strong against the rupee, you could actually live extremely comfortably for not too much money. You can have – and people do have – huge mansions, with swimming pools, Jacuzzis and the works. Outside, however, there would probably be a half-built road, unless you were willing to pay for it. There may well not be regular electricity, and you would have to fund your own electricity generator. These were all typical indications of state failure and bad governance. Pakistan was ripe for rebellion.

Contrary to crude stereotypes, Pakistan is a truly diverse, rich and cultured country. There is no single ethnicity called 'Pakistani', rather the country is made up of various languages and ethnicities, among them Punjabis, Baloch, Sindhis, Pashtuns, and Kashmiris, as well as others. Many of these ethnicities and languages span neighbouring states too, accounting for a rather stunted *Pakistani* identity. Rather than describing 'Pakistan', the political entity you see on a map, it is more accurate to describe *Pakistans* in the plural. The country has not only deep ethnic and linguistic diversity, but also vast political, class, cultural and delightful culinary differences. One legacy of the postcolonial partition is that entire provinces are split down the middle, half in Pakistan and the other half in India. Many older Pakistanis still have first cousins across the border, and in Karachi a powerful political bloc has emerged seeking to represent the *muhajir*, or those who moved across from India after partition.

More than any sense of shared heritage therefore, what held this country together by its artificial seams was the dream of its ailing founder, Muhammad Ali Jinnah, and a collective fear of what could have happened had Muslims remained a minority in India. Jinnah wanted to create a safe haven for a Muslim minority in a Hindu-dominated subcontinent. In turn, he envisioned a country that would safeguard other minorities too.

In 1947, Jinnah succeeded in outmanoeuvring almost everybody to gain independence for East and West Pakistan, but died shortly after achieving his dream. Having lost its founder so early on, Pakistan has been locked in unrelenting ethnic, intra-religious and linguistic sectarianism ever since. Troubles came to a head when the Bengalis of East Pakistan succeeded in gaining a majority of seats in the national parliament, and wished to form a government. The Punjabi-dominated West refused to accept the results. Disaster struck in the form of civil war, and the Bengalis seceded from West Pakistan in 1971 to form modern-day Bangladesh.

After this war, the founding idea that Muslims could look after each other better than Hindus seemed under threat, and it was left to the army of West Pakistan to encourage the Islamisation of Pakistan as an overarching national narrative, in a sense to glue the country together using politicised religion as a new form of national identity. In 1977 General Zia took over in a coup and did exactly this. Pakistan has never been the same since. Of course, confusing as it is for most outsiders, there are as many Muslims in India as there are in Pakistan, so what exactly should form Pakistan's national identity is a question that vexes the nation to this day. And for all my teenage idealism back at Newham, of Muslims bonding exclusively on nothing but Islam, things began to look a great deal more complicated on the ground.

Arriving into this quagmire in 1999, believing we had all the answers, I knew that I would have to learn Urdu fast, the one language that can be understood by most Pakistanis regardless of which province you are in. I hadn't grown up speaking Urdu – speaking English at home as a first language – but had heard it a great deal, and so was familiar with its basics. We were met by Rabia's uncle at Lahore Airport. A friendly, wealthy yet generous, genteel man named Dr Abdul Qayyum, he had travelled far and was excited to receive us. Uncle Qayyum was a well-established and respected dentist in a town called Raheem Yar Khan, which sits almost directly halfway between Karachi and Lahore. He wasn't a member of HT at this stage, but was a deeply religious Salafist, sporting a huge grey beard and a warm smile. After the conversion of his seven nieces to HT, Uncle Qayyum began to explore the Islamist cause more closely.

To begin with, we stayed in Lahore with one of his friends, a member of Jamaat-e-Islami, a political Islamist group in Pakistan similar in thought to the Muslim Brotherhood. This friend, a businessman, didn't come across as particularly religious, but he insisted his wife wore a full niqab (face veil). He showed his support, I later learnt, not through piety but through funding. I eventually found somewhere to live in Lahore, an upper-floor flat in Nishter block, Allama Iqbal Town. It was fairly basic but newly renovated, and we kitted it out with some fans, carpets and pieces of furniture.

The reason I had been stationed in Lahore was because that was where Imtiaz Malik, the leader of HT in Pakistan, was based. He had failed to get the movement off the ground, and the leadership felt that he needed help. I immediately went to meet him. He was older than me – in his late thirties – but it didn't take long for my respect for his seniority to dissipate. He was a thoroughly unimpressive character, and I could immediately understand why he had failed to recruit people to the cause. Imtiaz suggested that the best plan was for me to recruit people in the Islamic department of nearby Punjab University. There was a certain logic to this: back in the UK one of the best ways of attracting recruits was to start with the students. Punjab University was the biggest higher education facility in Pakistan and the fact that I was a student myself would make it easy for me. There was just one flaw to the plan, which Imtiaz should really have known. The university was already a Jamaat-e-Islami stronghold. These were students who knew about Islam, who were studying Islam and who were going to be difficult to convert. Any of the departments at the university would have been better to enrol on than that one.

The best place to have started was the medical college. It was on the other side of Canal Road and here the atmosphere was different. I discovered that Arab medical students had been coming to study here for years: among these had been members of HT. When I arrived, I overlapped with a Palestinian HT member who had been running a few study sessions there. He was leaving, and I couldn't help thinking that this non-Pakistani had achieved more in a shorter space of time than Imtiaz had done in five years.

Within a few weeks more reinforcements were flown in from the UK. There was Irfan Wahid, who had been my supervisor back in London. Shortly after Irfan arrived, Dr Abdul Wajid also turned up. Abdul Wajid was one of the HT members who had been behind the original recruitment drive in British universities. He was a seasoned, experienced speaker and a good recruiter. Irfan didn't have Abdul Wajid's oratorical skills, but was a decent enough organiser and administrator. All in all, it felt like a strong, almost heavyweight team. I was excited about their arrival, and felt that together we could really do things.

I sat down with Irfan and briefed him on my views about Imtiaz and he listened carefully to what I said. But then, to my horror, he went to Imtiaz and apparently repeated all the accusations that I had made. I couldn't believe it: I'd tried to paint an accurate picture for Irfan because I wanted to help the cause; all Irfan appeared to have done was to use the information to curry favour with Imtiaz, and sideline me in the process.

I'd given up a lot to move to Pakistan – I hadn't told SOAS I had gone and had essentially given up my degree. I'd put my future career on the line, and was now faced with the position of having nothing to show for that sacrifice. That stung. But what really got me was something more fundamental. I was an activist absolutely committed to HT, who believed so passionately in the group that I would do anything the leadership told me would further our work. I had left my studies behind, and only months after my marriage, because of how blindly committed I was.

Irfan's actions, however, opened my eyes. I saw that rather than everyone in the organisation doing things for the good of the cause, it seemed to me there were baser instincts at work too. From now on, whenever I looked at Irfan, whereas previously I had seen a brother, now all I saw was someone who apparently liked to manoeuvre for position. For an idealist like myself that was a painful thing to recognise. Looking back, it was the end of my political innocence.

It was around this time too that Osman, back in the UK, had decided he could no longer remain a student of the group. He had never been a full member, but he finally broke his ties to the group. HT had become too controlling for him, and too inflexible of his enquiring nature. Secretly I began to empathise with Osman's reasoning and I decided that I would never give all of myself in the same way: there'd always be part of me that I'd hold back. I'd gladly give myself unconditionally to Allah, but not to HT. The thought process involved in leaving groups such as HT begins first at questioning an individual in authority, then the tactics, then the strategy, then the methodology and then finally by questioning the ideology itself. If I trace back the reasons that ultimately led to me leaving the group, this was probably the first, primitive and unrecognised seed.

This was the first time I had worked closely with Abdul Wajid too, and the man who had seemed such an able and committed recruiter from a distance, up close appeared to me to be power-hungry. I began to see him as one of those people: transparently overbearing in his desire to dominate, and in his self-belief that he is always the most capable in the room. Just as I had lost favour with Imtiaz and Irfan, Abdul Wajid now made it clear that he considered me an intelligence operative trying to cause dissent within HT's nascent Pakistan operation. His stance was certainly scary to me. The certainty with which he had apparently decided this made me ponder the dangers of a lack of accountability at the top of any organisation. What if such people did take over the country?

The one thing I could do was recruit. Our strategy for Muslim-majority countries such as Pakistan was a long-term one. We knew that since Zia's coup in the 1970s, the process of 'Islamising' Pakistan's institutions had been going on long enough. Islamist groups by this time, dominant on many campuses, already controlled the mob and were attracting hundreds of thousands to their rallies. The country's intellectual elite feared Islamist intimidation and continued to make concessions to them. Thanks to the way Islamist groups were able to hijack Jinnah's vision, thanks to the Afghan jihad and the policies of the ISI and CIA, thanks to the rise of the Taliban, thanks to historic concessions made by the progressive governments of Pakistan, and thanks to corruption and bad governance, our job of injecting Islamism into Pakistan's masses was already well under way.

However, we knew that the two power blocs that really mattered in Pakistan, the two sectors without which change could not come, were the intelligensia, and the army. And so instead of wasting our efforts trying to build a mass movement that was frankly already being done, we began targeting the upper-middle classes and the armed forces. These formed the bulk of people who actually ran the nation. If we could hijack the intellectual life of the nation and the armed forces, the masses would gladly follow our lead.

There was already a special team, coordinated by British-Pakistani HT member Omar Khan, working within the army, focused on recruiting Sandhurst cadets. Our job was to target the elite English medium colleges such as Lahore University of Management Sciences (LUMS), places that had previously been bastions of liberal thought, and we began visiting posh cafes on Mall Road, and yuppie youth clubs, and spoke in our perfect English, with our degrees from SOAS, the LSE, Imperial and Oxbridge, our arguments already well honed. Nobody had seen the likes of us before. We were Islamists, but we were clean-shaven, young, wealthy and mobile, we dressed well, we were Western-educated and yet we were calling for 'the *Khilafah*'. We swept such places clean within no time.

Personally, I put my head down and got to work in two areas – aiming to build supporters within Punjab University, and to set up the organisation in Raheem Yar Khan, the town where Rabia's relatives lived. In the meantime, another member arrived in Lahore from the UK: Mohammed Nawaz, a lecturer from Sheffield University. Ignoring Imtiaz's instructions, I helped him get a job at the political sciences faculty. I had also managed to recruit a highly capable student called Saleem from my university class, and handed him over to Nawaz for training. Saleem was a hafiz, one who had memorised the entire Qur'an by heart, and he became a very capable activist.

Away from Lahore, I was making real inroads in Raheem Yar Khan. I was travelling there on weekends, and in a short space of time I had set up three *halaqahs*. What is more, these *halaqahs* weren't full of students, but of older and more influential individuals. I managed to convert a member of Lashkar-e-Taiba (LeT), now a proscribed terrorist organisation. There was even a local Salafist mosque imam who joined us. Then there was the ever-smiling Uncle Qayyum, the friendly doctor with a huge grey beard. The beard mattered in the Pakistani context: it showed he was a serious and religious guy. And he was genuinely devout, in the good, pious sort of way. He would leave his house at dawn, walk to the mosque to pray, and once he'd closed his surgery in the afternoon, would be seen in the streets handing out food to the poor.

'Maajid *bhai* – my brother, we are instructed by our Prophet, *'alayhi salam*, to be kind to our neighbours. A neighbour is defined as everyone on your street.' He once told me, 'That's why I try to distribute food to my whole road, so I can get the full *sawab* – the blessings.'

For his piety, he was loved by his family, friends and neighbours alike, as he was by me. Uncle Qayyum and I were extremely close; he became the lynchpin for all that I was to do for HT in Raheem Yar Khan. I'd recruited his son, his brother and many of his friends. The people I recruited were all rooted in the local communities; they were exactly the pillars of influence that HT dreamed of bringing on board. With them you have a chance of changing the culture.

One day, I even got a call from an excited Uncle Qayyum: 'Maajid, listen, *bhai*, I've been approached by a man whose name is the "sincere one". This "sincere one" has been going around doing *tableegh* – advocacy for our cause, for around twelve years now, all alone, and has finally found us again! He heard about our work through some people he tried to recruit in Raheem Yar Khan, and has just arrived at my surgery. You must come and see him, *jaldi ajau*, come fast; he's a gift from Allah to our cause!' Word was surely spreading, and our cells in Raheem Yar Khan were multiplying.

All this was made possible just from visiting at weekends.

It helped, undoubtedly, that Rabia had relatives there: it gave me credibility. Rabia would often stay over at Uncle Qayyum's house with the rest of her family during the week, cementing these roots still further. Even so, considering my situation, and lack of advanced linguistic skills in Urdu, it was a major achievement.

Keen to ensure the continuity of this work, I asked Abdul Wajid to come to Raheem Yar Khan to see what I was doing. He was resistant and sceptical at first, but when he finally did come it was clear he was surprised. They might not have trusted me, but Imtiaz and the others could no longer deny my success. HT began to subsidise my weekend flights to Raheem Yar Khan, in the hope of creating a real stronghold, similar to the stronghold gained by Lashkar-e-Taiba (LeT) in a town called Muridke. For me, this was vindication. I knew that none of the others had achieved half of this, and they were now forced to swallow their pride and deal directly with my recruits.

Yet leaving was on my mind. In the midst of all this work Rabia had become pregnant. I was overjoyed, especially given everything that had been going on with HT: here was something precious that the group would have no part of. I knew that she wanted to have her baby back in the UK, and to be near her parents for support. That set a clock ticking for our return. I continued to recruit, but in the knowledge that we were thinking of and planning on returning to Britain. I wrote to SOAS to explain where I was, and what I was doing; this was the first time I'd contacted them, and I had no idea what their response would be. To my relief, it transpired that it was possible to extend your leave of absence to two years:

I could return to continue my course as though nothing had happened.

Looking back, it was a remarkable time to have been living in Pakistan. This was the turn of the century, when the democratic government of Nawaz Sharif was removed in a military coup, and General Musharraf took over. In a strange way, that period of military rule chimed with my own attempts to help HT infiltrate the military, and overthrow one dictatorship with another. The next time I returned to Pakistan, almost a decade later, the country would be democratically ruled again, and I would be campaigning to entrench democratic culture within the country. Pakistan's story, by chance, would echo my own.

It is difficult not to see that period now as the run-up to 9/11. Nobody could have foreseen what was coming, but we all felt the strength of the movement: the way that the ideas of Islamism and Jihadism were spreading and taking root. It definitely felt as though we were part of something big: that we were almost on the verge of taking over. The Taliban in Afghanistan, the Sudanese government, these seemed to be just the start of something that the West was yet to pick up on. In those days the Taliban believed Pakistan was an Islamic state already, and had no gripe with the country. I remember meeting a senior Taliban commander in Raheem Yar Khan, in an effort to convince him that Pakistan was an illegitimate colonial entity. It didn't take long for the Pakistani Taliban to adopt our more revolutionary mantra.

Lashkar-e-Taiba (LeT), the group responsible for the Mumbai attacks in 2008, were another fledgling organisation that, like HT, were working to garner support. Although they were Salafist in creed and jihadist in their methodology, in terms of ideology there was little to differentiate them from what HT taught. In fact, so similar were some of our ideas that the group were using HT's own literature as part of their recruitment drive. Because all of this was so new, the authorities were still to recognise the threat that these groups posed.

In the same way that before the Newham murder, no one took the warnings seriously from the likes of Peter Tatchell, so the Pakistani authorities did little to stop the spread of these organisations. For example, in those early days LeT were holding their annual conferences – their *ijtima* – out in the open in their stronghold town of Muridke, which I attended. I remember seeing some of Omar Bakri's followers, from the now-banned al-Muhajiroun, in attendance there too. I think I caught a glimpse of the fiery Abdur Rahman, from the heady Newham days. Abdur Rahman would later go on to be convicted under the terrorism law for an offence in the UK. It said everything about how the threat was perceived then that the keynote speaker was General Hamid Gul, the former head of Pakistan's feared military intelligence, the ISI.

CHAPTER FIFTEEN

Caliphs in Copenhagen

When I returned to the UK, it was a little as though nothing had changed. I had my place to do my degree back at college. My father was under the impression I'd seen sense and come back to continue my studies, and so welcomed me upon my return. As for my position in Hizb al-Tahrir, my troubles with Imtiaz followed me. They sent an excoriating report to the UK leadership about my probably being 'an agent', and how I was not to be trusted. By this time Nasim had gone off to set up HT in Bangladesh, and the new UK leader was a British-Indian called Jalaluddin Patel. Unlike Nasim, Jalaluddin hadn't known me; he hadn't witnessed that young, passionate sixteen-year-old B-boy wearing a bandana, walking with a limp and angry at all the injustice in this world, transform into a global Islamist recruiter. Jalaluddin had been raised under Abdul Wajid, and was shaped in that mould. I was given a local university role and had one of my former *dariseen* called Amir placed in charge over me with strict instructions not to trust me. I didn't envy Amir; by now my *da'wah* antics were known throughout HT and here was one of my former students in the embarrassing position of having to pretend to lead me. No problem, I thought, I managed this in Pakistan, and I can manage it here. Amir, to his credit, was an intelligent and independent-minded brother and he dealt with me sensibly. It didn't take him long to be expelled from HT for his independence.

There was, though, one very significant change in my life, and that was the birth of my son, Ammar, which means 'the one who will build great things'. We named him after the famous companion of the Prophet, loved by the Sunni and Shia – a son to the first martyrs of Islam, Yasir and Sumayyah, who were tortured to death by their slave master Abu Jahl of the pagan tribe of Quraish, then ruling in Mecca. Our son was similarly born to parents who were going to sacrifice everything for the cause, and in turn that is what I envisioned him doing as well. The original Ammar was eventually killed in Islam's first civil war, a general to the Prophet's cousin and son-in-law, Ali, may Allah honour his countenance, against the rebel forces of Mu'awaiya: the romanticism of struggle.

Rabia, as a member of HT, had diligently followed me to Pakistan when I wanted to go. But back in the UK, as we settled into our new life at a flat in Wembley, the first cracks in our relationship began to show. As any new parent knows, the experience of looking after a newborn baby is an exhausting one. The endless sleepless nights can take their toll on the best of relationships. It was a period when Rabia really needed me to dig deep and support her. Yet it was now that she really perceived to what extent there were three of us in the relationship: me, her and our ideology. I was so committed to the cause that stepping back to help her cope with bringing up our son would have felt a dereliction of duty. If anything, to ward off the temptation of staying at home in the comforting embrace of my wife and newly born son, I increased my campaign work during this period.

Cruel, selfish things are so much easier to do in the delusion of self-righteousness, whether religious or political. I crushed that woman's dreams pursuing an elusive '*Khilafah*'. Having denied her a honeymoon, I was now denying her my support during her most difficult time. But we were both incredibly young, only just into our twenties, and still full of this heady mixture of self-belief and ideological certainty. Whereas she had wanted to settle more into married life, I felt that I'd always been honest with her. She knew who I was when I married her, and what I wanted to do with my life. If I become the person you are asking me to become, I argued, then you would not have loved me in the first place. You would never have wanted to marry that person, so don't ask me to become that person now. And with those words I'd often leave the house, questioning my belief that an ideological bond alone was sufficient for a lasting marriage.

This work felt more crucial than ever: although 2001 was the point when Salafi-Jihadism tipped over into international prominence because of 9/11, the peak of the movement in terms of support and momentum was in fact a good twelve months earlier. If anything, by 2001, that impetus had already begun to slide a little. I did my best to take advantage of this surge of interest in Islamism. Back at SOAS I found another brother to tag-team on the *da'wah* with: Ashraf ul-Haque became my partner as Ed Husain had been in Newham College. Ashraf told me he had turned down an offer from Oxford to attend SOAS because he had wanted to follow in my footsteps. Having administered Ashraf's oath of membership, together we recreated the glory of those early days right there in SOAS, and managed to recruit another three *halaqahs* of new followers. As I guided and protected him through HT's machinery, we became inseparable, and bonded in our shared disdain for any incompetent HT administrators. Although we didn't advocate Jihadism in any of our teachings, the politicisation process we began set a number of students on this path. One of my recruits that year was Zeeshan Siddiqui, who was later arrested and detained in Afghanistan by US forces, having gone there to join the 'Jihad'. Upon being returned to the UK Zeeshan was placed under a control order, from which he managed to somehow abscond.

I was also given the opportunity to help recruit Pakistani soldiers. There was a group of army officers who had been sent over on a scholarship to train at Sandhurst. This was gold dust for HT: as I said, their method of taking a country was to infiltrate the military and instigate a coup. It turned out that one of these soldiers had links to HT through his relatives. Someone in his family ran a garage in Stepney Green, which I used to take my car to. The garage owner's son, Aftab, was an HT *daris*, and although not a natural recruiter, had managed to raise the interest of this soldier. The officers were about to return to Pakistan, and so I was brought in for an introduction, partly because I was good at recruiting, and partly because, despite Imtiaz's efforts, I had a great reputation from my work in Pakistan. My task was to give them a final send-off, with encouragement about how they should recruit within Pakistan's army.

I met them at one of Aftab's flats in Forest Gate, talked to them about HT and explained how they could be central to our plans of taking control of a country. Rather than them becoming HT members openly, I said their responsibility was to go back to Pakistan and support the group clandestinely and begin building cells inside the army. They should then wait, and prepare to take part in a military coup.

This was a high stakes plan, with severe consequences if it wasn't successful. In 2003, Pakistani journalist Ahmed Rashid reported in London's *Telegraph* newspaper that General Musharraf had led a purge inside Pakistan's army, rooting out what he described as al-Qaeda sympathising cells. He was right about the cells, but wrong about the affiliation: these were the HT supporters I had met in that dingy flat in London and incited to rise up. When I heard the news, I felt stricken: by this time we were in the world of the 'War on Terror', and there was little that they wouldn't have done in terms of torture to interrogate these soldiers. A few years later I met their British-Pakistani cell-instructor, Omar Khan, in London. Omar confirmed all this to me. He had been the secret military contact between HT and these soldiers, and had been arrested with them. He'd been beaten and had a gun put to his head during his interrogation before being deported back to the UK. The soldiers who'd remained in Pakistan were not so fortunate.

My *da'wah* responsibilities would have made the year busy enough, what with my degree and a newborn son to deal with. But that was only part of my work for the cause during 2000. HT would regularly hold rallies, and I quickly became one

of the key speakers at these events. We held events outside
the US Embassy and in Trafalgar Square, led marches down
the Edgware Road and ran speaker events in Hyde Park.
These weren't small affairs: the rallies would regularly attract
audiences of around three thousand. This was a different skill
from the careful analysis of leading a *halaqah*, but I loved
it. Some people get nervous about speaking in public but
I enjoyed pumping up a crowd, and relished the chance to
get our message across to so many people. The fact that the
gatherings were so large only reinforced our perception that
the movement was on the cusp of a major breakthrough.

On top of all this, I also answered the call to kick-start the
Danish-Pakistani branch of HT in Denmark. This was like
the jetsetting version of my work in Raheem Yar Khan in
Pakistan. I would spend the week in London, doing my studies
at SOAS during the day and the *halaqahs* in the evening, and
then on a Friday evening, I would fly out to Copenhagen and
spend the weekend in Denmark. This made my work for HT a
seven-day-a-week affair, and created a schedule that put even
further strain on my marriage.

Denmark had been pinpointed by the *qiyadah* as somewhere
they were desperate to develop, to help establish HT's roots
on the continent. For various reasons, the European chapters
had not developed as they should have done. The original
HT chapter in Denmark had come under the authority of
the European leadership in Germany, and had followed their
recruitment strategy of targeting first-generation immigrants,
who had gone to the country for economic reasons. The result
was that the European branches were almost entirely formed
of North African and Turkish people. In the UK, by contrast,

the focus had always been on those born and raised there, the angry younger generation: students at the universities, and disaffected youth. The German strategy had never included these people: they considered them layabouts, whereas the UK experience had shown that such individuals were prime targets for recruitment. Our brothers in Denmark had now decided to follow the UK model and HT was fast expanding there. But they were yet to see penetration of the young Danish-Pakistani community, which could have offered the organisation another bridge into Pakistan, as we had done from the UK.

Given my background and experience in both universities and abroad, I was felt to be the ideal person to turn this situation around. I quickly got into the routine of catching my end-of-week flight and being met at the airport by one Khalid Amin, a Danish-Palestinian, who would take me through a packed schedule of forty-eight hours of meetings and talks. Once again, I quickly made inroads into the community. I set up study circles and even met some Pakistani army recruits: they weren't officers like the ones from Sandhurst, but were still soldiers, ready and willing to support the cause.

What was striking about Denmark was how markedly different it was from the UK in terms of racism, and not in a good way. In some respects, it felt as if I'd stepped back in time to my teenage years in Essex: that was what the atmosphere reminded me of, and that was how far the country felt behind the UK in terms of race relations. In Britain, the issue had to some extent died down and society had moved on, whereas everywhere I went in Denmark people complained about racism. The lines on the continent were drawn differently. At the time, third-generation Turks born and raised in Germany were still only classed as guest workers. That sort of policy created a completely different atmosphere in terms of how people saw their identity.

The response of the minority communities in Denmark to racism had been exactly the same as mine had been in Southend: violence. The potential recruits I met all had stories of serious criminal activity: these were former gangsters, former drug dealers. While Southend had been all about knife culture, here everyone had grown up around guns. I was told many tales of shoot-outs with police, attempted armed robberies, and on more than one occasion a shirt was lifted up and I was proudly shown a bullet wound or two.

Because of my background I was able to relate to these recruits in a way that the other recruiters failed to. The potential recruits were interested in my journey, and how I'd gone from anger to espousing revolutionary Islamism as the solution. I was fortunate, perhaps, to have been travelling to Denmark at the height of the Islamist fervour: that level of interest certainly made recruiting easier. I succeeded in seeding the growth of the Danish-Pakistani branch, and felt proud of how I'd spread the message in Britain, Pakistan and now in continental Europe. It's sad, but the HT branch in Denmark is known as one of the organisation's more extreme chapters to this day. Eventually, the German government would impose a ban on HT activities, and in 2006 the Danish chapter's spokesman Fadi Abdul Latif was convicted for hate-speech and inciting violence.

Given all this commitment to HT, it is perhaps not surprising that my studies suffered as a result. When the results came in for my exams, I had passed the sections on law, but failed my Arabic grammar, much harder than law in case you're curious. Without passing in Arabic, I couldn't go on to the next part of my course: a year studying Arabic in Egypt's beautiful city of Alexandria. To Rabia's frustration, rather than having some time off over the summer, I had to spend it revising in anticipation of re-sitting the exam.

I got a job as a security guard at London's Royal Festival Hall. It was a job that allowed me to man the box that opened and closed the barrier to let cars in. I sat in that box and revised my Arabic from nine to five each day, occasionally interrupting my flow to admit cars. The other security guards couldn't believe their luck – who would want to sit in that box all day? But full of dreams of reviving HT in Egypt, I focused on my studies. I was concentrating so hard that once I even managed to bring the barrier down on my finger. It split it open, and the scar remains visible till this day.

But the hard work paid off. I re-sat the Arabic module at the beginning of September 2001 and this time I passed. I could take up my place at the University of Alexandria, at their College of Literature's Centre for the Study of Arabic Language for Foreigners. Once again, Rabia and I packed our family belongings, by this time quite disillusioned with our relationship; she followed me again to another country. As our flight left, I watched London disappear beneath our plane, Ammar in my arms, I thought 'Twelve months and I'm back here, I really need to work on my marriage, for little Ammar's sake.' Little did I know that it would be many years before I set foot on British soil again, as an irreversibly changed man. Or that by the time I arrived in Alexandria, events on the other side of the Atlantic, on four different passenger flights, involving two towers, were about to change the world irrevocably.

CHAPTER SIXTEEN

The polemic

You drop bombs on my people while knowing full well that the level of 'collateral' damage – we call them innocent Muslims – will far exceed the damage to any 'legitimate target'. For you, killing our children en masse – and you still call it collateral damage – is an unavoidable consequence of pursuing your policies in our lands. To us, they are simply children. Don't you think we've been crying too, like you are now, for years? Do you think we felt no pain as you raped and plundered our lands, and bombed our cities? What lands, what cities, you ask? Your arrogance is only compounded by your ignorance. Look to Iraq. In order to remove Saddam Hussein, after the Kuwait war, you killed over half a million children because you could. Because you could! And because my people were too lost, too defeated, to be able to stop you. These are our children. We cry for them even as you feel absolutely nothing. What of Lesley Stahl's question on 60 Minutes posed to Secretary of State Madeleine Albright:

'We have heard that half a million children have died – I mean that is more children than died at Hiroshima and, you know, is the price worth it?'

Albright's callous response is etched in our memories, staining our innocence with her venom:

'I think it is a very hard choice, but we think the price is worth it.'

And you wonder why we are so angry? You wonder even now why, after all these years, as we speak these words, we are consumed with rage? The price of killing half a million children with your depleted uranium bombs is worth pursuing, but woe to us if we ever strike back! In your world, Albright's interview was barely mentioned: a Dow Jones search of mainstream news sources after the attack turned up only one reference to the interview in an Orange County newspaper. But in our world, in the hell we live in, this was major news. We will not forget our dead just because you have no feelings.

Is killing civilians justified only for your own foreign policy interests? You claim that, unlike us, you don't target civilians, that your intentions are noble, that you seek only humane concerns. How many deaths of 'untargeted' civilians by your hands entitle us to respond? Five, ten, a hundred, half a million? Are three thousand deaths enough to make you feel the pain of each and every mother you 'untargeted' with depleted uranium? If not, then know that our intentions in bringing you death can also be noble, we too shroud destruction in humane concerns. You do not have a monopoly on reaping devastation off the back of good intentions, and don't you dare claim such a thing, you arrogant monsters. You can support, fund and train dictators in our lands who have been torturing our brothers and raping our sisters in their prisons for decades, and yet you invade our countries, claiming to bring democracy? And you cite international law at us, while you wilfully ignore Israel's occupation of Palestine, as defined by the UN? We will never forget your friendship with Mubarak and Assad, your unconditional support for an occupying Israel, the way you used us as Mujahideen in Afghanistan only to turn on us once you'd got what you wanted. You chose your side and we have chosen ours.

We have come to know that no amount of civilised pleading, no amount of appealing to your humanity, for your mercy, no amount of playing by your rules in your game, will move you. You are stupefied in ignorant bliss while we bleed and secrete pus from every orifice. There is only one thing you people value and cherish, and that is your own lives, your own happiness and your own selfish oblivion. If inflicting upon you even an atom's weight of the pain we suffer at your hands wakes you from your stupor and forces you to listen to our cries as we drown, then I'm afraid we have finally decided that though it is 'a very hard choice, we think the price is worth it'.

This was powerful stuff, and it worked, but my polemic – a reflection of my instinctive response immediately after 9/11 – was only half the truth. How easy it is for a victim to construct a narrative out of half-truths, and inspire thousands in the name of righteous indignation. But the other side only saw half the truth too, and that was the problem. Understanding how I reached such a detached position is key to grasping the mindset of an Islamist, living his life on the verges of violence. I was an ideologue. That was the prism through which I saw the world. It was difficult for non-Muslim audiences to really understand where this sense of Muslim indignation had come from, but it was tangible, it was palpable, and the American-led invasions of Afghanistan and Iraq after 9/11 only served to cement these attitudes further. If America could bomb and invade in response to being bombed, why couldn't jihadists bomb and invade in response to our own deaths? And if the deciding factor was that one party was a state while the other was a loose grouping, surely the state should have been the more responsible one?

And while we in Hizb al-Tahrir disagreed with the tactics that al-Qaeda employed, most of us shared their sense of vengeance. Curiously, as seen from my above polemic, my position wasn't entirely detached from humane concerns. Rather, it was too attached to – indeed motivated by – humane concerns for Muslims alone, at the expense of 'the other'. If my efforts now can achieve one thing, let them build an understanding of the mindset that can make people so angry that they lose all empathy for others. Let them humanise even those who dehumanise others, so that the process of healing may begin. My above polemic may have been uncomfortable reading for many of you, especially for my friends who survived the 9/11 attacks, and for that I am sorry. The reality is, and it will help us not to pretend otherwise, there are still many people out there who think this way, whether we like it or not.

I have since visited Ground Zero on a number of occasions, and have been honoured to speak there upon invitation by the 9/11 Memorial Trust's board. It was a humbling experience, and I would be a strange person indeed if I had not been deeply moved by visiting the site. Stalin once infamously said that a single death is a tragedy; a million deaths are a statistic. That's what my response to 9/11 became. It wasn't about individual people, it was about the overall picture, and by this time I was so consumed by the suffering of 'my own people' that I had no empathy left for the suffering of those I accused of causing it. There is a lesson there, I believe, for the more hawkish elements among Western societies too.

Although my initial response to 9/11 might sound shocking in a Western context, in countries like Egypt and Pakistan it was reasonably common. In an eerie reversal of my Westcliff history teacher's request for a show of hands, I remember an Arabic class I attended a couple of weeks later. The Egyptian teacher asked everyone what they felt about the events in America. The class was full of students from SOAS and other foreign universities, and many expressed their disgust at what had happened. The Egyptian teacher, however, had a different view: she explained to the class how happy the ordinary Egyptian was that these events had occurred. She described how it was about time that the Americans got a taste of their own medicine. Many of the foreign students were taken aback, but across the Arab world and Muslim-majority societies, this was actually a fairly normal response. Echoing Malcom X's famous line, many believed these were America's 'chickens coming home to roost'.

As I digested the events of 9/11, my overriding concern was not for the victims and their families, but that this was going to play badly for HT, and for Islamism. I wasn't convinced of the attacks on an intellectual level, though my objections had little to do with the human cost involved. Back when I was at Newham College, the global HT leadership had been critical of Omar Bakri's aggressive policies for bringing heat on the group. That was the fallout of one murder – this was the killing of several thousand in the heart of New York, not to mention the huge symbolism of taking out the iconic twin towers. The heat that was going to be turned on Islamism was exponential: it was not just going to be felt by bin Laden and al-Qaeda, but by all of us for years to come.

We had specific concerns too about how the Western response would affect long-cherished HT projects. As it became clear that Afghanistan was going to bear the brunt of the US reaction, HT was about to lose what was considered a key link in the chain to developing 'the *Khilafah*'. From my starting point a few years earlier, HT had begun to put down serious roots in Pakistan. The same was true in Uzbekistan, where our organisation formed the country's largest opposition group, with hundreds of thousands of followers. HT was considered such a threat that the Uzbek President, Islam Karimov, had resorted to extreme torture to halt its spread: a future British Ambassador there, Craig Murray, would eventually resign, citing how Karimov was boiling our HT brothers alive in an effort to crush the group.

HT's vision was to rise to power either side of Afghanistan, in Pakistan and Uzbekistan, after which the Taliban would act as the bridge in building the first modern, nuclear-armed Islamist superstate. During 1999 HT even sent a delegation of senior Arab members from Palestine in order to offer the Taliban just such a partnership for our future 'nuclear *Khilafah*'. In those days, the Taliban had not yet come to believe that Pakistan was a *kufr*, un-Islamic state, and they politely refused to cooperate with HT. It didn't take long for our *da'wah* to change the Taliban view on Pakistan, and by 2009 they had usurped large parts of the country in the north. What 9/11 did, by precipitating the NATO occupation of Afghanistan, was destroy this dream of a Central Asian '*Khilafah*' at a stroke. We had always been critical of Jihadism for being the wrong way to go about bringing about an 'Islamic state', and the events of that morning just seemed to confirm how Jihadism had scored an own goal.

A couple of weeks after I had settled in Alexandria and begun my course, I made contact with HT in Egypt. Exactly as in Pakistan, Egypt in the 1970s witnessed the rise of state-sponsored Islamism, just as the decade before had witnessed the rise of socialism in both countries. President Sadat released thousands of Islamists from the jails of his predecessor, Gemal Abdel Nasser, in an attempt to shore up support for his new regime against the 'Godless' socialists. He even ennobled himself as *Ra'is al-Muslimeen*, President of the Muslims. But Sadat would soon learn the hard way that Islamism was not a beast easily tamed.

Having been founded next door in Palestine, HT had been operating in and out of Egypt since the late 1960s. Taking advantage of Sadat's Islamisation policy, HT managed to gain critical mass and planned a coup in Egypt as early as 1974. This failed attempt became known as the Case of the Technical Military Academy, or *Qadiyyat al-Fanniyya al-Askariyya* and a Palestinian HT member named Saleh al-Sirriyya was the inspiration behind it. The attempt led to the loss of many lives and the virtual obliteration of HT cells in Egypt. But HT didn't give up, and in the late 1970s a Jordanian member of the group named Salim al-Rahhal took up the task of reviving the group's call in Alexandria.

Because of the Military Academy case, HT was by now on the radar of Egypt's security establishment, so in 1977 al-Rahhal set up a new organisation called Tanzim al-Jihad, or the Jihad Organisation. Al-Rahhal was, by all accounts, a highly capable and dangerous man. Around eighty of his armed followers were discovered later that year in Alexandria raids. Eventually, considered too dangerous to remain, Salim al-Rahhal was expelled from Egypt. But, as we were taught inside HT, ideas are more dangerous than people, and al-Rahhal left his disciple Kamal Habib in charge in Alexandria, while a man named Abdus-Salam Faraj began expanding the Cairo branch of Tanzim al-Jihad around 1979.

Still focused on the military strategy, Kamal and Faraj managed to find Abbud al-Zummar, a military intelligence officer who joined Tanzim al-Jihad in 1980. It was this core of Islamist activists at the helm of Tanzim al-Jihad, founded by HT member al-Rahhal, who went on to assassinate Anwar Sadat in 1981. Echoing the Bolshevik and Menshevik split before Lenin's revolution, Tanzim al-Jihad in turn went on to split, forming the larger and more prolific al-Gama'a al-Islamiyya and the smaller yet more sinister Jihad al-Islami, led by one Ayman al-Zawahiri. Zawahiri later merged his group with bin Laden to form al-Qaeda, and the rest, as they say, is history. Thus the snail's trail becomes clear: the traceable effect that Hizb al-Tahrir has had on the world of Islamism as we know it.

Back to Egypt in 2001: our job was to revive the original HT organisation in the country. My contact began with an email, which gave me a phone number to call. I went out and rang the number from a call box. The voice on the other end gave me instructions to travel to a town called Kafr el-Sheikh, where I met a man called Hisham and we began studying in a *halaqah*, in the utmost secrecy. After a while, a meeting was arranged for me with Alaa' el-Zenati, the head of HT in Egypt. I met Zanati, and discussed my previous experiences in Pakistan, Denmark and the UK. He was sufficiently impressed to put me in charge of HT activities in Alexandria with immediate effect.

The fact that I was given a central role so quickly, and the fact that seeing Zenati involved so many clandestine contacts was indicative of what Egyptian society was like, and how little penetration HT had by this time. The memory of the Military Academy case, and the group's chilling effect on Sadat's assassins, lingered on for Egypt's Intelligence Services and they treated any hint of HT presence in Egypt as a 'code red'. Because the Egyptian state was so dependent on the military, they were particularly watchful of a group whose aim was to infiltrate the army, turning it on itself. The lengths that the state would go to shut down the organisation were enough to make you stop in your tracks and take a breath.

Since the assassination of Sadat in 1981, the country had been under Emergency Law, ruled with an iron fist by Sadat's successor Mubarak.

These Emergency Laws stayed in place right until President Mubarak's overthrow during the Arab uprisings of 2011, and gave the authorities sweeping powers to arrest and detain civilians indefinitely. They were a flagrant abuse of human rights that the United States and her allies put up with in return for the promise of stability in the region. Technically, HT wasn't a banned organisation in Egypt. But that was only because the Emergency Law worked the other way round: there was no natural right to association; instead a group needed the state's permission to do so. While some political parties had a permit to operate, HT had never had any such thing.

In Alexandria, there were two other HT members from the UK who had also arrived in Egypt. Reza Pankhurst I had known for several years by this point, having recruited with him at Cambridge University, and having encouraged him to travel to Pakistan to spread the message. Reza was in Cairo along with Ian Nisbet. Ian had converted to HT when he was a student at Westminster University. We all got on well, and Rabia and I would travel up to Cairo to meet their families on a regular basis.

Meanwhile, echoing Salim al-Rahhal in Alexandria all those years before I was born, I began the process of recruitment. Because of Egypt's State Security, the much-feared Aman al-Dawlah, it was all very surreptitious. I did not talk about HT on the phone, in case my phone was tapped. If contacting people by email, I would write the blandest of messages, like 'I am coming over for dinner'. I would meet up with people at prearranged places, and to begin with I was very careful about bringing HT into the conversation. It was more about befriending and getting to know people, to get a sense of their views.

One such individual was Ahmed Eid, a medical student at the University of Alexandria. Ahmed was very bright, someone with an almost photographic memory, and was already a very committed Salafist. Ignoring our tried and tested tactic of recruiting people from a secular background, my experiences in Pakistan had led me to believe that it was indeed possible to recruit Salafists. What I had overlooked was that Egypt was no Pakistan; whereas Pakistan was only just coming to terms with Islamism, Egypt had already lost a president to our ideology.

It was around December 2001 that things began to get serious. There was another British-Pakistani student on my course called Hassan Rizvi whom I had also befriended. Hassan was a young streetwise kid who had come over from the University of Exeter. Like most young British Muslims in those days, Hassan identified with Islamism even if he hadn't joined any group. We clicked immediately. On this particular day, we were out in Alexandria – we tried to mix regularly with Egyptians to help us improve our Arabic. Hassan had been in a mosque to pray, and as I met him outside I could see immediately that something was troubling him.

'Hassan bro, what's wrong?' I asked.

'The weirdest thing, man, someone gave me a message for you,' he said, looking puzzled. 'I was in the mosque, after having finished my prayers, when someone appeared next to me and asked if I was brother Maajid. He said he was a friend of Ahmed Eid's, and that he needed to talk to Maajid urgently. He said that you were in danger, bro.'

By now, I felt worried too, and was looking round to see if anyone was watching us.

'He wanted me to take him to you,' Hassan said. But though Hassan wasn't a recruit like me, he was street-smart enough to know what the score was. 'I said no way, bro, I refused. I mean, he could've been Aman al-Dawlah for all I knew. I said I needed to talk to you first. If you wanna speak to him, I've arranged a time and place where we can go together, tomorrow. But I'm coming with you, bro, just so you know I've got your back.'

As Hassan was telling me this, something suddenly hit home. It might just have been coincidence, but I hadn't seen Ahmed for a few days. There might have been any number of reasons for that, but I couldn't recall having seen him around. Had he been picked up? He was the one person in Alexandria I'd discussed HT with, but our conversations had just been between the two of us. I thought about it, and decided that it was unlikely to have been the secret police who had been talking to Hassan: if they had wanted to find me, it would have been easy enough to have done so.

The next day I turned up at the prearranged meeting place with Hassan. He didn't have to come, but I was glad of his support. We stood there waiting, when a car pulled up, and we were told to get in. We were driven round Alexandria for what seemed like an age. Then the car pulled up behind another vehicle, and we were told to get out and get in that one instead. Driven round the city again, we switched vehicles a second time. Eventually, we were put in a taxi van and driven to the outskirts of the city.

A while later the taxi van pulled up and we got out. Ahmed's friend was waiting for us, and he apologised for driving us around.

'We had to be careful,' he said. 'We had to make sure that you weren't being followed.'

By now, my head was rushing. 'What's up?' I asked in my newly acquired Arabic. 'Where is Ahmed? Is he OK?'

'He is OK now,' the friend said. 'He was arrested and tortured. He has just been released and wanted me to warn you.'

'*Subhan Allah* – Exalted be Allah! What? . . . Why?' I asked, as my heart started to beat fast and my brow broke out in a cold sweat. 'What's he been arrested for?' I suspected the answer.

Ahmed's friend looked at me gravely. He must have seen what the Aman al-Dawlah had done to his friend, and knew, as I did, that it was his association with me that caused it. 'Ahmed wanted me to tell you that Aman al-Dawlah know all about you. They know that you are a member of HT, they know your life history. They know about you recruiting in Pakistan and about your desire to establish a *Khilafah* here in Egypt. You need to know that Hizb al-Tahrir is considered by them the most dangerous organisation to have ever come to Egypt. They hate you more than they hate the jihadists.'

It was the word 'Pakistan' that really took me aback. Yes, I'd discussed HT with Ahmed, but hadn't gone into my time in Pakistan. That information could only have come from Aman al-Dawlah. How on earth did they know about that anyway?

'Ahmed wanted me to tell you', his friend continued, 'that they are preparing a major case against you; they will arrest you and put you on trial. That was why he was tortured, to gather information for the case against you. He tried to protect you as best he could, *akhi*.' Ahmed's friend emphasised the point about the trial again. 'They're not talking about deporting you, but incarcerating you. *Akhi* Maajid, you're from the UK, your jails are not our jails. Do you understand what that means? *Wallahi* – by Allah, Maajid, do you know what might happen if they find you guilty?'

I nodded. At this moment my mind started to drift to the obscure, the way it does when it senses pending danger.

'Where are we, by the way?' I heard myself mutter.

'We're in Abu Keer, on the outskirts of Alexandria; it's an old village famous for its fish. But back to the point, Ahmed wanted me to tell you, as a friend, that you should leave Egypt immediately. You should get out while you still have the chance. *Allahu ma'ak* – May Allah be with you.'

Ahmed's risk, in getting this message to me, is what we called in Egypt *Gad'ana*, a very chivalrous thing to do. It touched me deeply, and I still hold this gesture close to my heart for the courage it must have taken him to warn me. Here was a man tortured for information on me, and yet he further risked his safety, and that of his friends and family, to warn me in advance. To know Egypt's Aman al-Dawlah like I do now, is to not read these lines lightly. What Ahmed did could have forfeited the safety of any one of his family, his mother, his sister, his brother, and subjected them to torture, rape or even death in retaliation. Such loyalty, such brotherhood, is hard to come by. It was in moments like this that Islamism seemed to be the only bond that could inspire such chivalry in the hearts of men. The easy option would be to get himself free through setting me up, or failing that, to have nothing more to do with me. I was grateful to his friends, too, for putting themselves in potential danger by coming to talk to me.

I replayed what Ahmed's friends had told me, over and over in my head, blood pumping through my temples at a speed I didn't know was possible. This was a serious situation. The time had finally come, all those years of preparation, the romanticism of struggle, and now it was my time to struggle. I knew, too, that I couldn't just pick up the phone and ring Nasim back in London for his advice, or try to make contact with my other HT members in Egypt. There was a strong likelihood my phone was already tapped: there had been clicks on the line ever since I arrived in Alexandria. There was a good possibility I would be followed, and lead Aman al-Dalwah to the whereabouts of other activists. Whatever I decided to do, I only had Allah to rely on, *Allahu Musta'an*.

I thought hard about leaving the country. But if I was being watched as Ahmed was suggesting, how would I get past airport security? Surely they would just stop me at the border? As fortune would have it, Rabia and Ammar were already out of the country, having gone back to the UK to see family. I decided it was too dangerous for them to return, and got a message to them, without giving anything away, that they should stay in the UK until further notice. Rabia immediately knew the code for what it was; we had rehearsed this moment over and again between us, and she spent weeks in prayer worrying for my safety. As for myself, I decided the best course of action was to lie low. I stopped all HT activity instantly, and without notice. I steered clear of my flat, and moved around instead, staying with friends until everything had calmed down.

Over the next few weeks, I was living on the edge of my nerves. The fact that I was crashing on different people's couches didn't help – bad nights of sleep punctuated by being woken by every new creak and groan of the floorboards. But as the days turned to weeks I began to relax. It was the Christmas holidays: I had no classes to attend; Rabia and Ammar were away; and I couldn't do any HT work. It might seem an odd scenario under which to have a break, but for the first time in a long while, that's exactly what I did. I hung out with Hassan, and with a Japanese student in our class, Hiroshi Ito, who'd converted to Islam as 'Abdul Azeem'. Hiroshi couldn't speak English, so we'd talk to each other in classical Arabic. I finally felt I was making friends again, instead of getting close to people merely to recruit them.

Towards the end of the holidays, about a month or so after the meeting with Ahmed's friends, I felt confident enough about the situation to test the waters. I decided that I would try to leave the country to see what would happen. So Hassan, Hiroshi and I caught a coach from Alexandria to Cairo, and went to catch a ferry. The security here, I thought, might be less rigorous than at the airport. To my huge relief, I got through border security without a murmur. We took the ferry across the Red Sea to Aqaba, and drove over to Amman. From here we caught a taxi over the Allenby Bridge into Jerusalem, where we stayed in the Old City for a night. We were going on an adventure.

Being in Jerusalem, or al-Quds, was like taking a walk through an ancient history book. I remain mesmerised by the sheer majesty of the place. I remember tracing the steps of Jesus 'alayhi salam through the old city, eyes welled with reverent tears. I recall being incredibly humbled by the fact that I was walking in the footsteps of Prophets. I saw the Mosque of Omar, the Prophet's companion and Second Caliph of Islam, built on the footsteps of a church because Omar refused to enter the church to pray, from fear that his followers would later convert it into a mosque. So they built the mosque on the footsteps anyway.

And as we entered the Al-Aqsa compound, into Islam's third holiest site for Friday prayers, I became overwhelmed by emotion. The sheer significance of where I was, the purity of the place, and the fact that each brick, each slab, was currently suffering due to the conflict overcame me. We could see bullet holes in the sacred walls. We prayed there, salat al-Jumu'ah – our Friday prayers, right there under the green dome of the Al-Aqsa Mosque; right there where the seal of Allah's Prophet Muhammad 'alayhi salam led all other Prophets in prayer on that night known as Israa. Muhammad 'alayhi salam then ascended to Jannah – Paradise, from the very rock beneath the golden dome of the Qubbat al-Sakhra, right there, where I broke down and kissed the floor and begged Allah to forgive my transgressions against Him, my wife and my son in case I never saw them again. My own group, Hizb al-Tahrir, had been founded in this very mosque in 1953. Filled with an all encompassing sense of awe, from that day I dedicated my heart to the lands of Palestine.

It felt so good to be away from Egypt. For those couple

of days, it felt as though the suspicion and the stress of being watched was falling from my shoulders. It's difficult to describe the experience of living in a police state if you've never lived in one, but because someone might be watching you or listening, because you can never quite be sure, there's an inbuilt tension in how you go about your life. It's only when you leave the country, and feel this tension disappear that you realise how wound up you've been. It's an insidious situation: hard not to check your actions or feel paranoid, even when you're doing nothing wrong. Ironically, I felt more relaxed in Israeli-controlled al-Quds than I had been in Egypt.

While I was still in al-Quds, I took the opportunity to reconnect with HT and met the members after the Friday prayers in the Al-Aqsa Mosque. I introduced myself to Issam Amireh, a senior member. I told him about my background, my studies in Egypt and my HT activities in the UK, Pakistan and Denmark. He suggested that I should return to al-Quds after I had finished my year in Alexandria, to study with him for a while. This would have been a huge honour, and I readily agreed. We discussed the situation in Egypt, but not in detail – there was little he could have done to help me with Aman al-Dawlah. For those golden couple of days, I could see my HT career stretch out in front of me: studying in Jerusalem, returning to Pakistan to recruit, and cementing my place in Islamic history by helping to bring about 'the *Khilafah*'.

I returned to Egypt by the same route. Again, there were no problems at border controls. In retrospect, and in relation to what happened next, it does seem strange that I got in and out so easily. It might have been because they'd deduced from my return ferry ticket, and that I didn't have any possessions with me, that I was planning to return to continue my studies. Equally, it might have been a mistake on their part. Just because Aman al-Dawlah were ruthless in their actions, it didn't mean that they were competent in everything they did. Theirs was perhaps a more scatter-gun approach to keeping tabs on people.

It might also have been that there was a tightening of security after my return. After all, this period was the immediate aftermath of 9/11, and the situation in terms of policy was still quite fluid. At this point, no British citizens had been tortured in a foreign country as part of the War on Terror. I was a member of a group that was perfectly legal in the UK, and it seemed out of the question that I wouldn't be supported if I was arrested.

However, things were starting to change. How far and how deep the intelligence sharing was between countries after 9/11 is hard to say. But the fact that Aman al-Dawlah knew all about me suggests it was happening. The timeline is important here: by early 2002 the Taliban had been defeated, and the focus on military operations was giving way to the interrogation of captured prisoners. For the first time, your citizenship wasn't an issue. Neither were such niceties as the Geneva Convention. None of this was official, and a lot of it is conjecture, but it may have been that, in those weeks after my return from al-Quds, I became fair game to the authorities. Maybe they'd had the green light that the British government wouldn't intervene. The only way of finding out what happened would be to get hold of the Aman al-Dawlah files: when Mubarak was ousted in 2011, the headquarters were ransacked and the paperwork stolen. Whoever has taken those files has the answer: maybe one day I'll find out.

Whatever the truth, I returned to Egypt less worried than I had been a month or so before. I was so relaxed about the situation that I gave the all-clear for Rabia and Ammar to return to the country. I was still careful to maintain my distance from other HT members – I didn't go and see Reza, for example, or go back to recruiting. It was as if the situation was back to normal. Little did I know that this was the calm before the storm.

CHAPTER SEVENTEEN

Welcome to Egypt, we do as we please

The banging on my door came at three o'clock in the morning on the 1st of April. I was awake, as I'm sure they knew. Thinking about it later, they'd probably followed me all evening. My last night of freedom was spent with Hassan, enjoying the cafe culture of Alexandria. It is a beautiful city, far more so than Cairo on account of its coastal setting. There is an unmistakable quality to Alexandria at night: the intoxicating smells of coffee and shisha smoke, intermingling with the cool crispness of the sea air. I was lucky in a way to have wandered the streets underneath the stars that night: it would serve to give me a shard of civilisation to remember in the months and years ahead.

They must have already been there when I said good night to Hassan, and made my way back to the flat. I must have walked straight past them, as they gestured to each other and sent a radio message that I had returned. Did they sense me, as I tiptoed through the dark and sleeping apartment, careful not to wake my son, my wife or her friend Zahra, who was staying with us? Did they see me as I stepped out onto the balcony, soaking up one last look at the glistening skyline before bed? Did they hear my one-year-old son stir before I did, his restlessness and murmuring giving way to needy cries? I tiptoed over to Ammar's cot and picked him up, held him against my shoulder and rocked him gently. In those days he would wrap his little hand tightly around my index finger as I soothed him with Ayat al-Kursi, the sacred Muslim prayer, *Allahu La ilaaha illa huwa al-Hayyu al-Qayyum* . . .

A famous poet once wrote that the world would end, not with a bang, but with a whimper. My world ended with both – the whimpering of my son and the bang at the door. It was the sort of noise that rings louder in your soul than in your ears, as the bottom of a size twelve police boot kicked at the door, again and again, and the double lock I had taken to using offered some resistance. Even before I saw the soldiers I knew instinctively what was happening. Even before little Ammar started weeping, clinging to my arms from terror, I knew what had happened. And then . . . the door, I thought tangentially, I must save the door. I calmly walked over to the door, in a haze, and opened it before they could kick it down. There was after all nowhere to run to in this high-rise flat. Nowhere left to hide. As the soldiers burst into the flat in full armour, protective vests, carrying stun grenades and machine guns, I rushed back to shelter Ammar from the terrible sight. First they secured the area, checking to see if any resistance would meet them, and then they zeroed in on me, all guns trained on father and son as they barked orders in Egyptian Arabic at this

24-year-old father trying to shelter his crying little boy from the barrels of sub-machine guns. I stood subdued, not moving, just praying to heal Ammar's fear, chanting God's name in rhythmic tones gently in his ear, *Allahu Allahu Allahu Allah*. In the background, I could hear them approaching the bedrooms. They will storm in on my sleeping wife, I thought. I don't care what they do, I will not let them wake Rabia with their guns. I lifted a lead-heavy foot and started moving.

'Maagid Nawaz, where are you going?' a voice asked in accented English, with the Egyptian pronunciation of the 'j' as a 'g'. In front of me, the phalanx of machine guns gave way to a smartly dressed man in a suit. He was young, in his early thirties, clean-shaven. His dark hair was combed back. I knew instantly that he was the one to fear. He was the *zaabit* – officer of Aman al-Dawlah – and he didn't need a machine gun to assert his authority.

'Are you Maagid Nawaz?' he asked.

'I am,' I replied.

The *zaabit* nodded. He knew this already.

'You need to come with us.' The way he said 'need' made me flinch.

'Look, I opened the door, I let you in, I've got nothing to hide. Can I please just wake my wife? You can follow me in if you like.' I said as I was trying to calm Ammar.

'OK, let's go.'

And he followed me to the bedroom door, as I walked in and woke Rabia with a low, trembling voice.

'Rabia, wake up, it's me.' It didn't take much, she was up immediately, wondering why Ammar was crying. 'You have to get up, it's time, they're here.' Knowing instantly what I referred to, Rabia shot up, threw her long jilbab, or gown, over her body and quickly covered what modesty she could with her hijab.

'What, are they really here?'

'Yes, right by the door, you better wake up sister Zahra. Be strong for Allah's sake. I'm afraid I'll need to leave you shortly.'

I could hear a slamming of drawers and cupboards as I tried to keep calm. They were ransacking the house. Rabia rushed to wake her friend Zahra in the guest room as I walked back out to the sitting room. As Ammar still clutched to me in terror, I asked one last favour from the *zaabit*. 'Can I take this small Qur'an with me?' I asked calmly.

'Sure,' came the steady reply.

My immediate fear was not what they might find – I had no weapons of any sort – but what they might 'find': the planting of evidence.

'Wait here,' said the agent, as he left me guarded. Through the doorway, I could see that they were throwing my books into bin bags. I had HT literature in the house and plenty of it: enough to make my membership of the group incontrovertible. These soldiers, though, were just randomly taking handfuls of books off the shelves, and many of them were just normal books, readily available tomes about Islam and other subjects. That gave me, briefly, a flicker of hope, that these soldiers didn't know what they were looking for, and that maybe they might miss the most damning texts. They carried out bin bag after bin bag.

'You must come with us now, Maagid Nawaz,' the *zaabit* said sharply.

* * *

To travel to Egypt as a member of Hizb al-Tahrir, and to actively participate in recruitment, was always going to be a high-risk activity. It was a different situation from the one I'd come across in the UK or Denmark, and even in Pakistan the organisation wasn't banned until 2003, after Musharraf's purge of my army friends. Before I went to Alexandria, I'd prepared myself psychologically for what might happen. I discussed with the UK leadership the possibility that I might be arrested and tortured, and what my response should be.

The HT policy was clear. I was to give my name and that I was a member of HT. It was important to state that, to show you had courage and principle: to deny your membership, even to save your skin, was an affront to your beliefs, cowardice in the face of tyranny. This, though, was the only information you should give your interrogators: whatever they did to you, no further details of the group's activities were to be revealed. This remains, as far as I am aware, the group's policy even though it is a deeply unrealistic one. To give an interrogator that carrot – to stand there and say I'm in HT but I'm not going to tell you about it – is asking for trouble. Everyone has a threshold when it comes to torture, and the HT line is simply impossible to sustain. It would have been better not to admit membership at all and hope the interrogation didn't get any further.

It is worth adding, too, that HT's policy was particularly absurd given the group's response to someone being arrested. While members were told to stand tall, the group had an active policy not to support what they considered to be fallen soldiers. While the arrested HT member is interrogated and tortured, in the outside world HT would carry on as though that person was no longer their responsibility. Of course the group would make noises about its fallen members, but there would be no support officially provided by the group to the families. So while the HT member was under orders not to disown the group, the group would practically disown the HT member.

The reason that I was willing to put myself in such a dangerous position was because of the elements of HT's teachings. In the numerous *halaqahs* I had attended over the years, the importance of sacrifice was drilled into us. Stories were told and retold about Prophets, companions and martyrs who gave up everything in order to establish Islam. We were taught to believe that our struggle was so absolute that it was impossible to contemplate victory without blood being spilt. If that sacrifice was to be mine, I knew Allah would recompense me in the hereafter. I had considered the possibility of *shahadah* (martyrdom) and had reconciled myself with this outcome quite decisively. Never one to do things by halves, if the *shahadah* was in store for me it would not only be Allah's will, it would be my honour.

The final part of my preparation was to discuss with Rabia what would happen if I got arrested. As Rabia was a member of HT she understood why I was doing what I was doing. We discussed all the consequences of this happening, because the Aman al-Dawlah left no stone unturned when it came to extracting information. There were stories of wives and children being brought in front of arrested husbands, in order for him to watch them being tortured in front of him.

The one advantage that Rabia and Ammar had in such

a situation, ironically for me as an Islamist, was that they had British passports. We came up with a plan of action to follow if I was arrested: Rabia was to get herself to the British Embassy without delay and to make sure that she left the country at the first opportunity. My arrest would mean an uncertain future for Rabia and Ammar – as I say, Rabia would be given no support from HT while I was incarcerated. My sacrifice would be hers as well as my own. And in a certain sense, I'm still unsure who suffered more.

Now, as I was about to be taken away, I spoke to Rabia one last time, quietly and quickly, as they began tugging at my arms.

'Do as we agreed,' I said, looking at her desperately straight in the eyes. 'Do you understand?'

Rabia looked at me that final time, stricken with grief, and nodded. I knew she understood. She knew she had to get to the consul in Alexandria then get herself and Ammar out of the country quickly.

'Where are you taking him?' Rabia suddenly asked the agent. 'When are you bringing him back?'

The agent looked a little surprised at her questioning, but took it in his stride. 'In three days' time,' he said calmly.

'And how do I get in contact with you?' she asked. 'Who are you, anyway?'

The agent smiled, a little patronisingly at my wife. As if I carry a badge, it seemed to say. He wrote down a number and handed it to her.

'Thank you,' she said.

Her small triumph, though, was to be short-lived. The

number, when she tried it later, would turn out to be a false one. What she didn't know was that our phone socket had been ripped out. A number that wouldn't work, to be called on a phone she couldn't use. I later learnt that she had to go out into the streets at 4 a.m., knowing no Arabic, begging people to let her use a phone so she could call the consul.

Rabia's questioning, however, stirred up something within me.

'This is ridiculous,' I said. 'You can't just come in here in the middle of the night like this. You haven't told me what I am being arrested for. You haven't read me my rights. I haven't seen any ID. Do you even have a warrant to search my flat?'

The agent listened to my diatribe with a look of faint amusement. When I had finished, he laughed and shook his head, like I just didn't get it.

'Welcome to Egypt, Maagid. We do as we please,' he said with a sneer.

The calmness of his demeanour had finally cracked. Ammar's crying, which had been incessant, was the last straw. He came over to me and wrenched Ammar from my arms. It was a flash of temper, all the more brutal for the fact that it was the little boy who bore the brunt of it. To have Ammar's hand ripped away from me like that in those final moments was the most painful thing. He looked me straight in the eyes, bawling, his arms outstretched as the *zaabit* shoved him towards Rabia. That image is still scorched in my memory. This was to be my parting memory, and the last time I was to see him, or his mother, for a long, long time.

The *zaabit* then grabbed my arm, gripping it quite

aggressively, and I remember thinking that this was the first time since the police had burst in that anyone had touched me.

'Right,' he snapped. 'Let's go.'

There was no chance to say goodbye, not even a final glance back as he half pushed me through my front door, frogmarching me down the stairs to the police van below. She didn't know it yet, but that night Rabia was to lose her husband for ever.

CHAPTER EIGHTEEN

The *ghimamah* has no rules

The cold of the night air hit me like a smack in the face. I could see that the whole area had been cordoned off: there were more armed police standing at the front of my building, further vans and cars sealing the road. The *zaabit* spat an instruction in Arabic to a *shaweesh* – police conscript. *Kalbishuh* – cuff him, he said, and my arms were duly shoved behind my back. I could feel the sharpness of the metal scoring my wrists as I was shoved into the van. A heavy hand pushed me forward on the back of my head, and it was a balancing act not to stumble on the steps as I got in. A horseshoe of wooden benches ran along the sides. *U'ad* – sit, someone barked. I sat in the middle as the benches filled up with *shaweeshiya*, the van swaying each time another jumped in.

The *zaabit* shouted another instruction as the back doors of the van slammed shut '*ihna mashiyeen, ghammimooh*'. I didn't understand this but soon found out. The *shaweesh* next to me pulled out a rag, a dark, dirty, stained piece of cloth, and motioned at me to lean forward. It was a blindfold, and now, for the first time, as the gift of sight was taken from me, I began to feel petrified, complete fear, of the kind that cannot be described but only felt. The rag was wrapped tightly round my face, tied roughly at the back. I could feel the pressure of the cloth pushing against my eyeballs, the unpleasant odour battling the lingering traces of Ammar's baby talc.

Most of all, there was the unremitting blackness as the driver started the engine and began to pull away. It now dawned on me that in the back of this van, with heavily armed *shaweeshiya* surrounding me, I was powerless to use my hands to stop them if they attacked me, and I would not see it coming. This was helplessness. My remaining senses began to strain for any clues of sudden movement. The flicker of confidence I'd had in the flat seemed part of a different world. I was totally at their mercy, and I knew it.

The *ghimamah*, or blindfold, answered the question that the *zaabit* had ignored. I knew now that I was in the hands of Aman al-Dawlah. If they had been ordinary police I'd have been starting down the civil jurisdiction route. I'd be processed and deported, my rights as a British citizen granting me some semblance of respect. Egypt, however, was a country with two parallel judicial systems: the second, the Emergency Law track, wasn't bound by any rules. The *ghimamah* told me this. You don't blindfold someone unless you're taking them to a place that's off the radar.

My mind began wondering about life's finer details. The *ghimamah*. It's a filthy, torn piece of rag; it's not even a proper blindfold. That offends me. I'm worth more than a rag. Then . . . I wonder where it's been. I wonder how many other petrified souls have shared this yard of cloth. Their sweat and mine will now share a common foe. Then . . . actually the fact that it's a rag frightens me. Rags are unofficial, unaccountable. Real blindfolds have to be purchased and processed with receipts, in the cold light of day. Rags are free of rules. And now my body began to tremble, uncontrollably. As if the odour of my *ghimamah* had finally defeated Ammar's last act of defence for me, the scent of his baby talc on my neck, and the odour assaulted my brain, my nervous system. I am in deep trouble. *Subhan Allah!* I am in serious deep trouble. As it began beating its war drums my heart didn't want to surrender to the rag. Preparing to defend my body from whatever may come, I began breathing out, deeply, to try to calm myself.

I thought of my life. How odd my twenty-four years of life had been. Essex, Newcastle, London, Lahore, Raheem Yar Khan, Copenhagen, Cairo, Alexandria, Amman and al-Quds all flashed before me. I thought of *Tai Ammi* and her stories, Patrick, and the unintended path that his small act of racism had set that scared, lonely boy upon. I thought of my first girlfriend Sarah crying on that first day at Cecil Jones after I told her there were too many new girls to choose from. I thought of N.W.A, and 'Fuck tha Police', and my stomach turned as it struck me that only those with the luxury to speak could afford to be so defiant, and to get rich out of being so. I thought of the white friends I'd abandoned, my companionship with Sav and Marc, with Dan, who was stabbed for us; I thought of my crew, Chill, Ricky, Ade and Paul, and the mad times we'd had as every other girl wanted to get in on our scene. Had I really ever been that youthful teenage B-boy bopping to those beats in Southend's clubs? Then I saw Abi beating her womb, pleading with me not to go, not to go, and

I began to long for Abi's smile. I remembered Osman and Yasser, and how proud they were of my activism. I thought of Ed Husain at Newham, Uncle Qayyum in Raheem Yar Khan, Ash at SOAS, how are you all? And now I wondered if Rabia had managed to call that number, and knew instinctively that I would not be back in 'three days'. And so I prayed, I prayed and felt close to Allah in my loneliness as I begged Him to protect me from these *zalimun* – these tyrants: *Allahumm Inni aj'aluka fi nuhurihim* . . .

We stopped. I assumed we were still in Alexandria, but I had no idea. It was the middle of the night. Everything was eerily quiet. I assumed, again, that we were at the Aman al-Dawlah building. But we could have easily pulled up somewhere else: a disused factory, a deserted warehouse. My mind, now defeated by the odour of my *ghimamah*, was ready to suggest, in despair, any number of nightmare scenarios.

Presently, I was taken out of the van and guided into a building. Up we went, stumbling up some stairs that became impossible to navigate without the aid of sight. A door opened in front of me, and the cold slap of night struck me again. A second or two, and I worked out that I must be on the roof of a building. Why, why had they brought me up here? Pushed along, I was eventually guided to what felt like a precipice, the wind rushing against the front of my body, my feet sensing an edge that I dared not test. And then with rather more care than I had experienced until now, I was positioned into a spot and told to stand perfectly still. *Ya Allah*, the thought came to me as fast as the wind rushing past my hair. They're going to push me off the top of the building.

The *shaweeshiya* were laughing at me now: they'd done this before; they knew exactly what I was thinking. They could probably see my knees trembling, as I struggled to stay perfectly still . . .

'Don't move,' a *shaweesh* said, with a sneer. 'You really don't want to move.'

And with that, I could hear him retreat, his steps getting quieter as he crunched gravel behind me. I didn't dare move a muscle. I didn't dare feel anything. I didn't even dare to think. Focus on keeping still. Focus on keeping still. Nothing else exists. I willed time to move fast for me, I wanted this moment to be over, regardless of what came next, and as if to say 'who are you to ask me anything' time stretched out and took a yawn. It seemed to me that I was standing there for fifteen or twenty minutes, but it could just as easily have been two, or five.

Eventually, I heard the gravel crunch behind me again. I tensed up, petrified, wary that I might be about to get a shove. Instead, though, the *shaweesh* grabbed me and pulled me back. I tried not to buckle as he did so, the rush of relief loosening my limbs. Not that the relief lasted for long. When there are no procedures, there's no knowing what might happen next. They're softening me up, I thought to myself, as I was dragged back across the roof, barely able to walk from the tremor in my legs. That's what this is all about. To make me more susceptible, more suggestible, to weaken me. Come on, Maajid! You're not weak, you're never weak! *Ya Allah*, give me strength!

I was taken up some more stairs, and back inside. Through the darkness of my *ghimamah* I caught the glimmer of a lamp.

Positioned in front of what I assume to be a desk, a *zaabit* began to address me. I assumed this was the same *zaabit* who'd led the raid on my flat, but he was speaking Arabic now and, anyway, there was so much I was no longer sure of that it almost didn't matter. Everything was uncertain: where I am, who I was talking to, what is going to happen next. Reality was starting to fray at the seams.

'Maagid Nawaz,' my interrogator said.

'Yes,' I replied in English. 'That's my name.' I wondered if he could see through my attempts at trying to sound strong and confident.

My Arabic wasn't bad. Having been in Egypt for seven months I'd picked up the basics, but here I was struggling to understand every word of what my interrogator said.

'We know everything about you, Maagid. We know you are with Hizb al-Tahrir. We know you are attempting to revive this banned group in Egypt. We know you have tried to recruit people here, that your wish is to overthrow the Egyptian state.' He reeled off each statement like he was flicking dirt from his jacket. 'We know about your work in Pakistan, Maagid. It seems you think you're an important man.' He said the word 'important' with disdain. 'You know what I think, Maagid? I think you should tell me everything you know. That way, this will all be a little easier on you.'

There was a pause, as he allowed what he had just said to sink in. If it hadn't been for Ahmed's warning those few months earlier, I would have been shocked and scared at the mention of Pakistan. That's what he wanted me to feel, that stomach-churning sensation that there's been intelligence gathered against me: Aman al-Dawlah, ISI, MI6, he'd leave me to fill in the gaps. But thanks to Ahmed, I already knew they had this information, so it didn't surprise me now. 'Thank you, Ahmed', I thought to myself, 'for risking everything to warn me, you're a true brother. Look, you see, it's helping me already'. My prior knowledge gave me that fractional advantage, just enough to steel myself and respond.

'My name is Maajid Nawaz,' I said in English, sticking to my HT training. 'I am a member of Hizb al-Tahrir in Britain. I am here in Egypt to study.'

That response brought a fist down on the table. The slam sounded close. 'Don't you dare play games with us, Maagid!' he snapped in Arabic. 'I know you can speak Arabic.'

That flash of temper emboldened me. I felt in some small way that I had got under his skin. If I am to be defiant, it means I must stand ready for the consequences. *Ya Rabb*, my Lord, help me now for I am your humble servant.

'My name is Maajid Nawaz,' I repeated in English. 'I am a member of Hizb al-Tahrir in the UK. I have come from Britain to Egypt to study. I have nothing more to say.'

My use of English was deliberate. It was to emphasise where I was from. I wanted to remind the interrogator at every opportunity that I was a British citizen. This was the strongest card I had to remind him that he couldn't just treat me like he would other Egyptians. Or at least that's what I hoped.

'Tell me about Pakistan!' he shouted in Arabic. 'Tell me about your activities there.'

'I have been to Pakistan, yes,' I agreed in English. 'I have family there. It is perfectly normal for British-Pakistanis to visit the country to see their relatives.'

'Family,' he spat. 'What family?'

'Aunts, uncles, cousins . . .' I was careful not to mention my wife's family. I didn't want to give them any possible reason to arrest her as well.

'Yes, yes, yes,' the interrogator swatted my answer away. 'It's not family members I am interested in, it's members of Hizb al-Tahrir.'

He was, in retrospect, oddly interested in Pakistan, considering that it was nothing to do with Egypt. Later, when I had time to think things through, it did make me wonder about who exactly this was asking these questions, and for whom. As he snapped and shouted at me I stuck to my line. I continued answering in English, politely and firmly emphasising my British citizenship.

'Tell me about Hizb al-Tahrir in Egypt,' the interrogator changed tack.

'I am in Egypt to study. I am here in Alexandria as part of my university degree to study Arabic.'

Here the interrogator snorted; it's called a *shakheer* and is considered extremely rude. To Egyptians this indicates that you no longer make any pretence of social etiquette. 'Who have you recruited?' he asked. 'Who are you in contact with? Who else is involved?'

'I am a member of Hizb al-Tahrir in Britain,' I reiterated. 'I have nothing to do with the organisation in Egypt.'

'We'll see about that, Maagid,' the interrogator said. 'We'll see about that.' He sighed. 'If that's how you want to play it.' I heard a rustle behind me, from where another *shaweesh* must have been standing. 'I said that you had the chance to make things easier for yourself.' I felt the *shaweesh*'s hand grab my arm. 'But I can't help you now,' he said, as I was led away.

Taken back down several flights of outdoor stairs, metal steps at the side of the building, I began wondering if I was about to be driven off somewhere else. But instead we went back inside the building, down some more steps and into what I think was a basement. I heard the click of a key from behind me: my handcuffs were being taken off. Then the heavier clunk of a door being opened, and I was shoved forward, the door slamming shut behind me. Slowly, carefully, still blindfolded, I used my fingertips to take in my new surroundings. I felt cold bars on all sides and realised I was in a cell. As I finally sat down, legs aching for respite, I began to rub my wrists where the handcuffs had been.

I was kept in that holding cell for hours. Again, I can't be completely sure of timings: your perception of time melts away in such circumstances. And then I heard a shout, more like an appeal, someone asking to be taken to the toilet. And in broken Arabic. With pangs of rising guilt, I realised it was Hassan. Later on, another call: this time it was Hiroshi. Then I heard the voice of Yusuf el-Qadi, an Egyptian friend of ours, and a Muslim Brotherhood activist. Hearing their voices seared me in a way that the interrogator's questions had failed to do. They have arrested my friends. They have arrested my friends because of me. None of them had anything to with any of this. I had never raised the matter of HT with any of them. I sat there, too scared to call out to them, and wondered what they would think of me if they knew the truth.

Eventually, we were given some food to eat; one slice of bread and a small round blob of white, extremely salty cheese. A bottle of water was passed around the cells, from which we were allowed a swig. After what must have been the rest of the night, the guards were suddenly all action: the cell doors clanked open and one by one I could hear the shuffling of people being marched outside. It was my turn and the guard snapped at me to hold my hands out in front of me. Back on went the cuffs, and I was dragged out into the daylight.

The coldness of the night air was now a distant memory, and the heat from the sun washed over me. I was shown into the back of a van, only this time there were no benches, just a metal floor onto which I was shoved with Hassan, Hiroshi and Yusuf. It was a closed van with metal on all sides except for a couple of tiny square windows, covered in a metal mesh. The door slammed shut and the van pulled away.

As there were no *shaweeshiya* in the back of the van we were finally able to talk to each other. We had cautiously removed our blindfolds, keeping them round our necks.

'*Subhan Allah*, are you all right?'

'What have they done to you?'

'What did they say?'

It was Yusuf who was doing the apologising. He was the Egyptian and we were the foreigners, and he felt that acutely. 'I can't believe they are treating you like this,' he said as the van sped along an unknown road to an unknown destination. 'I am so sorry.' Yusuf had naturally assumed that it was his membership of the Muslim Brotherhood that was to blame. I said nothing. His insistence that it was his fault only made my guilt even worse. I knew from the questions that this was a HT case, and they were there because of me. But anything I told them would inevitably be used against them, forced out of them through torture. If my friends had mentioned that they knew I was with HT, it would only make matters far worse for them. The questions would keep coming: so he has spoken to you about it, then? You have joined HT too? *Maagid* has recruited you to his cause, has he? Their best hope was to remain in blissful ignorance of my beliefs. The interrogators, I hoped, would soon realise that they knew nothing and just let them go. And so I suffocated my guilt and my overwhelming desire to apologise, in order to keep them safe.

The buzz of the Alexandria traffic began to disappear. It became clear that we were being taken out of the city, driven out into the desert. They shot people here, I knew. Took them out into the middle of nowhere, and never brought them back. The van, meanwhile, was getting hotter and hotter. The desert sun was baking down, turning the back of the van into an oven. Our clothes were soaked through with sweat, I could feel mine clinging to me with their wetness. Heat and sweat, heat and sweat. The saltiness of the cheese we'd had, and the fact that we were sweating so profusely, made us all desperate to urinate. The sheer pain in our bladders was reaching dangerous proportions, but where to go, and how? Soon we felt the van pull over to the side of the road. But it was for the driver to go, not us.

The van started up again. Yusuf banged on the partition wall.

'We need to go,' he said. 'We need to use the loo back here.'

'Do it in the back,' the *shaweesh* shouted back. 'We're not stopping for you.'

The van drove on. We were in that van for maybe four or five hours, and there was no way in that heat you could hold on. There was a spare tyre at the opposite end to the doors, and we decided to take turns and just do it there. The urine went everywhere: all over the steel floor, where we were sitting and standing. The van stank with the putrid smell of sweat, urine and heat. Degraded and humiliated, there was nothing we could do.

As the journey continued, we came to the conclusion that we were being taken to Cairo. From the distance we'd travelled, it seemed the most likely destination. Yusuf kept on apologising, which just made the situation worse. In the heat of the van, feeling guilt over Yusuf's constant apologising, I kept quiet and tried to pray. *Ya Allah, Ya Rabb al-'arsh al-'azeem*, Lord of the majestic throne, grant me the strength to pass this test of yours. I remembered my lessons back in London, about how our struggle would not be achieved without shedding blood. Sacrifice was an honour bestowed on a chosen few. I am thankful to Allah for this opportunity to be tested and counted as one of His true servants: for the chance to prove the depth of my *eeman*, my faith. Allah will never fail me: I must not fail Him in return.

There was the noise of a city now. The van stopped and started amid the hustle and bustle of busy streets. 'Cairo. We're here', I thought. The driver pulled the vehicle over, and as I swallowed hard I heared the door of the van being opened.

'Where are we?' Yusuf asked.

'Don't you know?' the *shaweesh* laughed, as he began guiding us out. 'This is al-Gihaz.'

Al-Gihaz. The name sent a shudder through me. Aman al-Dawlah headquarters in Cairo – 'The Apparatus'.

'My brothers, pray that Allah comes to your aid,' Yusuf struggled to speak, while his face changed to a colour just off yellow. 'This place is a torture centre.'

A murmur. A groan. My arms are grabbed by a guard, my handcuffs roughly removed. A *ghimamah* was tightened over my eyes again and then, unceremoniously, my hands were pulled behind my back and tied together with another piece of rag. Another rag, another place of lawlessness. I winced as the cloth burned my wrists. Official procedures, like the handcuffs, were being left at the door. Manhandled down some steps, away from the sunshine and down into darkness, I was led into the underground cells of al-Gihaz, to await my fate.

CHAPTER NINETEEN

Number forty-two

I will never forget al-Gihaz. It is the sort of place that remains etched on your memory for ever. The sort of place that still, a decade later, I can recall with disturbing clarity as it wakes me up in the night, slipping insidiously into my dreams. The piling of the bodies. The heat and cold. The begging screams from the torture room at the end of the corridor. The waiting. It's the sort of place that when you first enter, you cannot quite believe it exists. Something from a film. But it's real all right. If only my mind could come to believe that it wasn't.

Itnain wa arba'een. Number forty-two. That was who – what – I'd become. My last vestige of identity and dignity were stripped from me as I was shoved down those stairs. I heard with mounting horror my fellow prisoners being called and taken down the corridor, the crackle of electricity. I heard the prisoners being dragged back, the 'schlump' sound as their near lifeless bodies were deposited back in line, the faintness of their whimpers and murmurs as they lay there, recovering.

I was only a number. This was the only order in that

cretinous hellhole, the way the numbers called out ratcheted up, ever closer to my own. Each individual torture session varied, but each must have been between thirty minutes and an hour in length. The wait for our own turn was over a drowsy, sleep-deprived day and night. I was at least sure of that, because I could hear the call to prayer, the *azan*, drifting in from outside the building: the morning *azan* is longer, with an extra line – '*al-salatu khayrun min al-nawm*, prayer is better than sleep'. When I heard that, I thanked Allah for letting me live through another night, for being with me, for preventing me from losing my mind. I'd heard that call twice since arrival, so I knew I was into my third day of imprisonment. Even in the abyss of that building, my faith was giving me answers, was helping me to keep myself strong.

The crackle of electricity was getting closer. So too were the beatings. The roll calls continued day and night, and anyone who didn't answer or forgot their number was beaten there and then. The more people came back from their interrogations, the greater this number was. The sound of beating a helpless, crying man is sickening. Others were made to stand for hours on end for such insubordination as failing to answer to their number. If they didn't stand still, or if their legs gave way, they were punished again. Some prisoners, while their hands were still tied at their backs, would have their arms pulled back and lifted from behind, to hang by the edge of a door from the rope on their wrists, until their will or their body gave way and their arms dislocated from their sockets.

In a cell behind me, within earshot, I heard a guard march in and order a prisoner to sit up. There was a scuffle.

'If I tell you to do it, you do it,' the guard leered.

'Please,' the prisoner begged. 'Please not that.'

'Did I say you could speak?' the guard snapped. The prisoner, by now, was whimpering. And with a snorting *shakheer*, the guard barked: 'Put it in your mouth . . .'

'Number forty!' My moment was coming closer as I struggled to remember my prayers. But my attempts to focus were interrupted by the brother next to me, the brother I was leaning against, who by this point was gently beginning to cry.

'Brother,' he whispered to me, '*akhi*, I'm next. I, I don't know what to do.'

'Sssh,' I said quietly, trying to listen out if a guard was nearby. If anyone heard us trying to talk to each other, we'd both be beaten.

'Help me, *akhi*,' the prisoner whimpered. 'They're going to torture me, I know they are and my number's next. Help me for Allah's sake.'

But what could I say to this brother of mine to ease his pain while I couldn't even find a way to comfort my own soul? Poor man, he's next; at least I have another few minutes for myself. Let me try to help him.

'Calm yourself, my brother,' I gently whispered. 'You need to be strong now. Remember you are here *fee sabeelillah*. You will be justly rewarded for the sacrifice you are about to make.'

The prisoner, number forty-one, continued, 'But I don't know if I can do this. I don't know if I'll be able to get through.'

It was painful, heartbreaking to hear a proud man broken like this. His sobs were the sound of someone whom al-Gihaz had worked its twisted magic on. He was a wreck. The only thing I could think to do for him was to recite for him, to recite a passage from the Qur'an, in the hope that it would give him the courage he so desperately needed. Slowly, and ever so quietly, so low that only he and I could hear, I willed my voice to utter the sounds of Allah's words. It was a risk, I knew that, especially as it was our turn next to be called. If we'd been caught speaking, we'd have been accused of collusion, and any punishment meted out would have been much, much worse.

What I recited to him there, on that day of torture, before he was called upon to sacrifice himself *fee sabeelillah*, is a passage called *al-Burooj*: an ancient story about a boy and a king. It is especially pertinent for those who find their *eeman* being tested. The king demands that everyone in the village worship him. But a boy, who converted to believe in the one true God, refuses. The boy stands by his belief, and is persecuted by the king for it. Like the others in the town who stand with the boy by the one true faith, he is thrown into a pit and burned alive. It took the use of all my energy to get my voice out:

I swear by the mansions of the stars,
And by the promised day,
And by the bearer of witness, and those against whom
    witness is borne,
Cursed be the makers of the pit,
Of the fire fuelled, and by where they sat,
They will surely bear witness to what they did to the
    believers,

Persecuting them for no other cause, but that they
    believed in Allah, the Mighty, the Praised,
Whose is the Kingdom of the heavens and earth, and
    Allah is a witness unto all things . . .

I recited the entire passage to him in Arabic, in the low, rhythmic tones of recitation, or *qira'ah*. Swallowing after each line to catch my breath, and to control my palpitations, and calm my fear: wishing, hoping beyond hope that my words would somehow summon the very angels of our Lord, descended by His command in a righteous rage to protect us from these animals. Like a child, his crying slowly stopped, his sobs drifted further and further apart as he listened intently to my voice, to Allah's words. The beauty of each *ayah*, each verse, seemed to me to sparkle ever more in the grit and grime of this dungeon.

'May Allah reward you, *akhi*,' the prisoner said, as soon I had finished. 'I don't know who you are, but you are a good man. *Wallahi*, you are a good man.'

'Number forty-one!' the guard shouted.

'And so are you,' I whispered. And as I lay there, my *ghimamah* soaking up my tears and itching my eyes, the brother was hauled to his feet and taken to be tortured.

Now I was alone. When the numbers had been lower down, I did wonder if a phone call might come before they got to me. Perhaps, hope against hope, the British Consul would have found out where I was. The guards would have been told to get number forty-two up and out of there, before anything happened. But as the roll call got higher, I knew that there would be no hope of escape.

But I still had my *eeman*. Helping number forty-one – for I never learnt his name nor ever saw him again – had stirred me. It showed to me that for all my fear, I still had my core strength. I was not yet a broken man. I was not weeping and begging number forty-three for help. And I had a plan, too. For while I was lying there my hands had not been idle. Little by little, I had worked away at the rag behind my back. It was loose now. I was holding the knot in place with my fist: otherwise, my hands would be free.

All my life, I had been in situations involving stabbings and assaults, but not once had I been the one beaten. I had never been forced into a humiliating position where I had no choice but to take a beating. It had happened in front of me, for sure, but never to me. And I decided that I wasn't going to let it happen now. Somewhere in the vicinity, I could hear the tortured screams of number . . . brother forty-one. If they try that with me, I thought to myself, they'll have to kill me for the wrath I intend to unleash upon them. They may have guns and torture machines, but I've got surprise on my side. My hands are free. I braced myself, and decided that at the moment of torture I would jump on my interrogator. I would jump on him and simply bite down into his neck, and bite and bite until they would have to shoot me dead to make me stop. I would die fighting, without pain, without suffering, with glory.

It sounds surreal now. But al-Gihaz is a surreal place, and listening to the screams of grown men pleading for their torture to stop over forty-eight hours can do surreal things to one's mind. It's as if the outside world, the normal rules, no longer existed. The dehumanising nature of the regime turns even the most rational minds to their animalistic instincts. Like a tiger backed into a corner, I was seriously prepared to fight viciously, ruthlessly – to sacrifice my own life rather than suffer the indignation the other prisoners had been put through.

The screaming suddenly stopped. I heard the guards drag brother forty-one back, body limp, like a sack of potatoes, until they dumped him beside me. Stillness. My time had come. I was next. And I steadied myself in preparation for my number to be called. The anxiety at that moment is not something I will ever, ever wish upon my worst enemy. The seconds turned to minutes, and the minutes turned to irrelevance as time drifted out of the window with my mind running from the sheer inhumanity of my situation. The war drums of my heart began to gather pace, and I prepared myself for the last moments of my life. Be strong, Maajid, Allah is with you, be strong and embrace your martyrdom.

Itnain wa arba'een!

There it was. Number forty-two. My whole body literally shuddered. It is my turn. Number forty-two. Odd, I thought, as my mind wandered off into that all too familiar place of randomness. Forty-two is my age, twenty-four, but backwards. How strange. I wonder if I'll ever reach forty-two years old. I gathered the strength to speak. My voice came out weaker than I would have liked:

'*Na'am* – Yes.'

And I stood up.

CHAPTER TWENTY

Assalaamu alaykum, you've just come out of hell

To be asked to voluntarily walk towards your own torture is the cruellest of expectations. Why can't they just carry me? Each step is a personal betrayal. My body is convulsing in revulsion against my commands. Every instinct is screaming at me to turn the other way, but I am expected to walk on. Try standing in the middle of a highway watching an oncoming bus without flinching, that's hard. Now try voluntarily walking *towards* that bus instead of stepping out of the way: impossible. My legs are buckling under each step; but I force compliance and walk on. Guard, your chaperoning hand that helps me walk blindly to my own torture feels perversely merciful; for how could I avoid stepping on my brothers in the corridor were it not for you? Alas, without sight I cannot help but feel so disgustingly dependent on you. Now it is hard to breathe. Fighting to stay hidden away deep within me, even my breath fears coming out to face my torturer. My heart is attempting to escape the cage that is my chest, and my mind is beginning to shut down. I am in shock. Ya Allah, I need you right now. If any mercy I have ever shown to anyone has amounted to any value in your esteem, then send me your angels now to shield me from these monsters. I am trying to be brave for you my Lord, but the truth is I am scared. Help me my Lord, for I am very scared.

The interrogation room. I can hear my interrogator in front of me, his electrocution device crackling in anticipation. My whole adult life I've spent in preparation for this moment of agony. Training my soul to accept what my body cannot. Now, I am so tense and tight that my jaw begins to ache. What will happen next? Will he hit me hard to warm me up? Will he attack me without warning, as an indication that he is brazen? If I were him, if I had sold my soul to the devil in this way, if I was going to do unspeakable things to my helpless victims, that's how I would do it. In a terrible, unpredictable, twisted way. Why sell your soul only to be useless at being evil? My mind is racing. The possibilities are too many. Come on! Do it properly, man! I can't stand the wait any longer, just get it over with. But I waited, and waited, and it didn't come. Instead, I heard the shuffle of feet and the door close.

I had assumed that they would just attack you with the electricity there and then. What I learnt later, from other prisoners, was that there was a whole process to electrocution. They stripped the brothers naked, pulled them down onto the floor, pinned a chair on top of them, and while someone sat on that chair to hold them down, they electrocuted them via their teeth or genitalia, or both. At the time though, I didn't know any of this, else I'd have known I wasn't about to be electrocuted. But I didn't, so I just stood there, waiting for the impact, my hands ready to be released, preparing to pounce on my interrogator's neck and bite it until death came to me.

I heard the squeak of a chair, as someone sat down.

'Maagid Nawaz?' This was a different person from the one who had interrogated me back in Alexandria.

'Yes,' I replied. The effort it took to make my voice audible was a battle in itself. At this moment, I felt brave just by being able to speak without breaking down.

'So tell me, Maagid. Tell me about Hizb al-Tahrir in Egypt.'

I swallowed hard. Defiance in Alexandria, without having been subjected to forty-eight hours of listening to the brothers getting tortured was one thing, but now I saw, I heard, I knew what they were capable of. You will stand among the *Sahabah*, Maajid – the Companions of the Prophet, do not give up now. The *shaheed* (the martyr) will not die. Like a green bird flying beneath the '*arsh* (the Throne of Almighty Allah), you will live under His shade. You will be that happy little boy once again. Do not give up.

'My name is Maajid Nawaz,' I replied, in English, in whatever level of voice I could muster, which probably wasn't very loud at all. I was still remembering my training, but only just.

'I am a member of Hizb al-Tahrir in Britain. I am in . . .'

A pause as I gasped for air.

'. . . in Egypt to study.'

I could hear the quality in my voice: though the words I was speaking were defiant in meaning, the way I was saying them was pleading. I scolded myself. Be a man, what's wrong with you, is this how Yasir and Sumayyah, for whom you named your son, Ammar, behaved? Stand strong, man!

The interrogator said nothing. He let the silence unsettle me. Then, in Arabic: 'OK, Maagid. I think you should listen to this.' My interrogator got up and opened the door. As the door opened, the sound of screams flooded in from a nearby room. As I heard the screams and pleas, and tried not to listen, a terrifying recognition dawned upon me. The person being tortured was pleading in English.

Kallim 'Arabi! The interrogator shouted back. 'Speak Arabic!'

'I'm trying,' the tortured soul replied, attempting through the shouts in badly broken, barely understandable sentences.

My God, I thought. That sounds like Reza. They're torturing Reza Pankhurst.

Subhan Allah! My last trump card, my British citizenship, really did mean nothing to these bastards. If they're torturing Reza, then there's no reason they won't torture me. Poor Reza, how on earth was a man supposed to speak in any language, let alone a foreign one, through the pain of electrocution!

The door to the interrogation room slammed shut again. The interrogator sensed from my reaction that I knew who was being tortured. Now he was right up to me, lowering his voice with menace.

'You hear that, Maagid? You hear what we are doing to your brother? Don't think we can't do that to you. For your own sake, stop these games and start speaking to me in Arabic.' He was shouting at me now. 'Start talking to me about Hizb al-Tahrir . . .' He spat the name of the group out in disgust. '. . . Everything! I want to know everything about your group in Egypt!'

The next thing I knew, I felt his fist in my stomach. A big, deep, powerful punch, and it took all my strength for it not to knock me over. My mind went black and I struggled to breathe as the wind was knocked out of my lungs. Somewhere in my distant memory, somewhere during more innocent days, I remembered that I hailed from a place where someone called Patrick had done this to me. But I had survived, I had lived to tell the tale and see Patrick cower in fear before me many years later. And that memory brought me back up with strength and a renewed *eeman*. Allah is with me. I see it now. This is His sign! Allah never abandoned me. He has been with me all along. And now I knew what I needed to say next to my enemy.

'I have nothing more to say to you. Do whatever you want.'

And I loosened my hands in preparation for my attack. To this day, I find it hard to believe that I actually stood there and said this to him. There are many moments in my life, and in this story, I am ashamed of recounting. But knowing that I uttered this one, feeble, sentence on that day fills me with pride. Ammar will surely be old enough one day to read these words, and right here he will know that his father tried with all his strength and all his might to be a noble, honourable man. Because he was named *Abu Ammar*, named after martyrs. And the rest is for the world to judge.

My enemy paused. I could hear him pacing. Then, to my surprise, almost as an anticlimax to what I had just embraced as the inevitable, he said in a dismayed tone, 'I'm sending you back to your place. You have twelve hours to think about what you just said to me. And if, after those twelve hours, you still don't tell me the truth, be in absolutely no doubt that

I will torture you in ways you have never imagined. Is that clear?'

I said nothing. The interrogator came close again, close enough that I felt his breath on me. Behind him I could hear the door being opened, and more footsteps entering the room. 'You know, you've got such a nice face, Maagid,' he hissed. 'It would be a shame to have to ruin it.'

With that, I was shoved and manhandled down the corridor. The guard was laughing.

'Such a nice face,' he repeated. 'He likes you. You know what we do to people we like, don't you?' The implication was clear as he dumped me back down on the floor. And he left me with that thought, to fester and rot in the darkest corners of my imagination.

The beatings continued. The numbers kept on being called, higher and higher: up into the hundreds. I replayed in my head again and again the comments that the interrogator had said to me. *Such a nice face.* I remembered the pleas of the prisoner being assaulted in the cell behind me. What was going on? Why hadn't he just tortured me and got it over with? Why was I being spared in this way? I began to feel guilt, as if somehow I had escaped unfairly while all the others, even my brothers from the UK, were treated in the same, brutal way.

I had been in situations before where I had escaped by the skin of my teeth. Matt's stabbing by Combat 18 hooligans in Southend was meant for me. The murder conviction in Newham was almost me. Somehow, I had always managed to get away with it. Was Allah saving me for something else? But as the night continued, punctuated by the sharp screams and sound of electricity ripping through the souls of men, it was a hope I was finding it increasingly difficult to cling on to.

In my exhaustion, both mental and physical, I entered a sleep-deprived daze. I was in danger of losing it. The regular roll call prevented us from sleeping, and by this time it must have been three and a half days since my arrest in Alexandria. Alexandria, Rabia, Ammar, how long ago that all seemed now. How much had changed in these few days. I knew already that I would never be the same again, that Rabia had lost the Maajid who woke her gently from her slumber in order to spare her the ordeal of being woken by guns. Then it came. The phone rang. It was like civilisation was calling to catch up on the denizens of some type of underworld. Like a dream, I could hear it ringing down the corridor, fuzzy and out of focus at first. But when the guard started speaking I immediately zoomed in on what he was saying.

'*Aywa effandim* – yes, sir,' he said with a sharp formality. 'Correct, we have the five of them here . . . *Aywa*, I will, sir, right away.'

The five of them. My alertness returned. My mind was light with the possibility. The five of them – he had to be talking about the foreigners. I knew there was me, Reza, Hassan and Hiroshi there. I'd figured that if Reza was there, then Ian Nisbet was probably there as well. He's the fifth! My heart leapt at the thought that we were the five. Rabia must have got hold of the consul.

'*Itnain wa arba'een.*'

My number was called again. Taken back to the interrogation room, I was positioned to stand in the same place as before. The interrogator arrived. This time, though, he didn't sound as aggressive as before. Disappointed, perhaps.

'Maagid, well, well, *hazzak sa'eed* – you are a very lucky man.'

That was all he said. I was bundled out of the room again, and then, to my excitement, escorted the opposite way along the corridor. I could hear the screams from the torture rooms receding behind me, getting fainter and further away. A door opened in front of me. Thank you, Door, you are my door to life, to civilisation. I will owe you a great deal, Door. My apologies for stepping through you like this. Instead I should be garnishing you in celebration as my hero. Then, that sweet smell, the taste of fresh night air. The real world. Life. Civilisation.

Back in the police van, my new guard was an ordinary *shaweesh* again, rather than the state security *zaabit*. He spoke to me gently, '*assalaamu alaykum*, you've just come out of hell,' as he helped me up the steps into the van. There was no menace in what he was saying. It took me a second to recognise the tone. Then I realised. He was just being friendly.

CHAPTER TWENTY-ONE

The luxury of an audience

As I guessed, it was the foreign prisoners who were being taken away: Hassan, Hiroshi, Ian, Reza and I. Once the van pulled away, I broke the silence and started asking after the others. The relief of having just escaped hell itself overcame us. Each of us began thanking Allah to be alive, and congratulating each other on getting out.

I quickly discovered that apart from Reza, the other foreigners had also escaped electrocution. Reza was in a different place from the rest of us, and would remain there for the remainder of my talking days with him. Eventually, blindfolds and hand-rags removed, we pulled up at the Public Prosecutor's Office. To be able to see again, after so many days, was a newly liberating experience. I found myself looking at anything and everything. How beautiful the world suddenly was when the ability to look upon it had been taken from you. And we were given food – something to eat that wasn't a hard lump of salted cheese. We had pitta breads stuffed with *ful*, the sturdy staple bean mash of Egyptians:

and we wolfed them down, grateful for such small pleasures.

We were each assigned a public prosecutor. Mine was a different sort of person from my previous interrogators. There's an Aesop's fable about the sun and the wind, in which the two weathers have a competition to see who can get a man to take his coat off: the wind uses brute force to try to blow it off and fails: the sun makes the man feel warm and relaxed and he removes his coat. The more the interrogators shouted at me, the more I buckled down and prepared for a fight. It was just how I had grown up in Essex; that's how we survived back in the day. But in the warmth and civility of that office I felt comfortable talking to the prosecutor. His name was Walid Minshawi, a suited, rather obese, educated man. Minshawi spoke about how he'd visited London on many occasions, and that his sister lived there. He played his 'good cop' routine down to perfection.

'Do you know what they just did to us? They're torturing people down there!' I exclaimed.

'That's a shame,' Minshawi said, 'but if you don't cooperate with me, we'll have to send you back there. That decision is yours to make. If you refuse to cooperate, then I'll have little choice.'

'I need a lawyer.'

'Oh, that won't be necessary.'

'What about the British Consul?' I asked. 'When do I get to see him?'

'They know you're here,' he said.

The consul should have been allowed to make contact with his citizens within forty-eight hours. The Egyptians had been incompetent at best, mendacious at worst in getting back to their request. But in the warmth of that office, and the relative civility – when compared with torture – of Minshawi's approach, I began to talk. I answered his questions in Arabic and in detail. I explained to him why I was in Egypt, discussed my studies in Alexandria and emphasised at length that I simply wasn't there to propagate HT's message. Minshawi listened intently to my answers, then he looked across to the scribe and told him which points he wanted written down.

'But that's not what I said,' I would protest.

'It's OK, we're writing what you said, don't worry.'

I found myself constantly correcting how my answers were being recorded, telling the scribe what he should write. But Minshawi would just laugh in his cheery, rotund way, and carry on. After four hours of questioning, presumably at dawn, each of our prosecutors wrapped things up. Without so much as having the chance to say goodbye, Hiroshi, my al-Quds companion, was released into the streets of Cairo that very morning. The prosecutors must have realised that his only misfortune was to have befriended me. I never saw him again.

For Reza, Ian, Hassan and I the situation was somewhat different. We were handcuffed – metal, not rags, it's strange the way that such small details make one feel relief – and driven in a police van to what we later discovered was Mazrah Tora Prison. There we were placed in *habs infiradi* (solitary confinement) away from the main prison cell blocks.

After returning from hell itself, battered bodies lying over more battered bodies, the relief of having my own little space again was overwhelming. These cells were bare. They

243

had no bed, no blanket, no light, no toilet, no sanitation, but this was my space, alone, where no one was questioning me any more, a place without screams and electrocution, a place where I could rest my weary head without fear of being beaten for oversleeping roll call, and so right now, in this moment, it was home. I had been awake for the best part of four or five days, and been put through the most extreme psychological distress. I was still in the same clothes I'd been wearing on my night out in Alexandria, and I was spent. I took my shoes off, used them as a pillow, and just slept on that concrete floor.

As the week dragged on, going back and forth to the prosecutor's office, I became more acutely aware of my conditions. The fact that there was no toilet meant that I had to use a corner of my cell. I became aware of the cockroaches that covered the floor. And how hard the bare concrete floor was. And, having bitten on grit and insects in my food on more than one occasion, how tasteless the gruel being pushed through my cell door each day was. And how ever so lonely it was to be trapped in solitary confinement. At the end of these seven days, the public prosecutor handed me a statement to sign. How much correlation it had to the answers I had given I had no idea. It was handwritten in impenetrable Arabic, and I could make nothing out of it. I literally had no idea what I was putting my name to. But the thought of being sent back to al-Gihaz was too much to contemplate refusing. Walid Minshawi had his way. I signed it.

Only after the questioning had finished were we allowed to see the British Consul. Gordon Brown was a career civil servant in his late forties, well meaning and sympathetic, but it was probably hard to offend his hosts without incurring diplomatic consequences. We were the first international political prisoners to be held in Egypt, or at least the first British ones, and no one was quite sure what the rules of engagement were. In the post-9/11 world particularly, it was unclear what was and wasn't permissible. From that initial meeting, it was clear that our case was of a different dimension from the ones that usually came across his desk.

Brown apologised for taking so long to see us. 'We simply had no idea where you were being held,' he said. This, it turned out, wasn't the only information the consul hadn't known about: Brown had no idea as to why we were being detained or what charges we faced. He was as lost and confused as we were, and it was hugely dispiriting.

'What about our families?' I asked. Here, at least, there was a sliver of good news. Brown told me that Rabia and Ammar were safely back in the UK. But that was the only concrete answer we got. Cooperation between the British, American and Egyptian intelligence authorities was clearly going on in the wake of September 11th. A number of times in my interrogation with Minshawi, he had introduced details like, 'We understand from the British that . . .', or 'American sources tell us . . .' So even if the British Consul wanted to help us on a personal level, the line coming back from the mandarins in Whitehall was probably not to upset an important ally in the War on Terror.

The night after Gordon Brown's visit, we were taken out of our cells and blindfolded and handcuffed again. As if to remind us of our place, we were frogmarched into the prison offices and interviewed again by Aman al-Dawlah. I recognised the interrogator immediately as the one who had questioned me back in Alexandria.

'We just want to be certain you're telling us the truth,' the *zaabit* said. I asked him how long we were going to stay in prison.

'A week or two,' he replied.

'That long?' I asked aghast.

The *zaabit* and his colleague burst into laughter. They must have known that a week was nothing inside Mazrah Tora. Some prisoners had been detained for years, even decades, under Egypt's Emergency Law, without so much as a charge. These were the *mu'taqaleen*. At the time of my arrest, 25,000 *mu'taqaleen* lined Egypt's prison system, all political detainees. I realised much later on, only after befriending some of these *mu'taqaleen* in Mazrah Tora, how green I must have sounded to the *zaabit*, fretting over a week in prison.

We were kept in solitary confinement, in those sordid conditions, and bare cells, for over three months before we were ever charged. In the arid summer heat, it was difficult not to be overwhelmed by the sheer helplessness of my situation. The Aman al-Dawlah were the worst of both worlds: brutal, but also incredibly incompetent. I became consumed by this twisted combination of fear and boredom, which swirled round and round inside me until it became pure rage.

If driving to the African student's house that night of Ayotunde's murder had been my lowest moment, this was my darkest. With no one else to talk to or communicate with, with nothing else to do, my mind began to wander. My cell had no lights, so once it was dark, it was dark. And as I tried to sleep at night on that hard concrete floor, I found myself flinching and flexing in case of cockroaches. I missed Rabia, I missed Ammar, I began to miss Southend, and the life of that 'Click'-suit-wearing B-boy seemed a distant dream now. I may have only been twenty-four years old, but from now on I would forever feel forty-two.

My mind began screaming out for activity, pleading with me for attention like Ammar used to. Boredom was on the verge of defeating me. I looked around, seeking anything to keep myself occupied, but all I had were the small stones on the floor. *Tai Ammi!* What did *Tai Ammi* do when I was unable to sleep, back in those days that seemed so distant now? That's it. She would make up stories. Those oral stories that sent my mind on adventures in magical lands of beautiful princesses and noble heroes. Hey, stone, how are you man? I name you Freddie-Fred, and you, stone, I name you Johnny-John, you know, after the old way, like Flavor Flav of Public Enemy. Yeeeeah, bwoyy! Freddie-Fred, can you beat Johnny-John in a race? Let's see. Ready, get-set . . . go! And with a flick of my finger I would project the two stones, over and over again, across my cell floor, to see who won the most races.

And there were plenty of times in that dingy cell, during the darkest hour, when the only sound in the still of night were the crickets somewhere far off in the reeds, that my mind turned to revenge. I wanted absolute, pure and unadulterated vengeance upon Aman al-Dawlah. 'My name is Maagid Nawaz, I am a member of Hizb al-Tahrir!' Rubbish! Did that stop Alaa' from having his teeth and testicles electrocuted for weeks and months till I could hear him pleading and begging like a child? Did that stop Hisham from Kafr al-Shaikh being hanged by his arms till his joints gave way and he begged for mercy while his tormentors snorted *shakheer* at him like animals, like pigs? Did it stop the rape and electrocution of prisoners' wives right before their very eyes? Did any of it help Reza while he was tortured just for being unable to respond in Arabic? And why wasn't I tortured? Why was I spared this pain? Are they playing with my mind? Was Combat 18 playing with my mind? Where's Matt now? You took a stabbing for me. To protect me. What did I ever do for you?

Non-violence? Non-violence is only for those who have the luxury of an audience! You see, an audience is an amazing thing. If people fear what you may do, if they fear the masses you may incite, they listen to you before you do it. What they really respect is your propensity to hurt them. The more you can hurt them, the more they respect you. But if people laugh at your pain, and mock your suffering, and goad you and prod you knowing that you can do nothing, except sit back and say, 'My name is Maagid Nawaz, Maagid, Maagid, Maagid Nawaz, I am a member of Hizb al-Tahrir' . . . Maagid! Maagid! Then what do we have left? Our own government couldn't even give a damn. *La'natullahi 'alaykum* – May Allah curse you!

You preach non-violence while you fund Mubarak, and sell him arms. You train his men, and shake his hand with your bloodstained palms? Well, now I refuse to play by any rules. Let Nasim work for the *Khilafah*, he doesn't need me. But Walid Minshawi, vengeance upon you needs me. And the thought of vengeance upon your ilk right now is what feeds me. How many years do you think you can keep me? I am but young and still so full of fire, it will take you many years to defeat me. You underestimated the flame that burns within me. And even as you catch me and eventually subdue me, I will kill as many of you as possible before you take me. And you will come to know how I went crazy, because of the poison that your own hands fed me.

And in the confines of that solitary cell, this all made perfect sense.

CHAPTER TWENTY-TWO

The Penguin is hit by slippers

When we were finally charged, we came to hear about it second hand. Some of the other prisoners had been listening to the radio, BBC Arabic, and they caught the announcement. Immediately they shouted the news over the wall, and the *shaweesh* guarding our cell told us what had happened. A few days later we received another visit from Gordon Brown, and he confirmed the charges in detail. Hassan, it transpired, was not charged. He was released soon after and deported back to London. Reza, Ian and I had been charged on two counts: firstly, for propagating in speech and writing the ideas of a banned organisation called Hizb al-Tahrir; secondly, for possessing literature of said organisation. Additionally, Reza also had a third charge: for being in possession of a computer printer. At least Hassan, my second al-Quds companion, who had had nothing to do with anything, could finally go home.

If our situation hadn't been so serious, the charges would have been laughable. Reza was facing a prison sentence for having a printer. None of us had been charged with what would have made sense: for being members of a banned organisation, something that in our interviews we had all defiantly admitted to. Instead, the charges were somehow more insidious: they were to do with discussing ideas and reading books: the right to free expression. This wasn't about HT, or about Islamism, it was about something far more fundamental. It was about liberty, one of the basic tenets which civilised society is supposed to be based upon. Judge us by our Islam, and we will judge you by your freedoms.

The charges exposed Egypt, and the Emergency Laws of President Mubarak, for the police state that it was. It was a banana republic. We knew by now that our chances of getting off were non-existent – they could make stick whatever they wanted to. We were looking at years in prison. By charging us in this way, it stripped them of any sense of moral authority. It made us prisoners of conscience. It meant that Amnesty International could take up our cause. And for Western leaders, it created uncomfortable questions for their entire Middle East strategy; they were supporting a regime that was torturing and imprisoning British citizens for 'speech and writing'.

Gordon Brown, to be fair to him, looked embarrassed as he discussed the charges with us. I could see him clearly for what he was: a career civil servant in an impossible position, the man in the Whitehall chain who was seeing at first hand the human cost of the 'price worth paying'. There was a war on – the War on Terror. The first casualty, as the saying goes, is truth. I looked him in the eye and saw that he knew what we knew: Mubarak's Egypt was no great friend or ally; his was a state built on the opposite of what the West was meant to hold most dear.

The trial, if one can give such events that sense of legitimacy, lasted the best part of two years. It would run for a week or two at a time, then there'd be a wait of another couple of months before the next session was called. There were twenty-six defendants in all being tried at the same time. In the courtroom, all dressed in white because we had not yet been convicted, we were held in a cage in the corner, like animals. The cage was so cramped that we would have to take it in turn to sit on the few benches provided, while the rest of us stood squashed round the sides.

Our group was taken to the courtroom each day in a convoy of blue police vans; the other defendants, all Egyptians, were being held in a mixture of other prisons. Each of us would be handcuffed to a guard for the journey. But rather than go in silence, we wanted to show Mubarak and his acolytes that he had not defeated us. We would not go quietly, we wanted the world to see us, and the world was watching. Each time we went in and out of that courtroom, we let off a huge cacophony of chants, rallying and sloganising. The TV cameras, BBC, al-Jazeera and others, all of them loved the spectacle we were creating.

'*Usqut, usqut Mubarak!*' – 'Down, down Mubarak!'

'*Laa nakhafu lawmata laa'im, al-Khilafatu fardun da'im*' – 'We don't fear those who blame us, the *Khilafah* will forever be an obligation!'

We would shout these slogans in Arabic, all around Cairo's streets, as we were transported in those blue metal police vans in the scorching heat of summer, drenched in sweat. To speak so openly against Mubarak while under arrest was a shocking thing for Egyptians to behold at the time. Most would stand open-mouthed and gape as we passed, some would raise their fists in salute. Many broke down in tears of sympathy right there in the middle of the street. Anyone who caught a glimpse of our regular convoys in the streets of Cairo in 2002 will remember the sheer pandemonium we caused. After the total defeat of the jihadists in 1999, no one dared denounce Mubarak in public the way we did. Several years before the Egyptian people found the confidence to stand together in Tahrir Square, we were hoping to inspire the courage and confidence it would take for them to do exactly that. We wanted people in the streets to think, 'if they can do it from their prison vans, we can do it from our streets.'

If you remember that miniature Qur'an I took from my flat, the last thing I took before leaving Ammar and Rabia behind, well, that had somehow remained with me throughout my time in the torture cells. I would hold it up and wave it in full view while I shouted my slogans. It gave me strength, and built my *eeman*. We were not criminals. We were proud political prisoners. We stood for Allah and His messenger, we stood for justice against tyranny and we were blessed to be chosen by Allah, as the ambassadors of *eeman*. Sure enough, our actions reached the world's media – TV, radio, print and the nascent but rising Internet. The whole world was talking about the British political prisoners who claimed they had been tortured in Mubarak's dungeons.

The courtroom was packed. Our case was the first time that foreign nationals had been tried in a case involving torture.

This created somewhat of a media frenzy. And it was here, in the courtroom, that I discovered just how badly some of the other brothers had been treated. One of the brothers, Ahmed, described how his wife had been stripped and tortured before his eyes in order to force him to confess. His story, sadly, was far from unique. We quickly used those moments in the cage to announce to the world how we had been treated. Journalists became fascinated with our case: liberals, Islamists, socialists, all began to sympathise with what had happened to us, and news of our plight was spreading far and wide.

Everyone in that cage pleaded not guilty to the charges. But unlike our Egyptian brothers, we three Britons also admitted to our membership of Hizb al-Tahrir in the UK. As HT was legal there, we felt there was nothing to hide. In one of the subsequent court sessions, a letter was delivered from Jalaluddin Patel, the young HT leader in the UK who had tried to marginalise me after my return from Pakistan. The letter felt to me at the time like a sofa-critique of how we had all carried ourselves. According to him we should have pleaded guilty, have shown more defiance, and the Egyptian members should never have denied their affiliation to HT. We were disgusted. Jalaluddin, sitting in London, had the nerve to tell these men how to behave? We wrote back immediately: you are no longer in our chain of command; we fall under the jurisdiction of HT Egypt. Its leader is in this very cage with us, having been tortured non-stop for three and a half months. These brothers have watched their wives tortured in front of them. You have not the right or moral claim to tell us what to do, and in doing so you presume to violate our channels of communication. Do not write to us again. Thankfully, we never heard from the guy again.

Right away, you could sense just how much the system was stacked against us. The judge, whose name was Ashmawi, would sit at the top of the bench, right next to the leading prosecutor, Walid Minshawi. As the case was to be tried under Emergency Law, both the judge and prosecutor were appointed by Aman al-Dawlah. The defence lawyers, meanwhile, were sat down at the opposite end of the courtroom with the accused.

As our lawyer, the three of us chose a brave man called Ahmed Saif. Saif's political views couldn't have been more different from ours. Saif was a communist, which under normal circumstances would have been anathema to our Islamism, but he had our respect. Saif had been imprisoned many times under Mubarak's regime, and yet he still continued to speak out fearlessly. We might have held different political views, but Saif was every bit as anti-regime as we were. A couple of years later, Ahmed Saif would go on to become a key founding member of the Kifayah, or 'Enough', movement. Kifayah were a liberal collective that decided to break the taboo of openly challenging Mubarak's authority in public. As I mentioned earlier, hard to imagine now, but in those days in Egypt this was an absolute red line. Later on, while serving my sentence, I would read time and again of Kifayah's brave anti-Mubarak protests. They would gather openly in the streets, attracting only around ten or twenty brave souls, surrounded by hundreds of riot police, and most people would laugh at their delusions of change. But Kifayah became the collective that ultimately snowballed into the Egypt uprising, led by liberal youth, in 2011. History, it would turn out, was on Ahmed Saif's side.

Almost two years after our arrest, on the day before we were due to be sentenced, it just so happened that Egypt's Foreign Minister, Ahmed Maher, was on a state visit to Jerusalem. Maher was a short, fat man with a huge bald head and a pointed nose. He looked like the arch villain The Penguin from the Batman films, and we found this image of him comforting in our situation. As part of Maher's visit to al-Quds, he went to pray in the Al-Aqsa Mosque compound, the very same mosque I'd attended a few years earlier with Hassan and Hiroshi, and where I met all the HT brothers, and where I agreed with Issam Amireh that I would one day return, and where I left my heart. HT was founded in al-Quds and all over Palestine we had a strong force of brothers. When Maher entered the mosque, to his utter horror, and the TV cameras' delight, he was met by a large group of HT protesters, greeting him with a barrage of shoes and slippers hurled at him with abandon.

'Get out, you *kha'in* – traitor!' they shouted at him, as the slippers rained down.

'*Zalim* – despot! Agent of America! You torture our brothers in Egypt, and think you can come into our mosque and pray? *La ahlan wa la sahlan* – you are not welcome in this mosque, out!'

Back at our prison, as the radio announced the humiliation of untouchable Ahmed Maher, the brothers, young and old, Islamist, jihadist, liberal, everyone whooped and rejoiced in spontaneous celebration. *Allahu akbar!* Taste a fraction of what you have put us through, and see how you like it! The next day, Egypt's national papers were full of images of The Penguin being hit by slippers. It was a real day of victory for us. The Egyptian state would not let this one go, sure enough they took their revenge. In the wake of the assault, our sentencing date was delayed by another three months. When we were finally taken to court, the judge announced that he was dropping all the original charges against us, only to replace them with a single, new charge: *intimaa* – membership of a banned organisation. After two years of a painfully slow trial, this time round there was to be no new discussion, no new defence. There and then, we were charged anew, convicted and found guilty within the same session, on the same day.

'*Intimaa*' was a far more serious charge. Reza, Ian and I were all sentenced to five years in prison: the other defendants got a mixture of between five and ten years for their membership of HT. As these sentences were read out in court, familes began to cry, journalists began scrimmaging, and we rose up in defiance. Like lions roaring with pride, the courtroom was ablaze with our chants and slogans.

'*Allahu akbar! Allahu akbar!* We will never surrender!'

We began congratulating and embracing one another in the cage, and chanting and praying and prostrating in thanks to Allah for this opportunity to present our sacrifice for His cause. Ashmawi the judge, job done, rushed out of the courtroom in fear, and Walid Minshawi looked on in utter confusion. How can they be celebrating? If I were in their place I'd be crying. And we did cry, tears of devotion to Allah, tears of love, tears of piety, the romanticism of struggle, and we knew we would go down in history, and people would look to us and be inspired.

After two years, once the verdict was finally passed, in between frequent letters we began receiving occasional family visits. How can I forget that day, Ammar, when you first came plodding along, by now a three-year-old, not knowing your *Abu* except for seeing him in chains on television screens. It's been two and a half years, my son. Two and a half years since these *zalimun* first tore you crying from my arms. And you came dressed in trousers, shirt and tie, and extended your hand out to greet me '*assalaamu alaykum, Abu*' unsure of how formal I expected you to be. And I swept you up in my arms, not wanting you to see the tears welling in my eyes and I held you close for all the years I was unable to hold you, for the days in the dungeons when I thought I might never see you again. I was so proud of your mother who had kept the memory of me alive within you.

Your mother approached me that day, her radiant face so happy, so proud and smiling at the visage of her man who had proven his sincerity to Allah's cause. And instantly, just by holding her in my embrace for the first time since my arrest, all my pain melted away, nothing mattered any more. My *ghimamah* of darkness had been lifted and all I could see was the glow of your countenance. How happy I was on that day.

When Ash, my trusty HT protégé in SOAS days, came to visit me in Mazrah Tora I was naturally excited.

'Ash, what's wrong?' I asked.

'I don't know how to tell you this,' he said, 'but I've left the group. I've left HT.'

'Why, what happened?' I asked disappointedly.

'I don't believe in it any more,' he answered; and then in his typically irreverent way, 'It's all bullshit, bro, the whole damn thing, they're a bunch of muppets, clueless thick idiots, they're an embarrassment to Islam and Muslims.'

Ash went on to describe a disastrous national sticker campaign decreed by HT leader in the UK Jalaluddin Patel, opposing the Iraq War. But instead of having a phrase on the stickers that actually opposed the war, Jalaluddin thought it clever to use the phrase in bold 'Don't Stop the War', and then, in tiny small print underneath it, 'except with Islamic Politics'. This was Jalaluddin's uncouth doctrinaire attempt at convincing Muslims in the UK not to ally with the *kuffar* in the Stop the War Coalition. It goes without saying that the campaign was an absolute failure.

Ash explained how he had become disillusioned with HT members, then with the group itself, and eventually with the ideology. Instead, he had become interested in Sufi mysticism.

'You're a bright person, Maajid,' he said. 'I know for a fact that you'll work all of this out and come to the same conclusions that I did.'

My reaction was to laugh this off.

Ash, though, was insistent. 'In Sufism, you have a sheikh, a spiritual guide,' he continued. 'My sheikh told me before I came here that he'd had a dream about you. He told me that not only are you going to leave Hizb al-Tahrir, but that you're going to become a great leader for Muslims.'

'*Subhan Allah* – can you hear yourself, bro?' I said and laughed.

'It's true,' Ash said shaking his head. 'That's what I came to tell you, and that's why I came.'

I dismissed Ash's flattery as that of a friend overcome by emotion on seeing his one-time HT mentor in prison. But even so, there was something about the confidence with which Ash spoke that struck me.

Life doesn't stand still just because you are in prison. During those years my parents' relationship finally cracked, and they divorced. By the time Abi came to see me she had met a friend, who accompanied her to Egypt on prison visits. He was an Englishman, a non-Muslim and they were not married. For the first time since my incarceration, my liberal upbringing was on public display in front of the top cadre of Egypt's hardcore jihadist scene, and I was torn: They're not married, he's a *kafir*, this is *haram*, prohibited. But he's come all this way to look after Abi, he's waiting outside the prison in the desert heat, from fear of offending me. This is a noble man, like Dave Gomer, like Mr Moth. And so I found a solution.

'Can I conduct an Islamic rite, the *nikah* ceremony, to legitimise your relationship before Allah? It's just some prayers before two witnesses,' I asked Abi.

'If it makes you happy?'

'But he'll need to embrace Islam first – pronounce his *shahadah*, the testimony of faith. I can teach him what to say,' I said.

'I just want you to be happy.'

In this way, right there in the visiting area of Mazrah Tora prison, I supervised the conversion and Islamic *nikah* ceremony for Abi and her partner. I asked him to repeat after me, '*Laa ilaaha illa Allah* . . . There is no God but the One God, *Muhammad ar-rasool Allah* . . . and Muhammad is the Messenger of God.' As my two witnesses I called over two of my prison friends, Omar, a Dagestani, and Hisham, a Dutch-Egyptian jihadist, famous for flying into monumentous fits of rage against the prison authorities. I don't think Abi or her partner quite understood what the witnesses to their *nikah* were in jail for. Equally, I don't think Omar and Hisham quite understood Abi's and her partner's views. As far as my jihadist friends were concerned, I had just successfully converted someone to the Islamist cause. They were overjoyed and sharing a few sweets around the visiting area.

'Maajid's mother and her partner have just embraced Islam,' they announced with warm smiles across the room. The implication being, of course, that by virtue of being in this relationship Abi had not already been a Muslim. Hisham, the Dutch-Egyptian jihadist, embraced Abi's partner in a long, tight hug. Looking him in the eye, Hisham then explained in earnest how he must never compromise on his new faith, to always remain strong, and to remember to fight the enemies of Allah wherever he finds them. The Englishman nodded in sincere agreement, and Hisham hugged him again, apparently in the belief that he had just witnessed the creation of another martyr for Islam.

CHAPTER TWENTY-THREE

'Monocracy'

Mazrah Tora, where we would serve out the remainder of our sentence, was no ordinary prison. Originally built by the British back in the days of the protectorate in order to hold political prisoners, it stayed ever true to its purpose. Over the years Mazrah Tora has held some of Islamism's most well-known ideologues. This was the prison where Sayyid Qutb, the ideological godfather of modern-day Jihadism was held. It was at Mazrah Tora that Qutb wrote his seminal *Ma'alim fi al-Tariq* or *Milestones*, which was to see him executed in 1966, instantly turning him into a flame that would light the sky for thousands of future Islamists.

The manuscript for *Milestones* was smuggled out of this prison by a young devotee of Qutb's at the time, a member of Egypt's largest Islamist group, the Muslim Brotherhood, Mohammed al-Badei. By the time I got to Mazrah Tora, Dr Badei had again been imprisoned along with many of the Brotherhood's leadership in the case known as 'The Professors', *Qadiyat al-Asaatiza*. By now he was a member of the leadership of the Brotherhood, serving on their Office of Guidance – *Maktab al-Irshad*. During those days we became close, exchanging many stories about his friendship with Qutb.

I remember how Dr Badei used to enjoy interpreting the inner, mystical meanings of dreams, known as a *ru'ya*. One dream in particular sticks in my mind the most. I told him that I had seen myself among the Prophet's Companions, all dressed in white robes, sitting in a gathering in Paradise. They all had thick black beards and were laughing and enjoying one another's company. In walked the Prophet, *'alayhi salam*, and we all immediately stood up in reverence. It was time to pray, and so we straightened our lines and waited for the Prophet to lead us. The Prophet looked to me and motioned for me to lead the prayer. My heart pounded. In utter fear I protested, 'How can, how can I lead the Prophet of Allah in prayer? *Ya rasulAllah* – O Messenger of Allah, I can never do such a thing.' The Prophet, *'alayhi salam*, simply turned to me and smiled. 'Don't fear,' he said, 'and do as I ask.' I did as I was commanded, but as I stepped forward, in total bewilderment, and began my prayer, I awoke before I could commence. Dr Badei felt that this dream was a great sign.

'Only Islam's first caliph, Abu Bakr, was ever nominated by the Prophet, *'alayhi salam*, to lead prayers in his presence. *Ya* Maajid, *Bashhir*, glad tidings! Your dream means that one day you will become a great leader for Muslims. And you see, as he told you in the same dream, you had no need to fear from leading your own Prophet in prayer. You awoke before you could actually lead him.'

Badei went on to become *Murshid al-'aam*, the Supreme Leader of the Muslim Brotherhood. After Mubarak's removal in 2011, the new Egypt is practically ruled by his group. Among other Muslim Brotherhood prisoners there were Dr Essam el-Aryan, their spokesman at the time; and Abdul Monim Abul Fatouh, an Islamist presidential hopeful. The Brotherhood were not revolutionary or militant Islamists, and as such their members usually attracted shorter sentences, typically two or three years.

There were also many members of al-Gama'a al-Islamiyya, which until its ceasefire in 1999, had been Egypt's largest terrorist organisation. This was the larger faction that broke away from Salim al-Rahhal's Tanzim al-Jihad after the assassination of President Sadat. Following their ceasefire, the majority of Gama'a's members signed up to what became known as the *muraja'aat* or 'revisions', essentially renouncing their former militancy. However, they remained Salafists in doctrine and non-violent Islamists in ideology. Among their number, with us throughout the holy month of Ramadan, was one of their founders, Sheikh Salah Hashim.

There were still prisoners at Mazrah Tora who had been involved in the assassination of Sadat back in 1981. The main assassins had been executed, but those involved in the plot and still incarcerated included former Egyptian military intelligence officer Lieutenant Colonel Aboud al-Zommor, his cousin Tareq al-Zommor, who were held in our wider prison complex, and in our block Dr Tariq and Salah Bayoumi.

Some of those executed in this case had been sent to their deaths back in 1982 by a then public prosecutor called Maher el-Guindi. As the years progressed, el-Guindi had gone on to become the governor of the province of Giza. One day the prison was alive with commotion. 'What is it, what's going on?' I asked. Maher el-Guindi has been convicted for bribery and corruption, I was told. He would be joining us here in Mazrah Tora, to live among the remainder of the Sadat case, those still left alive after he sent their colleagues to the gallows. An extremely odd scenario unfolded that week in Mazrah, as some of the assassins of Sadat sat in conversation with the public prosecutor who had led the case for their convictions some twenty-two years earlier.

'That man was a bloodhound, supervising interrogations over brutal torture, and I never stopped my *du'a*, my prayers, that one day he too would see justice as we have,' Salah Bayoumi said to me that day. 'Allah never raises anyone high except that he brings them down again. You watch, Maagid, one day my Lord will place Mubarak in here too, *bi iznillah*, with God's permission.'

There were other jihadists too, such as those accused of supporting Ayman Zawahiri's group Islamic Jihad, such as a British-Egyptian named Akram who we befriended and helped to make consular contact for after he narrated to us tales of his brutal torture. Soon, a number of new foreign nationals began to arrive. They had all been convicted in the case known as *Qadiyat al-wa'ad*. These foreign arrivals were a new breed of global jihadists, raised under the shadow of bin Laden's al-Qaeda. Internationalists, extreme in their views, fully trained and dangerous, they cut an intimidating spectre. There were two Dagestanis, built like Russian bears, one of whom, Omar Hajiyev, was a witness to Abi's *nikah* ceremony, and the other was Ahmed. Omar was a professional bomb-maker. Having learnt his trade in Chechnya and Afghanistan, he had been making his way to Gaza in an effort to train Hamas in

265

his deadly skill. He had been sentenced to seventeen years in jail, but after the mass prison breakouts during Egypt's uprising I often wonder what became of him.

Finally, at the other end of the political spectrum, there were leading liberal political prisoners and even those accused of homosexuality from Egypt's infamous 'Queen boat' case. A blue-eyed well-off Egyptian called Sharif was the most visible prisoner accused in that case. Being held in the same prison block, imagine if you can the dynamics between the jihadists and those from the Queen boat case. Two of President Mubarak's more high-profile liberal rivals were head of the Tomorrow Party, presidential candidate Ayman Nour, and sociology lecturer Sa'ad el-Din Ibrahim. Nour had stood against Mubarak for the presidency in 2005, finishing second; in other words, he won. As his reward, he was duly accused of fraudulently acquiring signatures to register his party, all one hundred of them, and sentenced to seven years' imprisonment. His criminal conviction meant that he was barred from standing for president again.

Dr Ibrahim had written an article denouncing Mubarak's plans to groom his son Gemal as his successor. In the article, Ibrahim argued that Egypt must not become a 'monocracy', a *jumlukia*, a hybrid phrase from the Arabic word *jumhouriya*, a republic, and *mulkiyya*, a monarchy. Ibrahim's was a seminal piece that shifted the liberal mood in Egypt against Gemal Mubarak ever taking the reins of power after his father. This infuriated Hosni Mubarak. Ibrahim's eventual conviction for 'bringing Egypt into disrepute abroad' shocked the world, especially the Americans, and was crucial in shifting US policy towards pushing Egypt for more reform faster. Together with

Ayman Nour, the injustice Ibrahim faced went on to feed the growing liberal discontent that eventually led to Egypt's uprising, and Sa'ad el-Din Ibrahim became recognised as one of the liberal intellectual godfathers of this uprising. Many years later, as I addressed George Bush's presidential conference in Dallas, I was to be reunited with Sa'ad el-Din over a video link, and as the conference looked on, we conversed for the first time about our days together at Mazrah Tora prison.

All of these figures, like me, were imprisoned on one side of Mazrah Tora. In the same way that Egypt had a parallel judicial system – the official one, and the Aman al-Dawlah one – so the prison was split down the middle. On the opposite side to us was the criminal block, separated by guards. The split personality of the prison was emphasised by the dual command of the place: as well as the prison governor, there was an Aman al-Dawlah *zaabit* assigned to our side. The name he used, probably fake, was Mohammed 'Ashwawi.

From time to time, Aman al-Dawlah would embark upon sporadic crackdowns against the Muslim Brotherhood, and because there were so many of them, the criminal blocks on the other side of the jail would have to be cleared out. We were all then stuffed into these group cells to make space, thirty or more people at a time: there'd just be row after row of beds with inches of space in between. These crackdowns would last for months, and while they went on, all the hard-fought-for privileges we'd gained would disappear.

The more people they shoved into those cells, the more the tension ramped up. Two or three prisoners had recently died before us in custody; one was my cell-neighbour for a while, a man called Hisham. Whenever that happened, we prisoners would take to banging our cell doors all night in mourning. It was a macabre and eerie spectacle: loud metal clanging would echo throughout the prison, punctured sometimes by wailing and cries of mourning, tempered other times by the murmoured sounds of desperate prayer. Now, as the air was already thick with pent-up anger and the cells already overflowing, Aman al-Dawlah announced to us the arrival of yet more prisoners. Tempers boiled over. Overcrammed, and frustrated, all of us swarmed out of our cells in a rage and, in a direct challenge to Aman al-Dawlah, refused to go back in. The prison sent in the riot police. The brothers, well versed in prison rebellion, were skilled at causing a commotion, and had everyone whipped up into fervour. I was right there, standing in the middle, pumped and determined not to take any more. When they arrived, the riot police were an intimidating sight. Fully armoured, they banged out a warning rhythm on their shields with their batons as they marched towards us in rows.

Focused fully on the approaching batons and shields, determined to stand my ground, I was too enraged to turn around and look at what was unfolding behind me.

'Enough! *Kifayah!* We've had enough! We're not animals, you cannot stuff more people into these cells!' I was shouting at the top of my voice.

But as I turned, to my surprise, I saw that all the Egyptian prisoners had retreated back into the cells! Their fervour had been nothing more than hot air. Or maybe it was called experience: they'd been there before, and didn't want to go there again. And now, outside alone, enraged, desperate and just plain fatigued, I turned my anger away from the approaching batons and drumming shields, and began shouting at the prisoners instead.

'Traitors, cowards! Where have you run to? Come and fight, you cowards!'

The brothers looked upon me pitifully. Rather than being a one-man force feared by the riot police, they saw me for what I was: a desperate and tired young man who just wanted to go home. Some of my friends came back out then, and gently held me close to calm me down, and guided me back to my cell before I was beaten black and blue.

'*Akhi* Maagid, there's no point. It's going to achieve nothing, we just have to exercise *sabr* – be patient. You cannot defeat Aman al-Dawlah like this.'

Except for when we forced their hand, we didn't benefit from much British government intervention in that prison. In fact, 'liberating' Iraq rather than liberating tortured British prisoners in Egypt seemed more of a priority for British politicians. Back in the UK, our local MPs David Amess and Stephen Timms kept the issue alive in Parliament, and our lawyer Sadiq Khan MP did whatever he could, including visiting us once in Mazrah Tora, but polite condemnations and stern representations don't carry well across the oceans. These years formed the height of Bush's War on Terror: the Iraq War was unfolding during my incarceration, and the West needed Mubarak's support. Indeed, Prime Minister Tony Blair had accepted a succession of free holidays from Mubarak at the exclusive Sharm el-Sheikh resort while we Britons were tortured in Mubarak's jails. (Blair later stated he made a charitable donation equal to the cost.)

But now and then through acts of pure desperation we were able to influence events. On one occasion, Ian had got into an altercation with a prison guard. The guard complained to the warden, and Ian was duly thrown into solitary confinement. Being the main conduit between us three and the warden, I went to see him to try to mediate on Ian's behalf.

'If I say Ian is in solitary, he's in solitary,' the warden snarled. 'And I suggest you back down immediately, Maagid. If you don't, I'll have you deported to another prison. I can set you up, have you killed by another prisoner, and no one will ever know. It's as easy as that.'

You're threatening to kill me? You're threatening to do to me what Combat 18 never did, what Aman al-Dawlah never got round to? You, a prison warden in Mazrah Tora, are threatening to kill me? You obviously do not know my Lord, Creator of the universe, Master of the heavens and earth, for he has shielded me in the harshest of battles, and against the worst of all odds, and I would be grossly ungrateful to Him if I now cowered before your threat. So I will resist you, like I resisted all those before you who tried to force me down, and I will win. Unified, we will all stand against you *bi iznillah*, and we will fight you with all our might and all our bodies, and our Lord will see you fall. Mr Warden, your time is up.

Immediately Ian, Reza and I launched a hunger strike. For eleven days and nights we didn't eat, insisting that the warden be investigated and charged with threatening to murder me. As the media attention piled on, the prison was plunged into tension. By the seventh day, with extremely low blood pressure, I became bedridden and unable to stand. But unlike the riot-that-wasn't, this time it was just the three of us involved, and we were determined not to give in. It often amazes me at how men in positions of authority so often underestimate the willpower of the desperate. There is an old tradition ascribed to the Prophet Muhammad, *'alayhi salam* – 'The prayer of the oppressed is never rejected' and whether by divine intervention or sheer determination, in my experience, eventually, the oppressed always manage to turn the tables. On the eleventh day the authorities cracked. The British Ambassador to Egypt came to the prison personally and explained that our demands had been met. (The warden was investigated and, ultimately, removed.) It was a rare, sweet victory in these harshest of years. But our most common prayer in prison during those years, which we shared with tens of thousands of other interned detainees, was to see Hosni Mubarak face justice during our lifetimes. My Lord does not fail me.

PART THREE

Radical

Start a huge, foolish project, like Noah ... it makes
absolutely no difference what people think of you.

Jalaluddin Rumi

CHAPTER TWENTY-FOUR

Where the heart leads, the mind can follow

In some ways, the most interesting story from my days in Mazrah Tora was the one unfolding inside my own head. Many political prisoners, and criminals alike, harden their beliefs and skills while incarcerated, coming out more committed than ever. For me, with its rich mix of prisoners, from the assassins of Sadat all the way through to the liberals and even homosexuals, Mazrah Tora became a political and social education *par excellence*. The studies, conversations and experiences I gained in Mazrah Tora, over months and years, were crucial in overcoming my dogmatic allegiance to the Islamist ideology. Having entered prison as an extremely idealistic 24-year-old, full of rage against society, over the course of four years, and for the first time in my life having nothing else to do but study, I came to re-evaluate everything I stood for.

It is important to understand that my change of views

wasn't an overnight process. Ideological dogma doesn't work like that: it's not like a tap you can just switch off. So ingrained was HT's cause in my very being, that it would be a process of years for me to work my way out of it. First emotionally, and then intellectually, then politically and finally socially, until piece by piece I had to reconstruct my entire personality from inside out. This is not an easy thing to do. Although I'd started this process by the time I left prison, I would return to the UK still a signed-up member of HT. It would be another year before I announced my departure from the leadership of my group, and more time still before I finally dropped the remnants of my Islamist baggage. That's the best part of five years to overturn the ideological convictions that had defined me for over a decade. This was the prism, the mindset from within which I had viewed the world: to unpick that, in descending order, until I questioned my fundamental religious, social and political convictions was nothing less than a paradigm shift, and in those days there was no one to guide me.

The starting point of my leaving had probably occurred back in Pakistan. My treatment out there had given me pause for thought about HT: not the ideas themselves, but the people who were in charge of the organisation. A similar moment occurred at the trial, with Jalaluddin's 'supreme command' that we should be more 'defiant'. I had plenty of time to think about these events, lying awake in my cell. Each time, it had been me who had gone forward, sacrificed everything for the cause, in Pakistan my degree and educational future, and in Egypt my body, yet each time there were idle hawks hounding me due to their own personal insecurities. This didn't challenge my faith in Islam, or initially my belief in the Islamist ideology, but it did make me question the capability, tactics and strategy of these figures. This, I believe, is the beginning of the process of leaving an ideological movement, for those brave enough to see their thinking through to its logical conclusion. Like an onion, you have to continue to peel back each layer and expose the next one, no matter how painful that process may be. My disillusionment with HT leaders and their tactics meant that, by the time I was sentenced, I was ready for some more serious thinking about my ideology.

The behaviour of HT members though was not the only factor that started me on this route. I believe that, where the heart leads, the mind can follow. After our conviction, Amnesty International adopted us as 'Prisoners of Conscience', and began campaigning openly and vigorously for our release. This came about through the tireless work of John Cornwall, a member of the organisation's Buckingham branch. It was John who insisted at Amnesty that our case was worthy of the organisation's support. Having been put away solely on the basis of our, albeit unsavoury, beliefs, we deserved to be adopted officially as Prisoners of Conscience. John, a frail Christian man in his eighties, who I did not know, campaigned for us with a passion not seen in most twenty-year-olds, and our story together eventually became the subject of an Amnesty video aired on television.

Not everyone within Amnesty agreed that they should be campaigning on our behalf. I learnt later that the subject of whether or not the group should support us became quite a hot topic internally. The counter-argument was that, although we had committed no crimes ourselves, the ideology that we preached advocated a gross invasion of human rights: once our version of 'the *Khilafah*' was formed, we advocated an aggressive policy of foreign invasion and expansion, the death penalty for apostates, 'rebels' and homosexuals, and a forced dress code for women. Thieves would be punished by having their hands cut off, and adulterous women would be stoned to death. Why should Amnesty campaign for our human rights, when, given the opportunity, we would deprive others of theirs?

There's no easy answer to this question. What if, prior to coming to power, Adolf Hitler had been detained for his not yet violent beliefs in National Socialism? Or what if, closer to my own story, Mubarak came to be tortured as Gaddafi was? The logical extension of supporting our case was that Amnesty should also, hypothetically, be prepared to campaign for Hitler if he were incarcerated just for writing *Mein Kampf*. Amnesty resolved this controversy in the manner of Voltaire, best summarised using the words of Evelyn Beatrice Hall, 'I disapprove of what you say, but I will defend to the death your right to say it.'

Biases aside, for me that's the only possible answer to arrive at. Any other stance makes a mockery of the universality of human rights. Even now, as I spend and expend my life campaigning against extremism, I would still want Amnesty to protect prisoners in a similar position to the one I was in. And I will defend people's right to read *Mein Kampf*, or Qutb's *Milestones*, even as I fight both far-right fascists and Islamists equally. But the devil is in the detail. Where I disagree with not just Amnesty but many human-rights groups is in their failure to highlight a clear and obvious distinction between a victim of human-rights abuses, and a champion of human-rights causes.

Any prisoner held solely for the non-violent expression of their beliefs, no matter how illiberal, has an automatic and unconditional right to our support as a fellow human being. However, not every former prisoner, once released, should be automatically hailed as a champion of human-rights, and placed on prestigious human-rights platforms as a spokesperson for human-rights causes. Keeping with the Hitler analogy, I will campaign against anyone who would want to torture Mubarak, for he remains a human being, but I would never extend to any one of the Mubarak regime's men a human-rights platform from which to address a young, impressionable crowd of student volunteers as if he were now some great champion of human rights just because (hypothetically) he may have been mistreated after the uprising. A human-rights platform must necessarily have a stricter tolerance threshold, by virtue of what it is.

Many human-rights groups have and do sadly blur this distinction when it comes to propping up Islamist and jihadist speakers on their platforms. Life is more complicated than that. Islam, Islamism and jihadists are more complicated than that. Just as the world is not a binary between Muslims against all others, it is also not a binary between America against all others. The long-term credibility of human-rights causes rests on the perception of principle, a perception damaged if populist causes are reduced to campaign binaries, whether during the War on Terror or later on during the Arab uprisings. In this, I gently agree with Gita Sahgal's principled critique from inside Amnesty's International Secretariat, making the above argument, for which she was suspended from Amnesty.

As a former Amnesty Prisoner of Conscience, and as someone for ever indebted to the organisation, my delicate advice comes from someone who discovered Amnesty's principles the hard way. Amnesty's support was a fundamental part of my political journey. I am, in part, the person I am today because of their decision to campaign for me as a Prisoner of Conscience. It's because of how much their intervention means to me that I do not want to see anything that might dilute that message; their work on human rights is too important for that.

Support for my plight from Amnesty was something that took me aback. It was its unconditional nature that humbled me: you're a human being, and so you deserve our support. There was something very powerful, and very pure about that premise. Like many ideologies, Islamism derived part of its power from its dehumanisation of 'the other'. It is easier to dismiss and do things to 'the other' if you consider them as unworthy: the Nazis and the Jews; the jihadists and the infidels. Throughout my teenage and young adult life I had been dehumanised and desensitised to violence. As I got sucked into the Islamist ideology, I in turn began to dehumanise others.

Amnesty's support challenged all that: instead of dehumanising people, it rehumanised them. I thought now of Sav and Marc, of Matt and Dan – stabbed for their association with me, of Dave Gomer and Mr Moth, of my mother's partner, these were bonds that were forged with non-Muslims who actually cared about my well-being. And instead of being fascinated with the afterlife and death, for the first time in many years I began to reconnect with life, and with humanity. This is not something you can teach, it is something you must live and feel. Where the heart leads, the mind can follow.

I began to see the other human interventions around me in a different light too. At 8.50 on the morning of 7 July 2005, three bombs exploded on London Underground trains in a coordinated terrorist attack. Just under an hour later, a fourth bomb was detonated on the back of a double-decker bus in Tavistock Square, right by my university, SOAS. In total, fifty-two people were killed and many hundreds injured. Sa'eed Nur had become many Sa'eed Nurs. Jihadism had finally struck London. From the distance of Mazrah Tora at the time, I felt revulsion when I heard the news. In contrast to my reaction at 9/11, and being already well on the way to rehumanising the world thanks to John Cornwall and others, I immediately thought of the human cost involved. Gone were my ideological acrobatics and Machiavellian justifications. This time I saw the plain and simple death of innocents.

That wasn't the view of everyone in the prison. Many, including Omar Hajiyev, my Dagestani bomb-maker friend and witness to Abi's *Nikah* ceremony, were initially proud of the terrorists' action. Omar was still at war and London was a legitimate target. Britain had taken part in the invasion and occupation of Iraq. There, they had bombed and killed thousands of 'our' civilians, and occupied 'our' lands. The government leading that action had been voted in by popular vote. Politically and theologically Omar was convinced that an eye for an eye was the correct and appropriate deterrent for these infidel *kuffar*. It was his job, after all, to train young jihadists in the fine arts of doing exactly that. Omar felt satisfaction at the fact that we Muslims were finally prepared and able to strike back. Here was a man fully and operationally capable of preparing such attacks himself.

Whereas before, I would have either quietly scoffed at *kuffar* suffering as not my affair, or toed the Machiavellian HT line that such acts were simply a distraction from our real goal, this time I actually felt the human cost involved. Compassion now moved me where once only anger had. So I turned to Omar and asked him: do you know where the biggest demonstrations against the Iraq War took place? From news clippings in old newspapers, I showed him pictures of the million-strong march of 15 February 2003 in London. The fact that the largest demonstration against the Iraq War was not in Egypt, Saudi Arabia or Pakistan, but in the UK, touched me. These were human beings in London, campaigning for other human beings in Iraq. Rehumanisation. Where the heart leads, the mind can follow.

Just because a government goes to war doesn't mean that everyone supports it, I explained to Omar. Democracy is not the same as a referendum, and there was no referendum on Iraq. And even if there had been, it would not have endorsed willingly killing Iraqi civilians. By your argument, I continued, you should blow up Turkey before you detonate a bomb in London. Turkey's a member of NATO, which supported the war as well, Turkey's a democracy too, and the protests there were nothing on the scale of those in London, so surely by your logic the Turks must have been more supportive of the war than the British. Omar shook his head: but the Turkish people are Muslims, we can't be killing our own people.

And I continued to push, so who you kill is less about principle and more about expediency? Human life for you is about political point-scoring? Then how is what you're fighting for any better than what you are fighting against? How can you feign disgust at Bush's war games when this is just a game to you too? Don't you see, if the Turkish population aren't a legitimate target for attack, then neither are the British people. Look – I pointed to the placards being waved on the march – here are Christian groups, Muslim groups, political groups, students, old-age pensioners, just people. *Ittaqillah, akhi*, fear Allah's judgement.

And we went on like this for an entire day, discussing theology, politics and war, until eventually Omar began to rummage his hand through his hair and appear extremely uncomfortable. So I stopped pushing. For a moment, I thought he might turn on me. I'd seen him wrestle in the prison yard with our other Dagestani friend Ahmed, and if he wanted to he could settle this in an instant. But Omar was no fool, certainly not unintelligent, and had grown very fond of me. A couple of days later, there was a knock on my cell door. Omar was back. Maajid, I've been thinking about what you said. I've decided you're right. I agree. British civilians are not a legitimate target.

On that day I felt that I had saved many future lives from the hands of this bomb-maker friend of mine (who after Egypt's uprising is assumed to be roaming free somewhere). And I was proud, proud for myself that I had achieved something small but worthy, and proud for him that he was humble enough to change his mind, and proud for the British people, who despite not succeeding to 'Stop the War', did not fail. Their campaigns, energies and lobbying may have fallen on deaf ears, but not here, not in Mazrah Tora and not with Omar; for here the price was worth it.

The rehumanisation Amnesty had helped kick-start was furthered by others in prison too. Ayman Nour was perhaps one of the inmates in Mazrah Tora whose views were furthest away from my own at the time. He was a remarkably interesting figure to spend time with in jail, his ambition and audacity being his most striking features. Nour had been prepared to put his head above the parapet and actually challenge Mubarak for the presidency when to do so was still a cardinal sin. That alone was worthy of respect, regardless of any other political disagreements.

Nour and I would spend time going for walks around the prison yard, and I would interrogate him about his thoughts, motives and dreams. I wanted to understand what motivated people to sacrifice for a cause other than Islamism. That intrigued me. For me, it was Islamism that allowed us to finally stand up to Mickey, allowed me to challenge the African students at Newham and allowed me to face my torturers with absolute conviction. But Nour and Sa'ad el-Din Ibrahim were prepared to face jail for liberalism, a Godless cause and the bane of religion.

But there was something of himself that Nour recognised in me. Nour, it turned out, had not always espoused such liberal views. To my shock, and to his delight, Nour explained how in his younger days he too had been a supporter of HT. Our paths had even crossed back in London, when he attended the same Wembley Arena *Khilafah* conference that shook the country with thunderous roars of *Allahu akbar!*

'What? But . . . *subhan Allah!* So why did you leave the cause?' I asked, genuinely interested.

And as we walked across the desert sand of Mazrah Tora's prison yard, Nour looked at me and simply said, 'I grew up.'

The way he said it caught me completely off guard. I grew up. The phrase made me pause. I had been expecting a long pseudo-theological justification for why he had left, but Nour never tried that, and he knew that if he had he would have lost, knowing my training would tear his arguments to shreds. He was too smart to get into that. Instead, he just left that phrase hanging there, and left me to think about it. Which I did.

While my heart led the way, through bonds with people like John Cornwall of Amnesty, Ayman Nour and Sa'ad el-Din Ibrahim, I also decided to nourish my mind. So I used my time in prison to study everything I could about Islam, the faith that I believed formed the basis of my Islamist ideology. And, as a nod to Abi's encouragement during my childhood, I decided to read as many English literature books as I could.

I became good friends with a brother called Mahmood. Mahmood was sentenced to fifteen years for being in the Cairo leadership of al-Gama'a al-Islamiyya, though he had since recanted his beliefs. Mahmood was a graduate in Arabic from Dar ul-Uloom, Egypt's most prestigious Arabic college. As a tactic of psychological warfare on top of his brutal torture, Aman al-Dawlah had intimidated Mahmood's wife into divorcing him. I spent many days perfecting my Arabic grammar, morphology and vocabulary in Mahmood's cell.

In return, I would try to help him learn some English. One of the difficulties that Arabs have in speaking English is that Arabic doesn't contain the letter 'p', and for some reason they manage to shorten the double-vowel sound 'ee' to a single 'i'. A word like 'please' therefore, typically comes out as 'bliss'. One day I was trying to teach Mahmood the difference in pronunciation between 'peach', 'beach' and 'pitch'. I said the words slowly and pronounced them heavily: 'Peach . . . beach . . . pitch.' Mahmood listened carefully, and then with all the sincerity a thickly bearded former jihadist could muster, proudly spoke my words back at the top of his voice, 'Bitch, bitch, bitch!' He looked at me in bewilderment as I burst into fits of laughter.

I found other teachers for my studies, too. I befriended a reformed member of Islamic Jihad, Momin, and Abdul Hameed – arbitrarily interned for five years – who was a graduate of Sunni Islam's most prestigious theological university, al-Azhar, as well as an exceptionally bright and perceptive theologian called Sheikh Nidal, also arbitrarily interned for around three years. All three instructed me well in ancient Islamic jurisprudence. It might sound strange, given how committed I was to the Islamist ideology, but I had never properly studied Islam, or the Qur'an. Islamism was a political movement before it was a religious one and many of its followers came from irreligious backgrounds. This was something that the Salafists have always taken us to task for. Sure, I'd read excerpts over the years, discussed specific passages in HT *halaqahs* where scripture was deemed to back up our arguments. But I had never attempted to study the Qur'an properly for myself.

So here, in Mazrah Tora, I committed half of the Qur'an to memory at the hands of another reformed member of Islamic Jihad, Ali Fiqih – sentenced to twelve years – who had an *ijazah*, a qualification in the art of *qira'ah* recitation at the hands of a master. To fully appreciate the ancient text of the Qur'an, one needed an exegesis, and understanding the dense theological jargon of these exegetes is a Herculean task in itself. This is what my various teachers helped me with. I began to develop a deeper, fuller appreciation of Islam than I had ever experienced before. That dark period of solitary confinement, when I had vowed to become a suicide bomber, now seemed like the thoughts of a distant madman.

During my incarceration, al-Gama'a al-Islamiyya, formerly Egypt's largest terrorist group, had also been busy publishing their *muraja'aat* of jihadist thought. These *muraja'aat* deconstructed the violent ideology of Jihadism, using traditional theology. Crucially, they were written and published by the leadership of Gama'a themselves. Here was, for the first time, an entire jihadist organisation admitting that it had got it so very wrong. Book by book, I devoured these *muraja'aat*. Though I had never been a jihadist, it wasn't hard for me to start seeing how the basic arguments used here could be extended to the very ideology of Islamism itself. And my mind started joining dots that even Gama'a hadn't dared to connect.

Reading classic English literature did for me what studying Islamic theology couldn't; it forced my mind to grapple with moral dilemmas. Upon our request, the British Consul would regularly send us books from the embassy library. I devoured the classics, but, in addition, focused on Tolkien's *Lord of the Rings* trilogy, reading it twice over. I couldn't shake the moral paradox that Gollum-Sméagol came to embody. Gollum was an evil creature prepared to do anything to get his One Ring back. Yet, as the story climaxed, it wasn't the hero Frodo who destroyed the ring. As 'evil' Gollum had done before him, Frodo eventually succumbed to the lure of the ring, making a last-ditch attempt to keep it. It was in fact Gollum who pounced at the ring, biting it off Frodo's finger, before accidentally falling to his death in the lava of Mount Doom, destroying the ring with him. An evil character had thus inadvertently achieved the good that the story's hero failed at, and saved the world. This moral complexity began to fascinate me.

I also read and re-read Orwell's *Animal Farm* and Golding's *Lord of the Flies*. *Animal Farm* made me ponder on life under 'the *Khilafah*' ruled by the likes of Imtiaz, Irfan, Abdul Wajid, Jalaluddin and their ilk. Golding's *Lord of the Flies* served as a stark warning about the tyranny that could arise from the most innocent of souls, with the best of intentions. Even the innocence of children was insufficient to guarantee against injustice, yet here we were working to set up a system that would install a ruler for life, run by people like Abdul Wajid, or Jalaluddin, and claiming to rule in God's name.

This combination of rehumanisation, studying Islam from its sources and grappling with moral complexity through literature, affected me in profound ways. Over the years, I began to re-examine everything I knew, and had been prepared to die for. Though we had placed establishing an 'Islamic State' and 'implementing' *shari'ah* as law, above even the most religious of rituals, I couldn't help noticing that not once were the words 'law', 'state' or 'constitution' mentioned in the Qur'an. When I thought about this further, it made historic sense. The Qur'an was an ancient text, while political ideas such as a 'unitary legal system', 'codified law', 'statehood' and 'constitution' were modern political concepts: they did not exist at the time the Qur'an was written.

I went back to look at what Islamists held as the last true example of legitimate government: the Turkish Caliphate or Ottoman Empire. Again, history was telling me a rather different story to that of HT. This Caliphate never had the sort of unitary codified legal system that HT was proposing to 'implement', with the *shari'ah* as law. Instead, justice was run under what was called the 'Millet' system – a pluralistic legal structure where the interpretation of *shari'ah* was left to local community tribunals. These would hear evidence and intepret *shari'ah* as they saw fit. There was not even any law obliging people to go to these tribunals – it was a voluntary decision. The Ottomans offered general edicts on administrative matters, but these were different from any sort of legal system.

The idea of a unified, codified legal system, and of having a judiciary subservient to that legal system, and of having a constitution that frames this legal system, and a state that protects that constitution by monopolising the use of force, all of these concepts emerged with the birth of the European nation state. These were modern, Western constructs. The Ottoman Caliphate, struggling to adjust, even initiated a reform process, known as the *Tanzimat* reforms, in an attempt to study how best to incorporate these new European ideas into their empire.

Throughout almost all of Islam's history a single interpretation of *shari'ah* was never adopted and enforced over society as a codified system of law. In fact, unlike in its English rendition 'Sharia Law', where we use *shari'ah* as an adjective describing the noun 'law', in original Arabic *shari'ah* is simply a noun. The specific 'adoption' of an interpretation of *shari'ah* as law by a ruler was not religiously mandatory, and it didn't happen in history. Unitary legal systems were a European idea, and worse, the desire to merge law with religious canons was specifically a Catholic pre-Reformation idea. This realisation had profound implications for my beliefs. Rather than justice – in the sense of legal consistency – being derived from Islamism, Islamism relied on Western concepts of justice to get off the ground. I buried my head in my hands as I slowly realised . . . we Islamists were the bastard children of colonialism.

I now thought about people like my trial lawyer, Ahmed Saif. He wasn't an Islamist; he was a communist. Yet there he was, fearlessly campaigning as a founding member of Kifaya – modern Egypt's first openly anti-Mubarak platform organised along non-Islamist lines. Ayman Nour and Sa'ad el-Din Ibrahim were liberals, from the opposite end of the spectrum, yet they too were passionate that Mubarak should go. I thought, too, about Amnesty International, and their campaigns for Prisoners of Conscience like myself. In each of these instances, they were driven by the same principles as me when I had joined HT: to fight for justice. Yet for all of them, their causes and beliefs had nothing to do with Islamism.

I had always been taught – and had passionately believed – that the presence of Islamism meant justice, and the absence of it created injustice. But now I began seeing things differently. What Ahmed Saif and Ayman Nour were campaigning for from their different viewpoints was undeniably just: having spent so long being detained at the president's pleasure, I had no doubt about that. The freedoms that Amnesty International were championing were something I'd learnt for myself to be manifestly just. Yet none of it was Islamism.

Through my studies I came across a tradition of the Prophet, concerning Najashi, the Christian Habasha king who protected the Companions by providing them with shelter as they ran from the pagan Quraish. *Malikun 'adlun la yuzlamu 'indahu ahad* 'A just king under whom no one is oppressed,' said the Prophet, *'alayhi salam*. Justice, from a Christian king, endorsed by the Prophet himself.

And as I started to decouple justice from Islamism in my mind, it was the beginning of the end of my belief in Islamism. If justice and Islamism were decoupled, then not only was it possible to have one without the other, it also meant that there were situations where the two might come into conflict. I'd only joined HT because of the fire that injustice had lit inside me. It was an uncomfortable recognition, and not one that I swallowed immediately. I shied away from its implications for a long time, retreating back into the comfort of my Islamist beliefs. But as hard as I tried to bury them, I couldn't shift the nagging thoughts I had in my mind. And where the heart leads, the mind can follow.

CHAPTER TWENTY-FIVE

No right to silence

Like the desert scorpion, Aman al-Dawlah still had one final sting to deliver us before we were allowed to leave Egypt. The Egyptian prison system is supposed to release prisoners after serving three-quarters of their sentence. Our release date – the marker of three years and nine months – had come and gone. Paperwork, we were told. Bureaucracy. In Egypt, one could never be sure if it was incompetence or something more sinister behind things. One only had to look at the tens of thousands of white-clothed prisoners arbitrarily detained – the *mu'taqaleen*, to witness the elasticity of the Egyptian justice system.

Then one day, out of the blue, a *shaweesh* came running into my cell:

'Maagid, they've arrived! They've arrived! Start packing your things, *inta murawweh* – you're going home!'

But does anyone ever leave Egypt's jails? What of my friend Ashraf al-Nahri, who completed a ten-year sentence, only to be taken on a round trip to al-Gihaz and interned again? I still remember the look of total sadness on his face. Have you ever seen total sadness? He left in the blue overalls of those with sentences, only to be processed and returned in the white clothes of a *mu'taqal*, arbitrarily imprisoned again with no respite. I went to him then, to make him a cup of tea, and to share words of comfort, perhaps a game of chess, because al-Nahri was a master of chess, and he had always been kind to me.

Put aside cruelty, put aside violence, even put aside murder for a moment, and consider justice. Justice, if it means anything, must mean to adhere to your own confessed principles. If you claim to stand for the rule of law and democracy, then stick to what you claim and be judged by it. If you claim to stand for death, and violent revolution, and armed struggle, then stick to what you claim, and be judged by it. These men stood by their ideology, they fought and in some cases killed for their cause, and they were judged by it. Killed, tortured or locked away. Now they have recanted. They have not only served their time, but they have renounced their past, because they trusted in your 'rule of law'. So will you now be judged by your principles? Or what else is left, but a return to lawlessness and vigilante vengeance? And so I didn't dare hope that I would be returning home. After all, this was Egypt, 'we do as we please'.

As word rippled through the prison that we were leaving, a succession of people came up to say their farewells, and I realised just how many friends I had made during my stay. Salah Bayoumi, convicted for the assassination of President Sadat, in prison since I was four years old, gave me a farewell present – a copy of the Qur'an with a dedication from him at the front. He began to cry as he embraced me and bade me farewell. His eyes carried the burdens of a tortured soul, confused about his own past and doubtful about his own future. As much as possible, I tried to keep my emotions in check out of respect for the many who had completed their sentences only to be re-interned as *mu'taqaleen*.

I had less respect for the prison authorities. We were taken in to see the prisoner governor, the one who threatened to kill me. He had not yet been transferred but was clearly worried about what was to happen to him. He asked us three to sign a prepared statement about our stay in prison. I read through the document. What a complete travesty it was. It went into farcical detail about how well we had been looked after throughout our stay. Each of us refused. I handed the governor his pen back. If you want to know what I think about Marzah Tora, we told him, you'll have to watch it on al-Jazeera, with everybody else.

The metal blue police vans came to pick us up. We were fully expecting a deportation order, to be escorted straight to the airport, put on a plane, and handed over once the flight had landed at Heathrow. Until we set foot on British soil, I refused to let myself believe that we were actually going home. As it turned out, Aman al-Dawlah didn't want to let us go without saying a special form of goodbye first. When the door to the van opened, I could see a guard holding my old nemesis, the *ghimamah*, a rag with which to blindfold my eyes, and my worst fears were realised.

This time, we were taken to Lazughli, the only Aman al-Dawlah building to match al-Gihaz for notoriety. We tried to protest. We explained to the guard that we had documentation, demanded to see a British representative, but he just laughed.

'No British here,' he said. 'Just Egypt. Now silence!'

Blindfolded again, and held in another torture centre, day turned to night and my dreams to darkness, as the terrifying backdrop of tortured souls continued without let-up. Scream after scream began to echo through the building. Four years had passed since our ordeal in al-Gihaz, but Aman al-Dawlah had not changed. They were still practising the systematic use of torture as their default interrogation device. Except this time there was a sickening, macabre twist to the torture. Penetrating through wild screams of agony we could hear the clear, distinct rhythmic sound of the guards listening to a recorded recitation of the Qur'an, as they tortured people. Such a flagrantly sacrilegious display could also be a twisted psychological trick – to say to the Islamist detainees, your faith won't help you here. Or perhaps in some sort of sociopathic way, they thought they were doing God's work.

I'll probably never know. But the latter is not as far-fetched as it might sound. Mubarak was keen to ensure that he had a religious, as well as a political grip over his country. The university of al-Azhar had long been the greatest theological centre of learning for Sunni Muslims. Under his rule, Mubarak decreed that its head would no longer be elected by peers, but be a political appointee. A pliant theologian, Shaikh Tantawi, was selected for the role. Tantawi, in return, would bring intricate theological justifications for Mubarak's rule, no doubt well researched and thoroughly argued. Anyone who opposed Mubarak's regime, Tantawi ordained, is to be classed as a '*khariji*' – essentially a reference to the early heretical outlaws who rebelled against the fourth Caliph of Islam. By such a classification, their killing and detention as rebels was justified by Tantawi's fatwa.

Since the subordination of al-Azhar to Mubarak's regime, the university has struggled to maintain the respect and prestige it once held throughout the Sunni world. I'd even learnt through my *shari'ah* studies in prison that some clerics relied upon an ancient juristic ruling, from the *Maliki* school, justifying the use of violence during interrogation. And right there, in Lazughli, while listening to Allah's words forming a backdrop to the torture of men, and though I was disgusted, my mind wondered off on one of its familiar tangents. Didn't 'our side' also glorify death, and the murder of innocents, by abusing Allah's words? Didn't 'our side' also use audio recordings praising God, as backdrop to footage depicting beheadings and mayhem? If these guards sincerely believe that by rebelling against their ruler, we are heretical *kharijis*, and that by fighting us they are doing God's work, then why not seek God's blessing while doing so? These were the dangers of meddling in religion to justify a political stance, even on the 'secular' side of the debate. And I remember thinking, why can't we simply argue our case. If I'm right, I get the credit. If I'm wrong, I get the blame. Let us spare Islam from the abuse of power-hungry men seeking to justify their political ambitions.

After some hours I asked to go to the toilet. A guard picked me up and escorted me through the building.

My mind was playing tricks on me. *My name is Maagid Nawaz, I am a member of Hizb al-Tahrir.* It's OK, I said to myself as I tried to ward off the nightmares of al-Gihaz, calm yourself, Allah is with you. You will get out of here.

As I came out of the toilet, I heard a quiet sobbing in the bathroom area, and turned to speak to a young man nursing his wounds.

'*Akhi*, what's wrong?' I asked, unable to see him through my *ghimamah*.

'I-I-I cannot stand,' the man cried. 'The pain. My feet, my legs feel like they are burning.'

'What have they done to you?'

'The electricity,' came his broken reply.

'You have been chosen to be tested by Allah for your faith in Him. Be proud of yourself, don't cry, *akhi*, you're a man now. You join the ranks of the heroes and martyrs of old.'

And then the guard returned. 'No talking! I'm warning you, we can do that to you too!' he shouted.

'I'm sorry, I'm sorry, I was just asking this brother where you had gone.'

Eventually I heard the morning *azan*. We had been in Lazughli all night, sixteen hours before we were finally processed. This time the blue van made no more unscheduled stops. British officials were waiting for us at Cairo International Airport, our passports and travel documents ready. An Aman al-Dawlah *zaabit* was to escort us all the way back to Heathrow on our British Airways flight.

'Any trouble,' the *zaabit* leant over to tell us, 'and I'll cuff you immediately.'

That was the last threat the Egyptian authorities threw at me. It was an empty gesture, and a pointless one. I was so exhausted after that sleepless, horrendous night in Lazughli that, as the plane took off, I fell into a deep sleep for most of the journey.

Egypt – and so it is that on this day the 1st of March 2006, after five years in your care, four of them at your expense, I bid you farewell. And despite everything that came to be, despite all the pain we shared, I cannot forget you. How could I? Blood, sweat and tears are not so easily removed from porous souls. I came to you a boy, those years ago, full of dreams, and passion, and rage, and lofty ideals, my soul at peace with God, my ideas at war with man. I leave you now, my hair grey, full of confusion, and questions and doubts, my soul warring with God, my ideas finding peace with man. Don't cry, my love, *habibti*, for though together we were stranded on a barren floor in anguish, and though together we banished insanity by embracing pain, our Lord will see us through, as He always has. And the spring that you planted in my chest shall carve its path and ripple through your streets soon enough, like a river bursting its banks it will flood your youth with hope. So prepare to rise again, for you are *Misr*, the land of the brave, *Ard al-Kinanah*.

As soon as we landed, and the Aman al-Dawlah *zaabit* melted away as if he never existed, we were met on the plane by officers from London's SO15, Special Branch.

'Are you going to read me my rights?' I asked wearily, as we sat in the specially built interrogation room at the airport. Having just come from one police state, I wanted to feel reassured that I hadn't flown back into another.

'You know, my right to remain silent and all that?'

The officer smiled at me thinly. 'Not here, Mr Nawaz,' he said. 'If you refuse to answer any of my questions, it's a criminal offence.'

'What? I'm sorry, how's that possible? Don't tell me you've done away with the right to silence?'

'Mr Nawaz, UK law no longer grants you the right to silence in any port of entry or exit in the UK. I'm afraid that I will need a sample of your DNA and you will need to answer my questions. If you do not, I will have to charge you with a criminal offence.'

'Then I demand access to a lawyer, or is that a criminal offence now too?'

Fortunately, we had a lawyer waiting for us on the other side of the gate. Stephen Jackobi of the group Fair Trials Abroad had been active in campaigning for our release, and was now with our families awaiting our return. Jackobi was friendly, but clear about the law.

'The officer is correct, I'm afraid,' he said. 'Since September 11th, the rules have changed: at any port of exit or entry into the UK, there is no right to silence. That's why they want to interview you now, rather than on the other side of the barrier.'

'So what should I do?'

'My advice would be to cooperate for now,' Jackobi said. 'You'll have to answer their questions.'

'And if I don't?'

Jackobi sighed. 'They'll arrest you. There's nothing I can do about that, I'm afraid.'

And so the interview began, and I answered their questions briefly and succinctly, as I was legally obliged to do, desperate just to go home.

'If you hear anything, or come across any information that might be useful, would you mind keeping us informed?' the officer concluded.

'No,' I replied. 'I have no intention of doing anything of the sort.'

After fours hours of interrogation, we were finally released. Stephen Jackobi had stayed there, to help and advise us. And not just on the legal side of things. He'd dealt with prisoners returning from abroad before, and in the short space of time he had, he wanted to brief us as best he could.

'I've got to warn you,' he said. 'It's going to be difficult. Don't think for a second that once you walk through that gate that all of this is over. To readjust to normal life after what you've been through is going to be really hard. You need to realise that it is going to test your relationships to breaking point. I've seen so many people come back and for their marriages to fall apart. The statistics show that most people in your position end up getting divorced or abuse their spouses. I don't want that to happen to any of you, but you've got to be aware that you'll really have to work at your relationships. Otherwise, you'll end up the same way.'

And as we stood at that airport gate, full of excitement, alive and alert, just about to be reunited with our families, I turned to Stephen Jackobi with a wide, warm smile on my face and a sincerity that I knew to be true, 'Don't worry about me, Stephen. I'm married to a loyal wife who I will embrace with all my heart. She's the mother of my child, and she kept me alive out there.'

And with a spring in my step, I walked out of that gate oblivious to the forces that were about to tear my heart clean out of my chest.

CHAPTER TWENTY-SIX

How many years did you fail?

I see you, London. Heathrow, immune from change during long spells of absence, oblivious to the distance of lovers, you seem to welcome me back with no less warmth than when I left. I see you, London. How I despised you and loved you. How I hated everything you stood for, and yet when deprived of your familiarity, your openness, how I missed you miserably. At once head of the colonial snake that poisoned my people, and snared my lands, yet also bastion of justice, the rule of law and fair play. And even now, as I rush to embrace you again, your boots stamp on my people in Iraq and Afghanistan, while I know that my boots are nowhere safer than resting in your green parks. Why do you confuse me so, beating me with one hand while drying my tears with the other? How I tried for thirteen years to rip you out of my soul, to deny you, to bury you, but how I've longed for you to claim me from the hell that I just returned from. London, I see you.

The media interest in our return was huge. We were greeted by the flashing of bulbs and shouts of journalists from every angle. I looked around, all I could see was a blur of people – where shall I turn, where are my family? Then I heard my dad's familiar voice rising above the din, shouting 'Maajid!' My mind instantly travelled back to when I was a boy, and I would make these silly little gifts for my dad, from the spare materials in his garage, in anticipation of his return from Libya every month. How long a month would seem in those days. And Dad would walk in, Stetson on his head, jeans, belt and boots on, and he would shout my name 'Maajid!' And he would scoop up my tiny little body and hold me in a huge bear hug. Instinctively, without even thinking, my body moved towards the voice I could hear, until I found myself embracing my dad with joy.

Next to him, right there by his side, I saw Rabia. She was crying.

And there I saw Abi, the womb that bore me, who I had hurt so much through the years. And I wanted to tell her everything, about the storm that was raging in my heart, about how I wanted to change, to make her proud again, about all the literature I had read, but there was no time. Then there was my childhood best friend, my protector and brother, Osman. I did you proud. I stood up for what we believed in, I fought them all the way, I didn't back down, just as you showed me. And Sorraiya! My God, you're all grown up, from nine to fourteen, what a difference! My sister, I'm sorry you had to grow up on a diet of torture, jails and anger. No child deserves that. I will try to show you a better way now, to heal our hearts together. And here was John Cornwall, my friend, my human friend. As I saw him for the first time, I felt like I knew him well.

But it wasn't just our friends and relatives at the gate. Elbowing and jostling for position as well were many members of Hizb al-Tahrir. No longer were we fallen soldiers who 'hadn't been defiant enough': at a stroke we were returning heroes, and the leadership wanted to bask in the glow of our media attention. Here was Jalaluddin, the man who had admonished me from the safety of his sofa, welcoming me back like he was my best friend. 'You are our heroes, brothers!' he proclaimed as he shook my hand and offered me whatever help I needed to settle back into the group.

I desperately wanted to see Ammar, who was waiting for me at my in-laws' house. So, as quickly as I could, I greeted family, friends and colleagues and got into a car with Rabia by my side. I remember holding her hand in that car, as I had done in the car journey home the day we were married. And she smiled at me now as she had smiled at me then. And we drove off together to see our son.

Ammar was now six years old, and had been running and messing around before I arrived. As soon as I opened the door and he saw me he stopped. His expression completely froze: it was such a shock for him to see me there. For a moment, as when I had first seen him in prison, I was worried as to his reaction. But as in prison, I needn't have been. He gave a little jump and ran over to hug me. I held him so tightly then and lifted him high into the air with a love that was deep and pure. We had a celebration meal, and then went back to Rabia's flat, our flat, which she had carefully arranged and decorated for my return. And that night, after I put Ammar to sleep, I slept awkwardly, bewildered, confused and not knowing how to express to Rabia the storm raging in my chest.

'Shhh, sleep now,' she said, 'there's no need to talk. We'll have plenty of time to talk.'

It didn't take any time for Hizb al-Tahrir to start seeking my involvement in the group's UK leadership. The brothers had organised a press conference for the following day. My mind was haunted with thoughts of all the brothers we'd left behind, of Akram and so many Egyptians who were languishing in jails for years well beyond their sentences. I owed it to them, to the world, to get matters off my chest, and to speak of the atrocities Mubarak's regime was committing in the name of stability. That day we addressed al-Jazeera, Al Arabiya, the BBC. As we had promised the warden, we told the world about Mazrah Tora prison and the brutal trangressions of Aman al-Dawlah. Later that week, I was even interviewed for BBC *HARDtalk* with Sarah Montague, toeing the party line, playing my role as an HT spokesman to perfection, desperately trying to cling on to anything familiar from my past to remind myself of who I was. During this period, I gave many talks for HT, spoke at rallies of thousands and even shared a platform twice with a member of the 'Outlawz', deceased rapper Tupac's former group. This man was called 'Napoleon', and after Tupac's death he had become a hardcore Salafi, disrespectfully declaring to all and sundry that Tupac was now burning in the fires of hell. And throughout this period, Rabia looked on with that same wounded look in her eyes, while I focused on the only thing I knew best: galvanising and rallying crowds.

In the weeks and months ahead, I took stock of my situation, and my self-esteem began to falter. I was now twenty-eight years old, still an undergraduate with no guarantee that I would be allowed re-admission, had a six-year-old son to support, no job to go to, and a four-year stint in jail as an Islamist political prisoner in a post-9/11 world. I began to panic. For the first time in my life I began to feel old. Not old in the conventional way, I was still only twenty-eight, but old inside my heart and in the depths of my eyes. The burden of what I knew and what my conscience was telling me about Islamism was heavy on my mind. My doubts kept growing, but the more they screamed for my attention, the more I sought to bury them away in denial. This is all I've known in my adult life, 'my name is Maajid Nawaz. I am a member of Hizb al-Tahrir.' What was I if not this? So I set myself some goals – if I could give myself something to aim for, then that might help lift me out of this trough.

My starting point was my degree. I went back to SOAS to see if they would allow me to continue my law and Arabic degree. They could quite easily have told me where to go. I'd done my first year and taken two years out, done my second year, and then was imprisoned for four years halfway through my placement abroad. Abi though, God bless her, had been persistent in persuading the university to keep my place open. To my relief two of my old Arabic lecturers, Muaz Salih and Muhammad Sa'eed, were still at the university and had kept the doors open for me. SOAS let me back in. I'd been arrested a few months before I was due to take my third year Arabic exams, so my faculty head said I'd have to pass those in order to be allowed back. As my one-year placement in Egypt had been extended by several years, my ability in Arabic was not in question. I took the exam, and got 97 per cent.

If I had just stuck to getting my head down and doing my

degree, things might have been fine. But HT asked me to join their leadership. There were two leadership committees by this point. After London's terrorist attacks of July 7th, Prime Minister Tony Blair had threatened to ban the group. In response to this, HT had created both a front leadership and a secret leadership committee. The 'executive committee' was the publicly recognised leadership, but the real power lay behind the scenes, in a 'wilayah' committee. This ruling wilayah committee was again led by Nasim; freshly returned from having set up HT in Bangladesh, he had been asked by the global *amir* to replace Jalaluddin due to the latter's extremely poor judgement. No wonder Jalaluddin had greeted me so fondly back at the airport, I thought. He'd obviously been brought down a peg or two. Because of my media profile, I was given a place on the front committee; and because Nasim knew me well and trusted me completely, he put me on the secret ruling *wilayah* committee too.

To begin with, I wanted to find a way to accommodate my changing views within HT. I felt the way forward was to hone my arguments, and convince other members to come round to my revised position. In that BBC *HARDtalk* interview with Sarah Montague, she had asked me what I stood for, and I replied that HT were calling for a 'representative Caliphate'. This led to a great deal of furious discussion inside the group. What did I mean by a 'representative Caliphate'? The Caliphate was 'the Caliphate'. There should have been no argument about that: this was the imposition of Islam on society.

But I had seen how people could change in prison. I had seen how someone's certainty to the point of death, could change to become regret and sorrow at lives lost. I'd seen how almost every facet of our ideology relied on modern European political philosophy, and that any Islamic legitimacy it had was at best only one view. I had seen how Islam could be abused to justify almost any political position, including torture. I remembered the character flaws of all the Islamists I'd come to know, both inside HT and others. It was fanciful, I felt, that just because someone was a committed Islamist, they would run things the right way. This came back to the decoupling of Islamism and justice in my mind. There needed to be some accountability, not only built into the system, but into the very formation of our ideology itself, which was, ultimately, a man-made construct.

Nasim actually began to praise me. He applauded me for my new ideas, and for my ability to think outside the box. This, he told the others, was how we were going to move the organisation forwards. But as the year went on, and the discussions continued, I became increasingly disillusioned at the slow response I was getting. My questions bore deep, to the very legitimacy of imposing any interpretation of *shari'ah* as law. After learning and studying how this had never been done, and nor was it commanded, I began to see such a goal as un-Islamic. How could I remain inside an organisation that I now believed was striving for a goal that ran against the very spirit of Islam?

As my doubts grew, I increasingly began to consider my HT brothers as ignorant of Islam, politics, and history. My mind felt as if it was going to implode. One wrong word, and I could be unceremoniously suspended from the group as a deviant. Then any legitimacy I would have to make reform arguments would be useless. I had to speak to someone. I turned to Rabia, who I could trust with my secrets implicitly. But although Rabia was the most moderate of those I had spoken to, ultimately, she was still an HT member. The reality now hit home to me like a blow to the head, my own wife would be a stranger to who I had become.

Who was I fooling? I'd spent most of my life recruiting from her family, I'd been responsible for the recruitment of her Uncle Abdul Rauf, Dr Qayyum's younger brother, who had been tortured in Pakistan's jails. Rabia's cousin, who joined HT after my recruitment efforts, had also been arrested in Pakistan and his mother had died while he was still incarcerated. I had argued a hard-line position to her entire family, bringing nothing but tribulation upon them. And here I was now, after she had just waited five years in the name of this cause, trying to convince her that my new ideas were correct instead. As the Prophet, *'alayhi salam*, had advised, 'Indeed there is a kind of magic in eloquent speech.' She was right. Why should she listen to me now?

'You were right then and you are right now,' she scolded, 'no one can argue with you, Maajid. You are always right. So what is the point of having this discussion?'

To my dismay, she was unprepared to even entertain the discussion. And so, miserable and lonely, I began seeking solace among new faces at SOAS, overly keen to make friends, overly trusting as I frantically searched for whatever 'normality' was meant to feel like. Lauren, Sergio, Maryam, Jeremy, Amira, I desperately sought out people who could remind me how to live my life again, for no recruitment purpose, just simply to have friends I could call my own. And then it was, in the junior common room of SOAS, that I met her.

Fatima Mullick was the opposite of everything I stood for. Or was she everything that Abi stood for? Proudly Pakistani, proudly female, her answer to the face veil was to wear her beauty brazenly, her answer to stoning the adulterers was to cite Rumi's 'Let the Lovers Be', her reply to Qutb was Khayyam, the mystical Persian sage. She embraced life in all its splendour where I had come to embrace the afterlife in all its austerity, and she despised the madness of men who cared more about whether their position in prayer was correct, than they did about spilling innocent blood.

She was a political science postgraduate, and she approached me one day with the question 'So, are you a PhD student?' She must have seen my salt-and-pepper hair, or perhaps she saw the age in my eyes.

'No, I'm an undergraduate.'

'Oh really, how many years did you fail?' she blurted out, laughing.

My pride was hurt. 'None. I was imprisoned in Egypt after 9/11. I served four years. I've just got back.'

Her face changed. 'I, I'm sorry, I didn't mean to . . . where are you from in Pakistan?'

'Gujrat,' I replied, smiling at her bluster.

'Oh, you mean Gujarat in India?' she asked, too flustered about whether she'd caused offence to think straight.

'No, there is another Gujrat, in Pakistan.' And after having caused her further embarrassment, and quite enjoying it, I decided to befriend this over-inquisitive politics postgraduate from Pakistan.

You see, I tried to recruit Fatima. Like the death throes of a dying body, I tried to project all my insecurities about my existential crisis onto her. I showed her my BBC *HARDtalk* interview and told her about how important it was that we Muslims know our identity properly.

And Fatima just looked at me square in the face as she said, 'I may not be able to argue with you, or respond to your points, but I know what you are saying is simply bullshit. And you know what, Maajid? So do you!'

And that was it. With those words the penny dropped. My mouth froze as I struggled to speak. Fatima had no idea she had just become the proverbial butterfly to unleash a whirlwind. And I had just found my new best friend, my rock of support among the confusion that was my life after leaving HT.

In the end, the timing of my decision was forced. While I had been in prison, Nasim had been in Bangladesh, setting up HT out there. He now needed to get back there to resume this work, which meant that – after Jalaluddin's inevitable fall from grace – HT UK would need a new leader. I had the media profile, the international experience, my Arabic and Islamic learning, I had cut my teeth the hard way and I had the intellectual ability. For Nasim, I was the ideal candidate.

The ball dropped. I could go no further. It was one thing to be arguing for my views within the organisation, it was another to be leading a group whose ideology I was feeling increasingly uncomfortable about. The timing couldn't have been worse. I was in the middle of revising for my final exams at university, but I had to make a move before anything was formalised. I called Nasim, friend to friend, protégé to mentor, and asked to see him alone at a cafe in London's Brick Lane.

This was one of the most nervous conversations of my life. I had been a member of Hizb al-Tahrir for over a decade. I had known Nasim since I was fifteen years old, and through that time he had been a friend and mentor to me through thick and thin. But I owed it to him to tell him my decision, face to face.

'I know you are preparing me to take over the leadership of the group, but it's something I'm going to have to turn down. In fact, I'm . . . I'm, I no longer believe in HT and I need to leave the group immediately. Please consider this my resignation.' I just blurted it out.

Nasim was completely astonished.

'We can work this out,' he argued. 'You have so much to give. Come to Bangladesh with me, we have a real chance of getting into power over there,' he said. 'We can run the country together, you and I.'

We sat in the cafe, going back and forth. It never got heated. It was more about sadness, and regret, and resignation. Nasim knew that I wouldn't have come to this decision lightly. He knew that I'd thought through the consequences, and that it would be unlikely we'd see each other again. In the end, as a favour to him, I agreed that I wouldn't announce my resignation for a fortnight. Maybe it was to give him the opportunity to tell the rest of the group himself, or because he wanted time to have another go at persuading me. If it was the latter, I didn't give him the chance. I had my phone switched off throughout the fortnight.

When the fortnight had passed I released an email to the media, rather than leaving it to the group to announce and twist the reasons for my departure. '*In the name of God the Compassionate, the Merciful,*' I began. '*Assalaamu alaykum.*'

I tried to keep my resignation as brief and as dignified as I could:

> *I have deemed it necessary to announce that, after serving in Hizb al-Tahrir for 12 years and since I was 17 years old, I have decided to leave the party and resign my membership effective immediately. I humbly request that I do not discuss the reasons for my decision at this moment in time, and ask that I be left to complete my much delayed final examinations. Forgive me for any offence caused.*

The moment I hit 'send', a dozen years of my life had come to a close.

I called Osman during this time. He didn't know it but he was the first person I told. I somehow felt that I needed his support. All those years earlier we had started on this journey together; he had left HT long before I did, I felt he deserved to know my decision. 'Good,' he said, 'don't worry, Islam is more important than HT.' He didn't yet know that it was precisely the modern *politicised* interpretation of Islam that I actually had a problem with, and I didn't have the heart to tell him.

I then immediately called Abi. As I told her my news, she broke down in tears of joy right there on the phone. 'Finally, finally, my son, I knew you would make the right decision. In my gut I could sense this was happening to you. I'm so proud of you, thank God, thank God!' She cried, 'All these years I've waited to hear this news coming from your lips, I knew you would eventually see the truth. How could you not? You're my son, it was my womb that bore you, I'm so proud of you!'

But my situation with Rabia was deteriorating day by day. I desperately needed the space to learn who I was, to construct myself anew, piece by piece. Every time she asked me to spend more time indoors, I felt suffocated as I tried to remove myself from everything associated with HT and their ideology. It was a terrible situation to be in. Guilt riddled my insides, and I felt as cruel, if not more cruel, than Aman al-Dawlah. But I needed to define myself again before letting anyone else in.

As much as she struggled to find the Maajid who was taken from her so suddenly in that Alexandria flat, there was no turning back for me. I had seen too much, learnt too much, to ever again be that same Maajid she married. In many ways I think I was a nicer person then, and like so many nice people who seek power, I wanted to force everyone else to be nice. It's called totalitarianism. Now I felt like a horrible person, full of guilt for what I could see was happening to my marriage, yet I no longer wanted the world to be nice. I just wanted everyone to leave everyone else alone. I just wanted to be left alone. And I began to stay at home less and less. Desperate to escape the claustrophobia of Islamism, my new prison.

But I had nowhere to go, nowhere to sleep. And so, I took to sleeping in the back seat of my clapped-out old student car, wrapped in a blanket, in my Renault Clio, parked outside my university in Russell Square, while my final exams were upon me. If those last days in Newham were my lowest, and if those spent in solitary confinement my darkest, then these here were my loneliest days. I still keep that blanket in the back of my car, just in case. Sad, lonely, confused and falling apart, I needed help to find myself again but couldn't rely on anyone to help me, because the only people who had walked through my hell now saw me as a traitor. I needed Abi, I needed home. While sleeping in that car I became certain that I would not be able to purge myself of Islamism while living with Rabia.

I didn't have the heart to tell her I was leaving her, face to face, as I had with Nasim. I knew it would only result in more futile debate. Instead, I left her a letter announcing my decision, and just left. After one of my final exams, Rabia turned up at SOAS with her family: her two sisters and brother-in-law seeking me out, trying urgently to reconcile. But I wouldn't speak to them. I didn't know who I was any more, how could I speak to them? It took all the will power I've ever known to turn away and run from her that day. But run I did. Having left my car at home for her, I got into a friend's car to leave, and pulling away, I could see Rabia running after me in the middle of the road, calling out my name, pleading for me to stop. As we sped off, I caught the look of anguish on her face. I hated myself for what I had to do on that day.

CHAPTER TWENTY-SEVEN

Civil-democratic intimidation

I spent thirteen years of my life as a member of Hizb al-Tahrir. Thirteen years as a deeply committed Islamist ideologue totally prepared to sacrifice all for my cause. My journey from prison, and my departure from the group, was not an easy one to make. After all, there were many reasons why I should not leave, and very few why I should. I profess to still not fully understanding how I got through this period for much was holding me back. Rage was a powerful factor blurring my judgement. Pulling myself away from the anger at what was done to us in prison was mentally exhausting. We were Amnesty International-adopted Prisoners of Conscience – how could Tony Blair holiday in Egypt, paid for by the Egyptian State while British citizens were being tortured there? How could the world protest at the atrocities of terrorists while governments behaved in a similar way? Wives had been stripped bare, and tortured in front of husbands. Children had been electrocuted. People would occasionally drop dead in our prison, succumbing to wounds from torture.

Thousands of men had been interned for over fifteen years without charge. From those interned, some had in desperation doused themselves in kerosene to set themselves on fire. I witnessed this all. Yet Egypt was the second-largest recipient of American aid, an ally.

Thus, the Islamist narrative of a clash of civilisations – *kuffar* against Muslims – echoed ever stronger in my mind. This was a war with no rules. Neo-conservatives had sent the message out loud and clear. The only voice heard was the voice of power, all the more reason for Islamists to seize the reins of such power. Abandon Islamism? And join what? Where was that counter-narrative? As an Islamist I enjoyed the backing of thousands of hardened men, many who had died for my cause. Where were the Muslim martyrs of pluralism? Why were the few who spoke out ridiculed or ignored?

I had married into Islamism, all my friends and many family members were Islamists. I would leave a global movement, having been a hero, to become an outcast. What would I say to Rabia? What would I say to her Uncle Abdul Rauf who – after my recruiting him to Hizb al-Tahrir – had his spine dislocated in Pakistan's jails? How would I face her cousin whose mother died from shock because he was not released from prison despite completing his sentence? I would have to look at these people in the eyes and say: it was all so wrong. I was so wrong.

But so what? Why should I be the only one to admit his mistakes? Is not winning the war more important than truth? This maxim, I knew, was also subscribed to by some on the left, the regressive left. For them, winning against capitalism was far more important than those they chose as allies. So

I watched as our ideology gained acceptance and we were granted airtime as Muslim political commentators. I watched as we were ignorantly pandered to by well-meaning liberals and ideologically driven leftists; how we Islamists laughed at their naivety. The critically acclaimed film *Persepolis* acutely highlighted this failure of the left in pre-revolutionary Iran. There, the left had joined Khomeini's supporters, believing his promises of a brighter future, only to be systematically purged after the revolution. Islamists are intent on replicating such a tactical alliance for the Sunni world. Why renounce Islamism if doing so would mean being denounced as a neo-con by 'neutral' non-Muslim critics who lend legitimacy to the Islamist-inspired clash of civilisations rhetoric?

But despite all of this, the one reason that I could not ignore, the one reason that grew deep inside me till it consumed me with guilt, was the realisation that I was abusing my faith for a mere political project. After learning in prison that Islamism was not the religion of Islam, but rather a political ideology dressed up as Islam, I no longer felt guilty simply for criticising a political system inspired by modern European constructs, while justified by seventh-century norms. And despite everything above that was holding me back, my desire for justice spurred me on. Ever since I had been a child I had found unfairness, injustice and oppression intolerable. And now, as I looked back into the years that had passed I saw more clearly than ever that we had used these grievances as a means of perpetrating our own injustice, not only against non-Muslims, but crucially against other Muslims too.

How we had used, even abused, people's grievances to suit our ideological agenda. What had the invasion and occupation of lands got to do with enforcing dress codes upon Muslims? Why should the solution to secular Arab dictators be Islamist Arab dictators? Why did foreign intervention mean that we needed to silence critical thinking and open debate by labelling it as heresy and blasphemy? In reaction to our own insecurities about our identity and position in the world, we – not anyone else but us – had become the real obstacle to progress for our own people.

But what was the problem with Islamism so long as it remained non-violent? Was it not the right of Muslims to adopt whatever ideology they chose? Of course, it was the right of Muslims to believe that one version of Islam must be imposed as law over their societies, just as it was the right of racists to believe that all non-white people should be deported from Europe. But the spread of either of these ideas would achieve nothing but the division and Balkanisation of societies. If the dangers of racism are apparent, even in a non-violent form, then it was the same for Islamism. Communalist identity politics, self-segregation and group-think are far more damaging to societies in the long run than the odd bomb going off here or there, because it is such a milieu that keeps breeding bomb-makers. It's odd that Hizb al-Tahrir in Arabic means the Liberation Party. We had hijacked the minds of the Muslim masses, and those minds needed to be liberated.

So, slowly, and alone, I began to unpick the last thirteen years of my indoctrination, concept by concept. Ideas that I had once held sacrosanct were unravelling in my mind as crude political deceptions. My whole character would have to change. Every moral frame of reference that I had built up in my mind required re-evaluation. I was not merely questioning jihadist terrorism as the Gama'a had done in their *muraja'aat* recantations. That was easy. No one really deserves a thank you for promising not to randomly kill you. No, I needed to go further. I needed to question the very basis of the ideology itself. The idea that an interpretation of Islam must be imposed as state law now seemed to me un-Islamic, counter-productive and anathema to what was fundamentally just.

This stifling, totalitarian victimhood ideology had taken the responsibility for reform away from our people, by simply finding satisfaction in blaming everyone else for our ills. My political grievances were still there, but I saw now that we no longer required Islamism in order to campaign against them. Islamism had in fact become one of the grievances that needed challenging. As I began to formulate this idea, the sheer scale of what we needed to do hit me. By now, Western governments, Muslim-majority governments, media, and hundreds of thousands of Muslim youth globally had all come to assume that Islamism was Islam. Leaving Islamism was one thing, but outrightly challenging it was another. But who better to do it than someone who knew the ideology inside out.

My head felt heavy as I took in the enormity of the task ahead. Most Muslims are not Islamists but the organised minority dominated the discourse. Islamism had been creeping upon Muslims for over eighty years now, and little had been organised to directly challenge it. Yes, certain Muslim associations have been stressing a tolerant Islam, but this was not sufficient. The good Islamist will merely co-opt that message into his political ideology, as we did. We tolerated the different strands of Muslim theology and we were well

319

disciplined when engaging with non-Muslims. By doing this, our aim was to co-opt everyone into our political goal, regardless of narrow sectarian concerns.

Unless all communities, but especially Muslim communities, stood together to reclaim the faith we would have no chance of challenging this ideology that had grown among us. It also meant that certain leftists and well-meaning liberals needed to stop pandering to a global totalitarian theo-political project. It meant, crucially, that normal Muslims needed to take a stand by closing their doors to Islamism.

Most importantly, Muslim leaders and theologians needed to be firm in the face of this ideological onslaught against our faith. And while theologians are especially responsible for leading the Muslim resistance against Islamism, Muslims could not be expected to do this if Islamism's twin, Islamophobia, was not also challenged. And though not all criticism of Islam is Islamophobia, there are those out there who harbour an irrational fear of Islam. Islamophobes and Islamists have this much in common: both groups insist that Islam is a totalitarian political ideology at odds with liberal democracy, and hence both insist that the two will inevitably clash. One extreme calls for the Qur'an to be banned, the other calls to ban everything but the Qur'an. Together, they form the negative and the positive of a bomb fuse. Until all of the above was put into practice, there was little chance of creating this counter-narrative.

These ideals, this counter-narrative: a respect for basic human rights, pluralism, individual freedoms, faith and democracy had to be reconciled with Islam not in the ivory towers of academics, but out there in the hearts of the masses.

To do that, we needed to permeate all elements of society with the counter-narrative: politics and policy, media, the arts, social media, academia and public opinion. We needed the backing of states, parties, coalitions and movements, and we needed ideas, narratives, leaders and symbols, all pooled together, just as Islamism had been doing since the 1920s.

For decades Islamist cadres had been busy branding and propagandising for their ideology at the grass roots of their target societies, while Muslim liberals either detached themselves in their mansions or embroiled themselves in the corrupt politics of their regimes. As Islamists, we would look upon these elite Muslim liberals as completely out of touch and detached from the sentiments of their people.

Was it any wonder then that Islamism had become the most effective social phenomenon among Muslims globally, in dictatorships and democracies alike? Dictators would either try to co-opt it, or brutally suppress it. Both tactics inevitably aided its growth. In democracies, electoral politics could only react to votes, and if the most organised bloc is the Islamist bloc, they will have their way, intimidating government after government with their opportunistic use of Islam to influence policy. Why were governments everywhere scared of upsetting the sleeping giant of Islamism? Why had they gradually succumbed to the Islamisation of their societies? Why did they not fear a similar internal democratic lobby? Where was the democratic intimidation? What I saw clearly now was the need for a radical new social movement, a Muslim Brotherhood equivalent, sitting above short-term party-political goals, which advocated the democratic culture among Muslim grass roots: a civic-democratic intimidation pushing for democratisation. Sitting in the seclusion of Abi's home in Southend, I realised that my quest for justice that began here was far from over. I knew now what had to be done, and I knew the cost of doing it.

CHAPTER TWENTY-EIGHT

The decade-late apology

It was on the site of the 7/7 attacks, appositely enough, that our counter-extremism organisation Quilliam came into being. Two years after the bombings, London life had moved on, and apart from the commemorative plaque in Tavistock Square, much had returned to normal. The London bus with its top ripped open had long been taken away, and its image was now a memory of history. Another number 30 continued the journey that bus should have completed, driving past a parked, clapped-out blue Renault Clio. Inside, an exhausted student was trying to sleep, curled up under a blanket on the back seat.

After writing Rabia that leaving note and moving back to Abi's, I had left my car to her. But in the period before that, in the weeks after leaving HT and during my estrangement from her, my car had become my home. I had my final exams to sit, and had to be in London rather than with Abi back in Southend. When I left HT, I also left my friends behind. My life had been so entwined with the organisation that my entire social circle had gone with it. I didn't have a job or any money, and so the car became where I went at the end of the day. I'd drive around until I found a space in one of the streets near SOAS – Tavistock Square, Russell Square, usually – and that would be where I spent the night.

But it wasn't all bad. My final graduation ceremony, ten years after initially enrolling, was quite a sight to behold. Due to dramatically over subscribing, SOAS had run out of seats in the main hall. The management arbitrarily decided that some of us, by alphabetical order, would receive our certificates and proceed to an overspill room to watch our own graduation ceremony via video link. I had waited ten years for this moment; my family were proudly in the main hall expecting me, and they had no idea that we would be denied seats alongside them. SOAS had just kicked the wrong guy out of his own graduation ceremony. Quickly, I rallied and organised the by-now extremely distressed students. We were outraged, and I spread word that I would refuse to receive my certificate unless they made space for us all in the main hall. The majority of students followed my suggestion, and those who simply wanted to get on with their day found it extremely awkward to argue against my reasoning: if prison couldn't stop me from graduating, I'd be damned if this would. We all began stubbornly announcing our refusal to cooperate, declaring a sit-in. The management had no choice but to cave in. Eventually a hasty compromise was suggested, we were told that we could sit on the stairs in the main hall, and we readily agreed.

It was a peculiar twist of fate that on that day Irene Khan, then Secretary General of Amnesty, was to receive her honorary doctorate from SOAS too. Irene was on stage to witness what happened next. As my name was called, I rushed onto the stage, and overcome with joy I hugged the university president and raised my hands in celebration. To my surprise, the students started cheering my name, and they rose in a standing ovation. As I embraced her, the university president asked, 'what did you do to get a standing ovation?'

'Oh you really don't want to know,' I replied laughing. My dear friend Amira Harb had been waiting her turn in line after me. Since that day Amira has never ceased to jokingly remind me how her turn on stage felt like an anti-climax after my little performance.

That year, before graduation, I had one of those moments when the universe seems to align itself perfectly. At just the time when all my HT friends were viciously turning on me – Traitor! Sell-out! Agent! – I bumped into someone from my old days.

'Maajid! *Subhan Allah! Habib* – my dear friend, you're back from Egypt. I saw your news on TV. How are you?' Standing on the SOAS steps, exactly where I had last left him, still wearing his trademark blazer, was none other than Ed Husain, now studying for his PhD.

Sometimes in life you can be lucky enough to find a friendship that survives being so long apart, despite the trauma in between. It had been ten years, but the bond between us remained as strong as ever. We both readily forgot that incident on these very steps when Tony Blair had come between us, and instead began talking of days old and new. Ed was in the process of writing his acclaimed book *The Islamist*, which would end up being published around the same week I left HT. Sensing that my thoughts had moved on considerably, he asked me to look through and comment on the Newham sections, which served as a reminder, if I needed one, of how far I had come. By this point I knew that I was going to leave HT, but hadn't broken the news to the world yet. In fact, the first version of *The Islamist* concludes with the speculation: which direction will HT go in, the moderate direction of Maajid Nawaz, or the hard-line one of Jalaluddin Patel?

The conversations and debates Ed and I shared in the back of my car during those depressing early days were critical to informing our joint direction for years to come. That clapped-out blue Renault Clio served us, and the world, quite well. For both of us, it wasn't enough just to leave HT behind.

'We need to reform the way we Muslims see politics, and revive knowledge of our traditional jurisprudence through the Sufi path,' Ed suggested.

'No, *habib*, trust me, everything, absolutely everything needs to be reformed, and that includes traditional . . . what I call medieval, jurisprudence. It simply doesn't address our contemporary problems.'

'But, that's . . . that's nothing short of a complete overhaul of the *deen*,' Ed exclaimed.

'Exactly. I'm talking about enshrining absolute freedoms, human rights, a respect for individual liberty, women's rights and reconciling modern scientific facts with Islamic interpretation. And I don't just mean in the lofty circles of academia or theology, that's all been done before, but actually out there, in the real world, just as we did for Islamism back in the day.'

'Yes, we can start doing *da'wah* for these values, just as we did back at Newham for HT.' The glitter in Ed's eye began to betray his excitement.

'Indeed! *Da'wah* for a religion-neutral space in the public sphere, *dhormo niropekhota*, I think it's called in Bangla. You know, it's so bad that in Pakistan's Urdu there is no appropriate word for secularism? They use *laa-deeniyat*, which implies no-religion. With such a translation, obviously Islamism will have a head start.'

'You do realise, there is a mammoth task ahead, Maajid, we will be roundly attacked,' Ed said rather too eagerly. 'But I have just the idea for how to begin. Let's start it all with a think tank, to lay the seeds for this idea globally, and let's call it after the Englishman who opened England's first mosque, to make the point that Islam doesn't always have to clash with society. His name was William Quilliam!'

And so it was, that in an old Renault Clio, parked somewhere on Russell Square in London, the idea for Quilliam to be the seed of this radical new thought direction was born.

What Islamism had done in Europe was to set Muslim communities back by an entire generation. It created a separatist agenda that became self-fulfilling. In an effort to protest discrimination, all it achieved was further segregation, and further social immobility created more discrimination, rather than less. When Omar Bakri Mohammed had left HT, he had founded al-Muhajiroun, which had protested in Luton against the bodies of soldiers returning from Afghanistan. In response to this, the English Defence League had been formed. Islamism, in other words, was in danger of making the situation worse, rather than better, repeating the cycle of racism, Islamist extremism, more racism, and more Islamist extremism. It is no wonder then that Omar Bakri's own daughter, Yasmin Fostok, grew so disillusioned with her father's rhetoric that in one monumental act of defiance she left home and became a stripper, declaring her profession proudly to the tabloid press with utter glee.

What exacerbated the situation was a lack of understanding about what Islamism was. Governments were allowing the Islamist narrative to drive the debate, and accepted their claims that they represented the majority Muslim voice. This simply wasn't true: Islamism was a modern political phenomenon with opinions that could be every bit as offensive as those held by far-right organisations – its anti-Semitism and homophobia, for example. But government and society instinctively resisted challenging this for fear of coming across as racist.

Official policy was a form of Orientalism. This paternalistically lumped all Muslims together as 'one community', the so-called 'Muslim vote', which required a 'native-chief' to speak on its behalf. Instead of being represented by their Member of Parliament, like everyone else, Muslims were encouraged to seek separate representation via an exclusively Muslim political umbrella. In a 'poor natives' sort of way there was the arrogant assumption that Islamism was a true expression of our authenticity, even if the so-called moderates tried to distance themselves from it. In a form of reverse-racism, liberal values were expected of the civilised white person, but the brown Muslim could not be held to those same standards, and should be judged by his or her own 'authentic' culture. This was a colonial 'poverty of expectation', which inevitably leads to segregation, low aspirations, patronising expectations, and cultural glass-ceilings, practically stalling Muslim social mobility and progress across Europe.

Ed and I wanted to expose all this. We wanted less separation of communities, and more involvement of Muslims in every aspect of society: to focus less on the differences and more on the similarities of cultures. Mainstream society, not just Muslims, bore a great deal of the responsibility to make this happen. The state could help here, but it could never drive the process: imposing ideas like democracy and human rights would only lead to resistance. Instead, the change had to come from within communities themselves – the flowering of more liberal ideas through civic debate and discussion. To be successful, our initiative had to be the exact opposite of neo-conservatism, a 'ground up' not a 'top down' process.

The shaping of these ideas into what would become Quilliam wasn't an overnight event. Ed and I had many discussions, and disagreed at times too, while fretting over where and how to begin. We weren't the first people ever to want to change the world. Coming up with ideas, in a way, was the easy part. The difficult bit was how to take them forward: how to turn our excited talk into action. What would the process actually involve? Where would the money to fund it come from? Where would we even start?

What we were encouraged by, right from the start, was the reaction to our ideas. Ours was the most visible and credible insight mainstream society had ever gleaned from inside Islamist organisations and the prisons that held them. Ed's book was published to a lot of media attention and discussion. In the wake of that, when I finally announced my resignation from HT, we went to meet Peter Barron, then editor of the BBC's flagship news programme *Newsnight*, who agreed to do an extended piece about my departure from HT. Late 2007, my story headlined the programme, and the producer Sara Afshar managed to secure over seventeen minutes airtime for the clip: they were so keen for me to speak that they allowed me to tell my story directly to camera, rather than via an interview with a journalist.

But it wasn't just the media who were interested in my story: the government was too. On the day the *Newsnight* piece was due to be aired, Ed and I were invited in to the Communities and Local Government department, or CLG, at the Home Office, to brief them about Islamism. As we entered the room we realised just how senior the meeting was: as well as Hazel Blears, then Communities Secretary, also present were Foreign Secretary David Miliband, Home Secretary Jacqui Smith and Charles Farr, the Director General of the Office for Security and Counter-Terrorism.

The last time an official had asked me about my political views, I was fingerprinted and had my DNA taken under caution in the interrogation rooms at Heathrow Airport. Here we now were, offering our opinions to three of the UK's senior most cabinet members. Later that week, after the *Newsnight* piece was broadcast, I received a rather bemused call from Abi. 'You'll never guess who came to see me after your story was aired on *Newsnight*?' she said between laughs. 'It was the Essex Police. They came to offer an apology for having arrested you at gunpoint all those years ago when you were fifteen. They saw it on TV and felt bad.' I burst into laughter. This was my 'green rucksack' moment with the police. My message was reaching people, but this time it was a democractic message, and I was encouraged.

This then was the genesis of Quilliam: our idea was to create the world's first counter-extremism hub for activism. We would create a platform from which we could directly challenge the dominant discourse of Islamism. We would speak, debate, lobby, brief, mobilise, galvanise, write, publish and organise in order to spread a counter-narrative to Islamism, hoping to inspire the mushrooming of our cause anywhere and everywhere.

The problem was money. Starting up something like this wasn't a cheap thing to do: there was the expense of running an office and hiring staff, the cost of travelling to conferences and countries to spread our message. We would travel around the country meeting with religious figures, former Islamists and government officials, trying to create a base for our organisation. I approached Muslims from the non-Islamist political scene, people like my stalwart supporter Iqbal Wahhab, and friends Nadeem and Tariq Shah, for advice and guidance. We wanted to get enough people on board to create a critical mass. But we still had no idea where the money would come from. We were both still students. Ed was still completing his PhD at SOAS; I – having completed my law degree at SOAS – had now enrolled for an MSc in political theory at the London School of Economics. And so, to begin with, Ed and I simply used our credit cards and student overdrafts to pay for everything, a sure way of accumulating thousands of pounds of debt. But this was our baby, and we desperately wanted it to work.

Eventually, Ed's book led the way. Someone who had read

The Islamist and had been impressed by our ideas gave us an introduction to a Kuwaiti Organisation called the Babtain Foundation. We met their representatives in London and explained our vision for Quilliam. To our delight, finally, they agreed to give us the seed money to get the organisation up and running. As a result, we were able to set up an office, and to hire a couple of other former Islamists, Dawud and Rashad, who joined us to form Quilliam's first office team.

In Jauary 2008, right behind Russell Square at the British Museum, to a great deal of media fanfare and public anticipation, Ed Husain and I launched Quilliam, the world's first counter-extremism organisation. I'm still amazed at the speed with which we managed to pull it all off – to go from a discussion in the back of a Renault Clio, to a fully fledged and funded organisation in less than a year, while studying for a postgraduate degree, was no small feat. Speaking and endorsing our work on that day were Lord Paddy Ashdown and Jemima Khan among others. But I was most moved by the speech given by 7/7 survivor Rachel North, who stirred the audience to tears recounting her ordeal of being caught up in London's bombings and the work she has done since to reconcile both herself and communities.

Not everyone from within Muslim communities, however, wanted to congratulate us for our work. Though he had long since left HT, and disagreed with them on many counts, my brother Osman, my childhood friend and protector, completely disagreed with my decision to make our fight against Islamism public. As did my cousin Yasser, also having left HT by now; he took Osman's view that challenging the ideology itself was one step too far. Our relationships inevitably suffered.

From all my closest childhood friends who had previously held me in such high regard for my commitment to Islamism, very few now agreed with my work. Out of these old friends, it felt to me that the most vindictive attacks came from Nas, the Greek. I remember feeling at the time that Nas began what seemed a personal campaign against me online, in the mosque that my *Nana Abu* founded, and in the local community. The only one who stood by me from the old converts to our cause, and who discreetly encouraged me in those early days, was our British-Kenyan friend Moe, who back in the day had been attacked by skinheads with a hammer. A particularly touching moment was when my non-Muslim school friends, led by Sav and including the likes of Marc, Jamie, Katrina and others organised a welcome home gathering for me in Southend. Despite all that I had done during my Islamist years, and the distance I'd tried to place between us, they still cared. Indeed, Sav had continued to write to me in prison, offering me his moral support. Such deep loyalty spurred me on further, and faced with a friendship like that I knew was doing the right thing.

Among Muslim communities across the UK, my name was dragged through the dirt. Ed and I were both targeted in a highly personal and organised smear campaign. Where Islamist rappers had once sampled my voice on their songs, their supporters were now declaring me an apostate. Such declarations are a necessary prelude for any attempt on a Muslim's life to be 'legal'. Islamist teams of agitators toured the UK with information packs about why my colleagues and I were heretics.

As all of this unfolded, I was still officially married to

– albeit separated from – Rabia. Any chance we had of reconciling matters was destroyed with the founding of Quilliam. From my side, I had left her home as a confused and emotionally vulnerable former-prisoner going through a fundamental crisis in identity for the second time in my life. I left because I wanted to rediscover who I was, and needed the clarity of thought that seclusion could bring. After having started the painful journey of my mental and emotional realignment, I felt that perhaps now I was ready to begin working with Rabia to fix our marriage.

Rabia had married an ardent, committed, fiery passionate Islamist, but the deal she was now getting was a liberal Muslim, moulded along Abi's lines. Worse, this liberal was intent on standing up to challenge everything he had once affirmed to her as sacrosanct. Despite our best efforts, and much heartache both ways, there was no putting the relationship back together again.

Rabia, if my running away hurt you, it was born from the hurt that was drilling through my entire being. When I rejected you, I was rejecting nought but my very own soul. I abandoned you, but had already abandoned myself. I no longer knew who Maajid was. If my thoughts confused you, it was but a fraction of the confusion befogging my mind. Now I had settled on something more concrete, something solid, something good, and I came back to show you what I had achieved, and would achieve, with my new mission, my new message. I came back to you whole again, knowing again what I wanted to be. To take that away from me would have destroyed me once more. I am nothing if I cannot strive for something. That's just the way I am. It's the way God built me, and despite being built for this particular disposition, I have come to believe that it is my curse, for it has caused me unimaginable misery. Perhaps only time will tell what, if anything, my vanity will produce. But likewise, time could have told what, if anything, would have healed between us. And now it is for ever too late.

After the divorce, being the most confused and miserable I had ever been, I also fought with my best friend Fatima over her plans to return to Pakistan. By now Fatima had graduated and was intent on returning home, as she had always wanted to do. But having just failed at one key relationship in my life, I wasn't going to allow my closest friend to simply melt away from me too. As we fought, back and forth we went about the future of our friendship, and in utter frustration I found my fist slamming against my bedroom wall. There was a sickly, smacking sound accompanied by the sensation of heat and blood rushing to my fingers. I knew instantly that I had broken the bones in my hand. Fatima began trying to soothe the pain with cold water and ice, and kindly laid me down and put me to sleep.

Rabia's reaction to my work was not atypical. We hadn't just made enemies of HT, but most Islamist organisations from all branches of Islamism. Ed and I were accused of apostasy, of heresy, and far worse. These days, a few years after founding Quilliam, such a reaction is harder to imagine. With the mushrooming of counter-extremism initiatives globally, with the debate being so much better informed, and with increased visibility for the liberal Arab youth behind many of the Arab uprisings, challenging Islamism is becoming increasingly common. But back then, death threats, and bomb warnings at our office, were a frequent occurrence, even from al-Qaeda sources directly. We had to install blast shields in the office, and went to great lengths not to advertise our location. Even now, we keep the office address off our literature and website, even now I continue to be cautious about my movements.

A month or so after the launch of Quilliam, Ed and I were in Denmark. Many years earlier, if you recall, I had been a regular visitor to Copenhagen, actively recruiting to build an HT chapter there. Now I was back, giving a critical conference speech in the town hall about the very organisation I had helped to set up. The raw recruits I had persuaded to join had been of a different persuasion to the typical HT supporter in the UK: many of them had hailed from a criminal fringe, drug dealers and gang members. After my speech, hosted by Fathi, a local Turkish-Dane, Ed and I went to Friday prayers at a nearby mosque. As prayers concluded, Fathi approached me inside the mosque looking very worried.

'Brother Maajid, there is a very dangerous man outside the mosque asking for you, please do not leave.' Naturally, being me, I went out to talk to him.

'Are you Maajid Nawaz?' he asked.

'Who are you?'

'Yes, you are Maajid Nawaz,' he said nodding, and cycled off.

The man was a well-known local drug dealer. As soon as he'd seen me, he put a call through. The next thing we knew, there were three cars full of young Islamist sympathisers, parked at the end of the road, waiting to attack us.

'Fathi, let me talk to them,' I argued.

'No, brother Maajid, I'm afraid you don't understand. These men, I know them, they have guns. You must leave immediately.'

Ed and I had to take shelter in the back room of an Islamic bookshop, and there we hid until a car came to collect us and evacuate us. This was Copenhagen in the year 2008, not Kabul in the year 2000.

Just as we thought that our day couldn't get any worse, we were wrong. While we were hiding from the Danish thugs, Ed's phone rang. It was our contact from the Babtain Foundation, to tell us that they had decided to withdraw our funding. I felt they were unhappy with some of the public statements we had made. At a stroke all our financial support had vanished – we had a huge bill to pay the British Museum for hosting our launch, and now we had no way of paying for it. Assuming we got out of Denmark alive, Quilliam was in danger of being closed down before it had even started.

CHAPTER TWENTY-NINE

Monkeys in a zoo

Ed and I coined a phrase in that hideout in Copenhagen, 'We don't do fail.' That became our mantra, our unofficial slogan. We weren't going to be intimidated from speaking by violent threats, nor for that matter by financial ones. Ours would not be the sort of organisation that tailored its message to suit its sponsors. If that was the sort of influence people thought their money would buy, then we were better off without their support.

We hit the same problem again with the next person to fund us. Our second backer was an Egyptian businessman who wanted to use Quilliam to promote a socially conservative version of Islam. We met him during our return from Denmark, and off the back of that one meeting he transferred a large donation into our account as a goodwill gesture and for that we were extremely grateful. Unfortunately, as with the Babtain Foundation funding, there were conditions. Rather than being a non-religiously aligned organisation with its focus on political rights, our backer wanted to become the public face of a conservative form of Sufi Islam. There were elements of our message he wanted adjusting, for example over civil rights for minorities and homosexuals. So we accepted the goodwill money, which cleared our debts, but did not take the relationship forward. Again, the funding ceased.

The other source of potential funding was through the government. This, in its own way, brought as many potential problems as private donors: it can make people suspicious of your message, and lead to accusations that you were little more than government agents. However, we had maintained good relations with the British government after that initial meeting in Whitehall: we had briefed them where requested, and they had continued to support us. If the various Islamist groups in the UK, the Salafists all over the world, and the 'Afghan Jihad' could receive funding from the British, Saudi and Pakistani governments respectively, we wondered why our cause shouldn't benefit from this sort of boost?

It did not seem unreasonable to try to formalise this relationship a little and see if any funding was available. We went back to the Office for Security and Counter-Terrorism and spoke to their head, Charles Farr, about our situation. Charles kindly agreed to support us via the government's Preventing Extremism programme. We met various ministers and were granted government funding, until such a time as we could find alternative sources of financial support. Charles Farr deserves credit for helping to get Quilliam onto its feet during these early days.

From these touch-and-go beginnings, Quilliam had started to gain real momentum. We were able to start speaking publicly, debating, commissioning reports, lobbying politicians, travelling to conferences, working the media, offering policy advice and consultancy. But very early on, we saw that it was not just Islamism we would need to tackle. Away from Muslim circles, the two dominant trends we would most often come up against were polar opposites, either that of the patronising 'Orientalism' I described earlier, or an anti-Muslim form of conservatism.

Both sets of people would often attempt to use Ed or myself to grind their own ideological axes. In their own way, neither group was happy with half of our message. When we were critical of Islamism, the 'Orientalists' got upset. When we raised the grievances in society that acted to fuel the Islamist narrative, the conservatives objected. As a way to describe this quagmire I came up with a phrase: 'trained monkeys in a zoo'. Both sides wanted to keep us as their pet monkeys in a zoo, to come to us for entertainment and benefit when it suited them, but to try to ignore us when our ideas went against their established ideological bent.

On many occasions after my talks, people – usually white liberals – would stand up and declare that I had no idea what it was like to suffer as a victim of society. They would assert that there was no way someone like me, educated, speaking articulate English and wearing a suit and tie, could ever understand people who felt so desperate that suicide bombing was their 'only' option. Terrorists' reactions cannot be separated from their social causes I was told; blame lies squarely on society. It was as if their brains were malfunctioning. I had invariably just spent half an hour telling my entire story, of violent racism and police harassment in Essex, and of torture and solitary confinement in Egypt, but because my conclusions didn't align with the angry 'monkey' they were expecting to see, it was as if they hadn't heard any of it.

'I am a pure product of these grievances you keep harping on about' I would declare, 'now deal with my conclusions'.

Among the regressive left, the 'Orientalists', we were attacked by the likes of *Guardian* journalist Seumas Milne. On the right, I was to be personally attacked by none other than America's arch-conservative Glenn Beck on Fox News. Beck took umbrage at the fact that I'd been working with Google's Jared Cohen and the State Department on the Alliance of Youth Movements project (AYM) and launched one of his typically high-voltage personal assaults on Jared and me. But we were nobody's lackeys, and just as we had shifted the debate in entire societies towards Islamism, we fully intended to do it again for our counter-narrative.

Our aim would be to criticise Islamophobia and Islamist extremism as openly as possible. We would defend the right of Muslims to practise their faith, even those who were conservative, while vehemently challenging the idea that any one version of Islam – even a 'moderate' one – should ever be imposed in any society as law. This position placed me on interesting sides of various motions. In *The Doha Debates*, hosted by Tim Sebastian, I argued on a panel that 'Political Islam' – the desire to impose a version of Islam as law – was a threat, while for an Intelligence Squared debate in New York I defended the religion of Islam itself as essentially one of peace, against Islamic-critic Ayaan Hirsi Ali.

Word soon spread and from my appearance on *Larry King Live* to my being interviewed one-on-one by al-Jazeera's Riz

Khan, Quilliam was fast becoming the recognised authority on challenging both anti-Islam and Islamist extremism globally. Our work now started to attract a critical mass of support across society. Among the media, America's flagship news programme *60 Minutes* profiled our work and my story. In the arts people like Jane Rosenthal, founder of the Tribeca Film Festival, helped to introduce our work at the Festival and to her friend Robert De Niro, or Bob as she calls him. On the technology side, when learning how best to use social media in order to galvanise support, my work on Facebook benefited from the early advice of people like Facebook co-founder Dustin Moscovitz. My use of Twitter to spread our message was a task personally assigned to me by its founder Jack Dorsey.

Politically too, the corridors of power were beginning to show immense interest. Soon after setting up Quilliam, I received an invitation to address the US Senate about our work. The invitation came from Senator Joe Lieberman, chair of the Senate Committee for Homeland Security, and I would become the first former Islamist ever to testify in the US Senate.

Being a senior former Islamist, however, is not without its problems. The State Department had sorted out all my travel arrangements, but a week before I was due to go, my visa had still not come through. At this point, I received a worried phone call from the Department of Homeland Security. There are problems with your visa, I was told. We're not sure we'll be able to get you one because of your conviction in Egypt. My conviction in Egypt, I replied, is exactly why the Senate have invited me to come over and talk! Back and forth we went, between Homeland Security and the State Department, with nobody sure exactly where the visa was stuck. Eventually, word got back to Senator Lieberman, who rang up the US Embassy in London, shouting as he instructed them not to embarrass him.

The night before I was due to fly my visa still hadn't come through, and by now I was resigned to the fact that it wouldn't happen. Suddenly, I received a call.

'Mr Nawaz? I'm calling from the US Embassy. I have your visa here.'

'Great. I've got to be at Heathrow early in the morning: should I get a cab and pick it up on the way?' I replied with relief.

'Actually,' the man said, 'I'm not at the US Embassy.'

I was confused. 'But I thought you said you were.'

'I'm with the US Embassy, but I'm based somewhere else.'

'OK, where are you based, I'll come to you?' I asked in bewilderment.

'Here's what we're going to do,' he said. 'I'll meet you myself at Heathrow tomorrow morning. I'll be waiting for you at the information desk of your terminal.'

'How will I know what you look like?'

'I'll be wearing a blue raincoat.' And with that, he hung up.

The following morning, I went to the information desk as arranged. There, sure enough, was a man in a blue raincoat.

'Good morning, Mr Nawaz,' he said, and handed me three brown envelopes.

'Is this my visa?' I asked.

'Sort of,' Blue Raincoat replied. 'We couldn't get you a normal visa, I'm afraid, but we are very keen for you come and speak. Do you know about the Mafia?'

'What about them?'

'Sometimes we have court cases where we need to bring people over to testify. But these people are convicted criminals and technically aren't allowed into the country. So what we do is to arrange for a parole visa. This allows them into the US under the aegis of federal agents. From a legal point of view, they're under arrest for the duration of their stay.'

'Right,' I said, taking the envelopes. 'So I'm on a parole visa, like a Mafia boss? I'm under arrest?'

'Technically,' Blue Raincoat was keen to assure me. 'Please don't be offended by that. We're not implying anything, it's just the only way that we could get you into the country to speak at the Senate.'

'Are there any conditions to being technically under arrest?' I asked.

'Yes,' Blue Raincoat admitted. 'You will have a 24-hour federal detail following you for the duration of your stay. But please, consider them your chauffeur service, rather than your arresting officers!'

It was one of those moments where my former and current lives grated against each other. Phrases like 'agents' and 'detail' and 'technically under arrest' were enough to give me a flashback or two from my time in Egypt. Heathrow, too, was where I'd been interrogated by Mr Blue Raincoat's British equivalents. But I took the envelopes and handed them over as directed: one to get on the plane, one on arrival in the US, and one to rule them all . . . well, actually for myself (which I still have). I'll say one thing for being on a parole visa: it does mean you get to leave the aircraft first. I was escorted off at the other end, fingerprinted and interviewed, before being handed over to my federal detail.

The federal agents, from Immigration Customs Enforcement, or ICE, took the hotel room next to mine. I had to inform them of my movements at all times. They were armed, and everywhere we travelled we were tailed by a further two cars. To begin with, the agents were quite suspicious of me. It was only after I'd spoken at the Senate that their attitude changed.

'I'm sorry, sir,' the lead agent, Bryan, said as he offered me his hand. 'Up until now, I had been under the impression that our job was to protect America from you. Now I realise that we are here to protect you from America!'

The speech itself was a defining moment, as it allowed us the opportunity to define Islamism, explain its causes and present the doctrine of civic challenge to the world; and this all went out live on C-SPAN, the American politics TV network and hit the news globally.

That visit was the first time I'd been to the United States, and I was determined to make the most of it, federal detail or otherwise. Sayyid Qutb, Jihadism's ideological godfather and author of *Milestones*, who had served time with Dr Badei in my prison Mazrah Tora, had visited the US back in the 1950s. Qutb's trip inspired him to write a book about his experiences, *The America that I Saw*, in which he was heavily critical of the 'licentiousness' of America. I wanted to challenge this, and created a rival version. I posted my 'The America that I Saw' as a video blog on YouTube, and argued for the positives I'd seen. Without those same freedoms Qutb had been critical of, I argued, Muslims would not have been allowed to ever build mosques in this country. Having spent some years in the same prison that held Qutb before his execution, I felt somehow connected to his radicalism. The radical message for the Middle East of his time was Islamism. How odd it was that by my time the truly radical idea for the Middle East, straddling dictatorships and extremism, had become grassroots democratic activism.

CHAPTER THIRTY

Visiting No. 10

As with our initial Muslim donors, it didn't take too long for our policies to differ from those of our paymasters. The problem was a report we wrote on the UK government's prisons policy, run by the National Offender Management Service or NOMS. This looked in detail at the problem of rising extremism in prisons and what we believed was the disorientated response of NOMS. Our critical report really didn't go down well at the Home Office, NOMS in particular reacted very badly, and a question began to circulate across certain government departments: why are we giving money to this organisation for them to be critical about us?

It wasn't long before another flashpoint occurred. This time we had written a report reviewing the government's entire 'PREVENT' strategy towards extremism. We had broken down, department by department, where we felt the failures were. Having learnt from our prisons report experience, and realising that this might not be a palatable message, this time we were very careful how we presented it. We didn't issue the report publicly, which would have been an easy thing to do. Instead, we sent it to the government as a confidential briefing, by hard copy alone, to ensure that an electronic version wasn't available to end up on the Internet.

In the end, though, that's exactly what happened. The report was leaked, scanned and uploaded online from within a government department. That department was Farr's Office for Security and Counter-Terrorism, the very department giving us our funding. We had criticised some policies in the OSCT, but had praised others. We were particularly critical of the view that government partnerships with non-violent yet otherwise extreme Islamists were the best way to fend off Jihadism. This was meant to be constructive feedback from friends to friends. The OSCT begged to differ. We were caught up in the political storm of a general election, with the political parties taking potshots at each other on such issues, as well as the economic downturn.

Matters came to a head over the Zakir Naik affair. Farr had been corresponding with Naik about bringing him to the UK to speak. Naik, not a terrorist, had been on the record and on YouTube videos both praising bin Laden and claiming 9/11 was an inside job. Farr took the view that these opinions, though extreme, were still non-violent and could therefore act as insulation from real Jihadism. Hence, anyone flirting with extremism would probably take Naik more seriously than a 'moderate' preacher. There was an internal logic to this view, but we disagreed with it and advised against it.

Though we stood against the banning of non-violent extremist groups like HT, we certainly didn't think that their legal status equated to an automatic right to endorsement.

Naik was free to come to this country and speak, but not with government support or endorsement. In our view, Muslims must not be treated as 'good monkeys' and 'bad monkeys'. The same standards of civilisation should apply to all, equally. If nominally non-violent racism, in the form of equally legal groups like the British National Party – the BNP, was not promoted as a solution to violent racism, then why were these same standards not applied to Muslims? Were we Muslims deemed too primitive for liberalism?

Eventually, UK Home Secretary Theresa May settled the debate by denying Naik a visa to enter Britain. Naik sued the British government for discrimination, and presented as evidence email correspondence between him and Farr, in which Farr assured Naik of his support. Farr was hugely embarrassed, and the press went to work. Ironically, this incident precipitated the beginning of the end for the 'Orientalist' view in government departments.

Soon after, I received a call from 10 Downing Street. The Prime Minister wanted to see me. David Cameron was due to give an important speech in Munich, distinguishing Islam from Islamism and extremism, and was requesting my advice. It felt strange indeed. Here I was, someone who had previously fought with all his might against everything this country stood for, and now I was called upon by the Prime Minister to provide expert advice on matters of critical national importance. I agreed to go.

Inside, Downing Street felt quaint: a traditional terraced townhouse, a very nice one obviously, but a house nonetheless, with creaky staircases and all those quirks. The mahogany leather waiting-room sofa was the same as the one we grew up with in our front room – my dad used to ban us from sitting on it in our jeans in case we scratched the leather. There wasn't the sense of grandeur or pomp that you associate with Parliament, the White House, or the American Senate: but an almost eccentric English charm, all of its own.

As well as myself, the other person called in for the private meeting was Paul Goodman, a former MP and shadow Communities Minister when the Conservatives had been in opposition. The Prime Minister came in: he was taller in real life than he seemed on television. It was a relaxed set-up – we were sat round on sofas, rather than the formality of a round-table discussion. Alongside Cameron, Paul and myself, there were various aides in the room as well: Ameet Gill, then the Prime Minister's speechwriter, Jeremy Heywood, the cabinet secretary, and others.

Cameron was warm and engaging. His people skills were unexceptionally exceptional. By which I mean: you don't get to be in a position of power like that without an exceptional level of people skills. I have met enough political leaders – George Bush, Tony Blair, Gordon Brown – to know that this is the norm. It would have been more of a surprise, in a way, if he didn't have these attributes. He was bright, as you'd expect, and well briefed. He didn't come across as someone who was 'winging' his way through the meeting.

The policy that the government was pursuing was, I felt, heading in the right direction. They were rightly flipping Bush-era neo-conservatism on its head. Restoring lost ground on civil liberties, while increasing the pressure on the civic challenge against extremism that we'd long argued for. Some time after this meeting, Parliament's Home Affairs Select

Committee convened to look into many of these reforms, and they asked me to testify. In this hearing I directly challenged Congressman King and reaffirmed my stance that the excesses of the US neo-conservative era must be reined in. Cameron's government had the same idea. They weren't interested in pursuing ID cards, for example, and had begun to curtail the process of detention without trial.

Cameron then asked what I thought should be done about Hizb al-Tahrir. When he had been leader of the opposition, he had asked Gordon Brown why he had not banned my old organisation as Tony Blair had promised after 7/7. Brown's response had been to quote me from my first *Newsnight* interview, as someone arguing that rather than banning HT a civic challenge should be presented instead. Now in government, Cameron asked me directly whether the group should be banned. Again, I explained my reasoning. Banning was not only illiberal, it wasn't the solution: far better to create a scenario where joining the group becomes a societal taboo, as with the BNP. An actual ban would only give the organisation publicity they didn't deserve.

Cameron was also interested in an idea that I had been espousing about the comparison between extremism and racism. I had argued that the two should be analogous in terms of public response. Why should extremist views, which went against basic liberties, be any more acceptable than racist or homophobic ones? I told Cameron that he shouldn't be afraid to criticise Muslims who were putting forward extremist views in the name of faith. There was a difference between holding those views and religious piety that was important for him to understand. Finally, we spoke about the Arab world.

I stressed that the old dichotomy pitting dictatorships against Islamism had to be abandoned, or else extremism would be the inevitable outcome.

David Cameron seemed genuinely impressed by what I had to say. When he eventually gave his Munich speech, it included almost all of my suggestions. I then got a further call from Cameron's cabinet secretary Heywood, sounding me out about taking a government job as a special adviser to the Prime Minister and Deputy Prime Minister on extremism matters. I went back in for another meeting, and we discuseed the idea at some length. In a typically civil-servant way, they wanted to first hear whether I was interested in the job before making me a formal offer. Their condition was that I leave Quilliam, but that's something I wouldn't even do for Rabia.

Sure enough, when our funding came up for renewal, it was withdrawn. We lobbied hard to have it reinstated; Tony Blair stepped in, personally encouraging people to help us; we even got supportive MPs to force an emergency debate in the House of Commons on the subject. They agreed to give us the outstanding money we were still due, but not any more than this. The government were battling with bringing down the deficit, and this was a bad time to get on the wrong side of the civil service. The week before Christmas 2010, I had to make seven painful redundancies at Quilliam. At our lowest point we were reduced from a staff of twenty-five to just four. Ed had to leave too. We agreed that we could no longer afford to pay two senior people within our organisation, and when an opportunity came for him to work for the Council on Foreign Relations (CFR) in New York, we both carried on until he secured the job. Having two people at the head of an organisation wasn't the easiest of affairs; there were times when our views naturally divulged, and Quilliam's messaging appeared conflicted as a result. Now, being left alone at Quilliam as co-founding chairman, with four staff and a revival to orchestrate, I set to work to shape the organisation more in my own personal mould.

It was an extremely difficult task, but we don't do fail. Peaks and troughs in life are what made me who I am. Losing our government funding came with a silver lining; we were able to reassert our independence. Cutting costs made us a leaner, more viable organisation. We know now that we have the strength to survive, even in the most difficult financial climate. We've come out of the worst of that, and for the first time we found reliable donors who don't demand favours or want punches pulled.

The peculiarity of the situation wasn't lost on me. It seemed that here was a government that had cut the funding for my organisation, primarily caused by our disagreement with Farr and his Office for Security and Counter-Terrorism, while they also appeared to want to hire me to give them essentially the same advice.

On one level, the job was everything I could have wished for: this was a position of real influence, where my ideas could be put into practice and make a serious difference. But did that advantage outweigh my loss of independence and my ability to speak out? If there was an area I disagreed with, as over NOMS and the prisons policy, I would not have the freedom to bring the issue to the media's attention. If I did take the job and then ended up resigning over such an issue, I wasn't sure that I would have an organisation to return to. I knew how much difficulty Quilliam was in, ironically enough, as a result of losing government funding. If I left, then the organisation would most likely fold without me.

I didn't want to see that happen. I felt the work Quilliam was set up to do, despite all our success on the media and policy front, hadn't really begun. Lyndon Johnson once famously quipped 'It is better to have him inside the tent pissing out, than outside the tent pissing in', but in Muslim-majority countries there was no tent, and that's what I needed to help build. As it turned out, Heywood may have surmised my dilemma, and they never pursued the formal offer further.

CHAPTER THIRTY-ONE

Khudi Pakistan

There was no doubt about it, through Quilliam we had paved the way for a global counter-narrative and had captured the imagination and attention of the world, from heads of state to arts and technology leaders. But I wasn't satisfied. I wanted to show how possible it was to actually take what we were popularising in terms of ideas, and put that activism into practice on a grass-roots level. By now my message had attracted the attention of the prestigious TED conference for global thought leaders. They invited me to speak on de-radicalisation and tell my personal story. 'That was last year's news,' I boldly told the conference organisers, 'I have something far more cutting edge to speak about.' Suggesting new topics here was a high-risk strategy, but I knew I wouldn't be able to deliver properly on any other topic. This bee was in my bonnet and it simply needed to escape.

I wanted to create a counter-extremism social movement for Muslim youth that would actually carry our ideas, brand our ideas, popularise our ideas among them, just as we had done with HT, but for democratic culture instead. Ideas, narratives, symbols and leaders . . . grass-roots democratic culture needed what Islamism had. I wanted to create a radical civic force in society that would intimidate politicians into democratising society, just as Islamism had intimidated them into Islamicising society. And I wanted to seed this work in a country that by 2010 everyone had given up on, Pakistan.

Pakistan, my old country of wandering Sufi mystics, where every woman is a *Sohni* and every man her hero, my old country of technicoloured food and beautiful literature, my old country of original folk music, qawwals and the most majestic voice, my old country of sharp wit, industrial ambition and intense passion. Despite all your trials and tribulations your people soldier on, they soldier on though they are told by all that they will fail, they soldier on against disaster, war, corruption and poverty, because within them is a resilient spirit, an innovative flair and a fierce desire to live, to survive and to prove to the world that they will stand up and be counted. Forgive me. Forgive me for I once went to weaken you even more, but through all your resilience I can now help with the cure. And so I went. I went to do what I could; fighting the very virus I helped to sow deep within your veins. Fatima had inflamed within me a desire to discover you once more.

Since the invasion of Afghanistan, Pakistan's troubles with extremism have gone from bad to worse. The Taliban had taken over vast swathes of the country in the north, suicide bombings were a daily occurrence and the Islamist ideology was fast overtaking its rivals in gaining the attention of the country's youth. This sad state of affairs is best exemplified by the ruthless assassination of Punjab's governor Salmaan Taseer in 2011, followed shortly after by the killing of minorities minister Shahbaz Bhatti. Thousands of people came out onto the streets in celebration of Salmaan Taseer's murder, merely because he dared to suggest reform to the country's colonial-era blasphemy laws. As a final crippling wound to a beaten body, Salmaan Taseer's son was kidnapped by Islamist extremists seeking to exchange him for his father's convicted assassin. The true depth of Pakistan's problem finally began to be witnessed by all.

Throughout this period, my old group Hizb al-Tahrir had been busy recruiting inside Pakistan's army. The army had experienced three separate incidents of HT-related arrests. The recruits I had met in the year 2000 in London had been discovered and arrested by General Musharraf in 2003. Then there was the 2009 arrest of four people including Colonel Shahid Bashir from Shamsi airbase. Most recently, Brigadier Ali Khan was arrested alongside four other officers in 2011. After this last purge, Pakistan's security forces started to clamp down heavily on senior HT activists. In August 2011, friendly Uncle Qayyum with the large grey beard, by now a committed HT ideologue, was picked up from Raheem Yar Khan by Pakistan's military intelligence and was held for nine months during which he states he was severely beaten. Dr Qayyum has since released a statement. Like me, he claims that regardless of the consequences he openly admitted to his interrogators that he was a member of Hizb al-Tahrir. Ammar had been visiting Raheem Yar Khan with Rabia when Uncle Qayyum was picked up and I couldn't help but blame myself for once again exposing my son to the brutal side of the

'War on Terror'. Matters were getting out of control, and the country desperately needed a counter-narrative.

Fatima had always tried hard to show me the other side of Pakistan, the side that I had either tried to destroy for so long, or had never seen due to having only mixed among the hardcore of Islamist circles. She began reintroducing me to Pakistani music, indigenous poetry, literature and history. As she spoke, memories of the days before it all went so horribly wrong would flicker in my mind: memories of *Tai Ammi* sitting by my bed reading those enigmatic stories, memories of my dad's devotion to Nusrat Fateh Ali Khan's legendary qawwali music and memories of a distressed young Abi drying her bullied child's tears, 'They're calling you a Paki, so what? Tell them you're proud to be a Paki', and through Fatima's words it finally all began to make sense. Abi had simply been telling me in her own way to proudly reclaim my identity. All those years earlier, she was trying to guide me to do exactly what the early American rappers had done: 'Yeah, we're Niggaz With Attitude, and if you don't like it, fuck all y'all!' Is my culture British, Pakistani, Arab, Muslim? It's all of those, and none of the above. I am what the hell I want to be, I will reclaim as mine whatever I feel like, and if you don't like it, 'fuck all y'all!' Fatima and I decided that everyday Pakistanis needed to reclaim Pakistan and Islam as their own. They needed to reintroduce a brave new Pakistan to the world, the Pakistan of survivors, the Pakistan of fighters, and we would do what we could to help the country achieve this. In doing so, our fight was with those who had hijacked both our religion and our country.

So it was that we founded 'Khudi' Pakistan: a Muslim

Brotherhood equivalent for democratic culture. I launched the idea from one of the world's most prestigious global platforms for thought leaders, TED global in Edinburgh. The starting point for Khudi was my thinking back to the work I had done in Pakistan with HT. I had seen for myself, and through my own efforts, how ideas and groups could flourish and set the intellectual standard for young people. The message was wrong, I knew that now, but maybe the tactics were right. Perhaps we could use the methods of the Islamist groups to create a counter-Islamist movement, to do *da'wah* for the democratic culture?

Since its inception, Pakistan has never had a social movement, working on a level above politics, to champion democratic culture. When I say above politics, I mean simply advocating the values that underpin democracy across all political parties, on a non-partisan basis. Democracy is more than just an electoral process: it's about the culture associated with it. Without freedom of belief one cannot set up whichever party they so choose. Without freedom of association one cannot join that party. Without freedom of speech, one cannot campaign for their party. Without human rights one cannot run opposition parties without fear of imprisonment. Democracy must, by necessity, be more than just elections. These ideas need to be embedded within any democracy for it to function properly: the democratic culture.

What groups like HT and activists like myself had achieved was to chip away at this culture. Among the young population in particular, there was no appetite for these democratic values. There were plenty of people out there promoting the opposite – and those extreme beliefs carried a certain kudos.

Being a young democrat, by contrast, wasn't trendy. It was in danger of becoming an outdated brand that no one wanted to be associated with. If that process continued, then as these generations got older and took power, democracy in countries like Pakistan was in danger of being eroded away.

This was a bold new idea that no one had ever attempted before. No one had considered turning the tables on Islamist groups by using their methods for democratic ends. It sounds a strange sort of inspiration, but I looked in detail at organisations such as Hamas in Gaza and the West Bank. In the space of less than a decade this group had managed to overtake the Palestine Liberation Organisation as the main source of power in Palestine. They had put down roots in the younger population in a way that the PLO were unable to counter.

The basis of Hamas's rise to power was in their clear and powerful message. They also promoted this message through values-based welfare work: they provided services like schooling and got involved in social relief. By combining these services with their message they were able to instil their ideas not just through sloganeering and campaigning, but through getting involved in the very fabric of society. What I wanted to achieve with Khudi in Pakistan was this, but for democratic culture. As the wise poet Rumi said: like Noah, my thoughts turned to starting a huge, foolish project, and it made absolutely no difference what people would think of me.

Khudi is an Urdu word originating from Persia. Used in the poetry of the famous South Asian poet Allama Iqbal and popularised by Pakistan's first major celebrity rock band, Junoon, the word roughly translates as self-empowerment or self-esteem. Using Islamist tactics again, I designed Khudi, ironically like al-Qaeda, to be an umbrella organisation, under which existing groups and campaigners could coalesce and pool resources. I knew we needed a powerful and committed leadership to kick-start the group. My choice was obvious; by now I was convinced it was the reason God worked to make her approach me that day and ask me how many times I had failed my exams: Fatima Mullick became the first national coordinator of Khudi. Together, we now needed to identify the best youth activists, recruit them and form our first leadership committee.

In 2009, with a BBC *Newsnight* camera crew in tow, and a security team watching out for attempts on my life, I embarked on a national counter-extremism tour of Pakistan, speaking at over twenty-two universities from Islamabad to Karachi, from Quetta to Kashmir. I used this tour to identify and recruit the leaders for Khudi. Across Pakistan, Fatima and I met thousands of frustrated young students, and through our interaction with them we carefully selected those who we saw could lead the way. The Khudi executive committee now comprises youth like Islamabad-based Ali Abbas, founder of the Pakistan Youth Alliance, or PYA. PYA is active across Pakistan in the field of disaster relief and emerged from the Lawyers' Movement that overthrew Musharraf's military rule in 2007. Another Islamabad-based member is the inspirational Imran, who heads our training and government relations. With intelligence and sheer determination Imran had risen from an illiterate rural family of thirteen to become the president of the debating society in one of Pakistan's elite schools. Then, based in

Lahore, we have Rab Nawaz, editor of our youth magazine *Laaltain*. Rab was the secretary of the University Students Federation, a movement that began at Punjab University to oppose extremism on campus. Their brave activities came to an abrupt halt when their leadership started getting shot by extremists on campus. Also in Lahore are the calm-spirited and humble Shabbir, and our committed web expert Umair. Together, this team manages two offices inside Pakistan, a network of thousands of volunteers and has attracted tens of thousands of online subscribers to Khudi.

Fatima and I began to travel as frequently as possible to Pakistan to train this core group in building a movement. We laid out the basic idea and ethos with them, gave them the vision, set up the structure and began to organise activities: student debates, a nationwide student magazine, democratic interventions with student wings of the various political parties, clean-up initiatives, media interviews, academic and political lobbying. Pretty soon the name of Khudi began to spread across Pakistan.

Still focused on the need to reclaim Pakistan we helped to set up the first International Youth Conference and Festival (IYCF) in the country, partnering with Miradore's Tepu and Adeel, our fresh young events coordinators in Islamabad. At this time, fewer and fewer people were willing to travel to Pakistan. Our aim was to try and help reintroduce Pakistan to the world, and to reintroduce the world to Pakistan. Having previously spoken at Google's Zeitgeist annual thought-leaders conference, I called some friends at Google and we managed to persuade Google's leadership to come to Pakistan and address our IYCF conference. This was the first time Google had ever sent an official delegation to Pakistan, including YouTube's then head of news and politics, Steve Grove, and from Google's philanthropy side Jay Boren. We also managed to bring in speakers such as Susan Gordon from Facebook platform 'Causes' and Marc Koska. Marc had invented the non-reusable disposable syringe, saving many lives in the process. At the top of our list, and to introduce Pakistan to her, I called in my friend, the godmother to activists, Stephanie Rudat. For a while, Stephanie had been working to coordinate and train democracy movements globally. She had been involved in the founding of the Alliance of Youth Movements and now ran a similar platform called *Think*Consortium. We wanted Pakistani youth to feel part of the global picture: the more plugged in they felt to that, the less isolated and susceptible to Islamism they would be. The conference was a major success, and we held a second in 2011, with the hope of many more such events to come.

As was expected, some people weren't as receptive to my new ideas as others. Islamist groups, in particular, didn't take kindly to what they perceived as a traitor coming in to campaign against them. The threat that Ed and I had encountered in Denmark is just as real in Pakistan. Right from the word go, we had to be extremely careful about our security.

The importance of this hit home, literally, during one of my trips. I was in Lahore, on the second leg of my national universities tour. After a long day of campaigning, I had slipped out on my own to a cafe for a coffee and shisha. I picked a cafe near where I was staying without really thinking about it. What I hadn't realised, but quickly did, was that this particular cafe was a meeting point for Pakistani members of HT.

As I was drinking my coffee, an HT enthusiast came to sit down next to me, uninvited, and started talking about 'the *Khilafah*'. I humoured the guy for a while, but he didn't take the hint and leave.

'Look,' I said, 'you're clearly from Hizb al-Tahrir. I'm afraid I am not interested. I am just here to drink my coffee.'

At this point, the guy started staring at me. 'Hang on,' he said, 'you're Maajid Nawaz, aren't you? You're that guy who is going round the universities, shouting his mouth off about us.'

'Yes,' I admitted, 'I am. But I'm really not here to cause trouble. All I want to do is have a coffee.'

By this point, two others, also uninvited, had come to sit at my table.

'This is him,' my original 'guest' explained. 'The one I was telling you about.'

'OK,' I said. 'I'm really just here to have a coffee. It's eleven at night, and I've been working all day . . .'

'Yeah,' one of the men said. 'Working to spread your lies about us.'

This wasn't good. 'Who is the person in charge here?' I asked. The trio indicated another man, sat on his own in a corner. 'All right,' I said. 'I'm going to go over and say "*assalaamu alaykum*" to him, and then I'm going to leave. I don't want to offend anyone here.'

I walked over to the man in the corner. His name was Tayyab Muqeem, a British Pakistani who, like me all those years ago, had come to Pakistan to help recruit for HT. His inroad into Pakistan was through teaching English via the British Council – a common HT technique that Nasim used to set up HT in Bangladesh. Muqeem had managed to get himself appointed as head of English at a private university called Superior College.

I held out my hand out to him. He refused to take it, saying instead, 'If you don't get the fuck out of here right now, I am going to knock you out.'

Startled by his reaction I persisted, 'I'm just trying to shake your hand, I only came over to tell you that I'm not here to cause any trouble.'

I heard a scraping of chairs behind me, and looked round to see the three men who been talking to me before getting up and walking over. Everything happened so fast. Before I could work out what was going on, Muqeem took advantage of the fact that I had turned away. He stood up and hit me on the side of the face. I had not been expecting this, and caught completely off guard I found myself falling to the floor. As I went over, I caught a glass, which shattered in shards all around me. Ever the stubborn one, I stood up again immediately to face Muqeem, extending my hand a second time. 'I'm not here to fight,' I said. At that point, before it could go any further, the cafe owner stepped in and ushered Muqeem out.

Since that incident, I have been far more careful in terms of my security in Pakistan. So far no similar attacks have occurred. But the fact that the menace is there shows, perhaps, how threatened the Islamists feel about our campaign. It is still early days in the country, but we now have an organisation that boasts two permanent offices, chapters in every major city, and a network of volunteers across the country. It is not an overnight process to change a culture, but in the short time Khudi has been up and running, we have already taken some great strides.

CHAPTER THIRTY-TWO

I will see your day when it comes

In London we had founded Quilliam as a hub to inspire the counter-narrative globally. In Pakistan we had founded Khudi as a practical example of what can be done; but ever-restless, I wasn't satisfied. If the inspiration for Khudi was the franchise model of the Muslim Brotherhood, then I would need to franchise it to other countries. Just as Islamism had spread, oblivious to borders, across the Arab world and throughout Muslim-majority societies, we needed the democratic culture to do likewise. As word began to spread, emails requesting guidance from young democratic activists in war-torn countries who had seen my TED talk began to arrive. Youth began to reach out to us from Yemen, from Iraq, and from Somalia; off the back of specific invitations I travelled to Nigeria, and for the THINKFest in Goa, India and Bangladesh, where our advice was needed to prevent further

HT infiltration of their military. It felt odd, even surreal, to be going to Bangladesh – the country where I knew Nasim had founded HT, and to be working directly against the fruits of his labour. I was now using everything I had learnt from Nasim against him; his protégé had turned into his nemesis. Even Europe, after England's youth riots of 2011 and widespread unrest in Greece due to economic hardship, looked as if it could do with such a movement. But I knew we couldn't expand too fast. We had to take it slowly, carefully and strategically. What mattered most was to instil clarity in the idea, and set up a strong, experienced team. Our answer to how and where to set up next was looking clearer, as with Pakistan, due to another childhood association in my mind, my father's work in Libya.

One of the senior activists and analysts at Quilliam is Noman Benotman. Noman is a former leader of the Libyan Islamic Fighting Group (LIFG) and back in the 1980s he fought alongside Osama bin Laden against the Soviet invasion. When the Soviets withdrew, bin Laden called a meeting of his Arab generals, to discuss what to do next. It was at this meeting that bin Laden declared his wishes to turn the war against the West. Most of the generals agreed to follow him. The exception was Noman; he told bin Laden that this was crazy. He said that he'd come to fight the Russians, not to kill civilians. He felt they should be focusing on rebuilding the country they'd fought for, not attacking the West.

Noman and his troops returned to Libya. He then entered a process of demilitarising the group, in a similar way to IRA disarmament in the Northern Ireland Peace Process. Noman acted as the conduit between the LIFG and the Gaddafi government. He struck a deal with Saif Gaddafi whereby the group would renounce violence in return for their members being released *en masse* from Libya's prisons. He worked to guide his former group through their own process of deradicalisation, eventually encouraging them to write books recanting their old jihadist philosophy. In many ways, Noman was a kindred spirit, and I was honoured to bring him to Quilliam.

When the Arab Spring swept into Libya, Noman was in Tripoli and in a difficult position. Here was someone who had been working to disarm the LIFG, and had made promises to Saif Gaddafi to do so; now, however, there was an urgent need for the same people to re-arm. Would they return to their old jihadist ways, or would they fall into place under a popular leadership? Noman knew in his heart that the right place to be was on the people's side, and through Quilliam we lent our weight to the people's campaign in Libya.

As Gaddafi's forces were marching to crush Benghazi, Noman rushed back to London and opened Quilliam's front against Gaddafi's regime. In back-to-back media interviews we exposed Gaddafi's crimes and urged Western support for the Libyan people. We used the contacts we had made through Quilliam's work with the government to put Noman in touch with the air campaign. Noman had access to information on the ground in Libya, which he was able to pass on, and senior members of the RAF would call upon us for advice and analysis as the campaign progressed. Noman was one of the key figures behind encouraging the former head of Libyan intelligence, Moussa Koussa, to defect, and was the first to break the news. Understandably, our activities attracted the wrath of Gaddafi's regime; they even hacked our computer system in an effort to stop us. Following the fall of Gaddafi, Noman has been working with Libyans to help them shape their new government. He is able to offer them the unique perspective of not only being close to his former comrades in the Islamist militia, but also that of the tribal militia, and is crucial as a stabilising force between these competing factions. Keen to continue his post-conflict work, Noman maintains ties with Libyan jihadists globally, even those currently held in Iraq's jails, in an effort to convince as many as he can about the need to democratise Libya.

But for any new government to succeed, what is eventually needed in Libya is an injection of the civic ideals and democratic culture that Khudi has been busy promoting in Pakistan. Libya has been under a dictatorship for so long that it is completely lacking in any experience of democracy. For civic values to flower in such arid conditions is a tall order indeed, and the danger of sliding back towards the familiarity of a more autocratic regime is a real one. True to the Islamist model that inspired me, I began dreaming of franchising our Khudi-style movement to Arab nations. Pakistan was once again beginning to export positive political ideas. The months and years ahead will tell how far we can push this model globally, but the romanticism of struggle remains ever alive in our hearts.

And then there was Egypt. Out of all the countries where the Arab uprisings occurred in 2011, it is Egypt, perhaps unsurprisingly, that I took closest interest in. From my time in prison I have kept my unusual mix of contacts. My lawyer during the trial, Ahmed Saif, had been a founder member of

Kifayah. He was there at the beginning, when you could count the number of protesters on one hand, and their protests were seen as a laughing stock. In my work for Quilliam, I had come across the leaders of the April 6 Youth Movement: the group that first sparked Egypt's anti-Mubarak protests. Again, no one had taken them seriously when they announced at a 2010 Alliance of Youth Movements conference in New York that they would lead a revolution against Mubarak.

So when everything began to come together on 25 January 2011, and the protests started to spiral, I was on the edge of my seat in anticipation. 'World you must watch Egypt' I tweeted, knowing from the conversations I'd had with protesters that this time, and considering what had just happened in Tunisia, it was for real. I was quick to do what I could to help the revolution. A crucial factor in how things developed was going to be the reaction of the West. President Mubarak had always enjoyed support from being a close ally of the United States and its allies. If Mubarak received their support now, it would be that much more difficult to dislodge him. If the West stood back, then his position would become untenable.

What I could do to help their cause was get the protesters' message out and into the Western media. I wanted people to know that this was a movement led by liberal, young Egyptians. I didn't want the protests depicted as being Islamist-led. They were not instigated by the Muslim Brotherhood and it was important that Mubarak wasn't portrayed as the lesser of two evils: for too long the argument had been that yes, he was autocratic and unpleasant, but rather that than the extremist alternative. What the Egyptian protests showed was something new and exciting – a third way of genuine people power: radical democracy. It's what we'd been arguing was possible for a long time. That was why it was so important that they succeeded: at a stroke it undermined the old dichotomy of secular dictatorship or Islamist rule.

I was quick to reconnect with the likes of Ayman Nour, the liberal leader who had told me to 'grow up' in Mazrah Tora prison. I arranged for him to appear live with me on al-Jazeera to make the protesters' case: 'I am very proud to have spoken to my former cell mate', I tweeted. I reached out to another former cell mate, the Muslim Brotherhood spokesman Esam al-Erian, to gain insights as to their plans, and spoke to Sa'ad el-Din Ibrahim for advice. I called my old lawyer Ahmed Saif. 'This is not the time for me to speak, Maagid, the time for our youth has finally arrived,' he said to me with extreme humility.

And so I called the April 6 revolutionaries, coordinating with them their message for Western media. I used Quilliam's considerable press outreach to immediately release a number of press releases, endorsing the protesters' demands, and reminding the media of my own story, and how despotic the Mubarak regime could be. Mubarak, beware the prayer of the oppressed! This was the moment I really appreciated Jack Dorsey's advice to get on Twitter, and for the first time I really understood its potential. Every time I tweeted a link or a comment, I got calls from journalists who were following me, wanting an interview.

I then got in touch with Mona el-Tewahy, a US-based Egyptian-American, a former journalist turned activist. Both of us were in contact with protesters in Tahrir Square, and

I felt a consistent voice in the Western media was needed to put forward their cause; we began trying to coordinate our response. What followed was a non-stop cycle of media appearances and newspaper interviews, phone conversations and articles. I was delivering body blow after body blow to Mubarak through the press, the corridors of government and in the court of public opinion. I became a regular face on CNN, Sky, Bloomberg and the BBC: I wrote opinion pieces for *The Times* and the *Wall Street Journal*. And I tweeted, of course, relentlessly.

We knew from early on that our message was getting across: we could tell from our server at Quilliam who was downloading our press releases, and could see that the British and other governments across the world were regularly doing so. Cameron had asked me about Egypt in my meeting with him at Downing Street, and in his speeches since then he had been rejecting the old binary of 'dictatorship or extremism' for the Middle East. The success of our campaign had not gone amiss; former President Bush eventually invited me to his home in Texas to share my thoughts on the future of Egypt. This was where we had that delicate conversation about the definition of torture. My green-rucksack moment had finally come for Hosni Mubarak, and this time it was through our democratic advocacy that we were bringing down the bully. 'Our lobbying works', I tweeted, when Western leaders began to distance themselves from the regime. 'Game over Mubarak.'

I wasn't naive enough to believe that when the post-Mubarak elections were held a liberal regime would take power. It was always clear that the Muslim Brotherhood was going to capitalise on the uprising in any new administration.

It takes time for new political ideas to filter through, and in the meanwhile democracy means respecting the choice of the people. It would be deeply erroneous to see this as an endorsement of Islamism. For me, the Muslim Brotherhood's success is a bit like how many analysts see the American invasions of Afghanistan and Iraq – not so much a reasserting of US power but an overstretch; and in Egypt, the beginning of the end of its fascination with Islamism. In the long term, now with room to breathe, the younger generation who began this uprising will move on to create other movements and inspire new trends, beyond Islamism. Already, reform wings and breakaway youth factions from the larger Islamist groups are emerging. Islamism is not the future. In time, people will realise how it is part of the past, the old order.

My prayers, our prayers, in Mazrah Tora that Mubarak sees justice were finally answered. *Ya Mubarak hashoof feeka yawm*, 'I will see your day when it comes,' was a regularly invoked phrase by many of those oppressed prisoners. It was a dream that kept us alive in the desert heat, a dream that one day he would be brought to justice. For Mubarak to be swept from power was one thing, for him to be arrested was another. But for him to be put on trial, wearing those same white clothes, sitting in the same cage we were held in, and sent to the same prison that we were jailed in: that was something else. Mubarak, his two sons Alaa' and Gemal, and his interior minister Habib al-Adly, all ended up in Mazrah Tora prison. Divine intervention, call it what you will. But my Lord is just. He never fails me.

Seeing Mubarak in that cage was a cathartic moment. It brought it all back – the torture, the injustice, the wasted years of my early twenties. It was hard not to be moved. I felt a whirl of emotions: delight and sadness, victory and closure, vengeance and inner peace, all at the same time. I'd be lying if I said there wasn't an element of revenge in there, but it was revenge of a righteous variety: a just one. Mubarak's defeat had not come about through violence, not like Gaddafi. The supposed 'strongman' of Egypt had not been taken down in a hail of bullets, or by a suicide bombing, or by an HT-inspired military coup. It had been achieved by peaceful, democratic means. By people pouring out on to the streets and having the courage to stand together. And I had played my part.

I remembered, too, how I had been rounded on by the Islamists when leaving HT: the way that the ideas I had been espousing through Quilliam and then Khudi had been criticised and ridiculed. At once, all my friends had turned on me, and I lost so much. Apostate, I was called. Hypocrite. Traitor. Sell-out. The people will rise up to prove how wrong you are, I was told. I looked at Mubarak facing justice and thought to myself: well, the people did rise up all right, but not for Islamism. The small democratic spark that ignited our hearts all those years back in Mazrah Tora, with Ahmed Saif and the Kifayah movement, with Sa'ad el-Din Ibrahim and Ayman Nour, had finally engulfed the streets of Egypt. The radical grass-roots democratic alternative is here to stay, and a small smile flickers across my face whenever I think about it.

*Here I am, back in Mecca. I am still travelling,
trying to broaden my mind, for I've seen too much of
the damage narrow-mindedness can make of things,
and when I return home ... I will devote what energies
I have to repairing the damage.*

Malcolm X (1925–65)
Letter to James Farmer

Epilogue

If you ever travel to London and happen to be walking along Blandford Street, just off Baker Street, you might stumble upon a boutique Italian restaurant called Il-Baretto. If you decide to go in – and I would advise you to – you may well come across a rather loud table of friends talking to Luigi Festante, the house sommelier. On that table you're likely to encounter Samir Imran, a South Asian art critic, or Arsalan Hyder, a trained prosecutor. On any given day you could catch Fatima Mullick or her sister Zehra. You may also happen upon Imran Amed, a leading fashion journalist, Jeremy Brown my barrister friend from SOAS, my cousin Raheem (Dr Nasir's son), now an aerospace engineer, or my grown-up sister Sorraiya. And on that table, invariably, there I will be, sat among my friends and family, all of us locked in one deeply engrossing conversation or another.

On one such evening, I found myself recalling a recent incident that I had written about in *The Times*, in an article that came about as the result of one of my tweets. I was alighting from my train home after work the day after the Norwegian right-wing terrorist, Anders Breivik, had committed his appalling massacre. There, on the platform, I caught a man racially abusing a helpless old grandmother in a hijab, walking with her young grandchildren. 'Go back to your own country! This is England, we don't want you Muslims here!' he shouted at the terrified family. England had been tense. The anti-Muslim English Defence League had been on the rise and Breivik had just taken their reasoning a stage further in Norway. Suddenly exacerbating the uncertain atmosphere was this man, terrifying Muslim children in front of me on the train platform. Perhaps it was the freshness of what Breivik had done, perhaps it was the visage of cowering children in headscarves and the memories of Bosnia, perhaps it was everything – my entire life – that flashed before me then. Whatever it was, I found myself instantly transported back to the Essex of my teenage years. Memories of 'paki-bashings' came flooding back, and I saw nothing but Mickey standing before me once again. Rage ripped through my mind as I hurtled towards this man, my voice bellowing out expletives and my eyes telling a tale of fury. In an instant the racist bully was transformed into a spectacle of fear. I didn't even need to lift a hand – the coward teetered away meekly in the hope that all could be forgotten. The family thanked me graciously, but as I started walking home my hands began to tremble in shock. After all that's happened, this is not over. The cycle of hatred is coming back around. Time hadn't healed me. Somewhere deep inside me lurked a menace, and it took a trivial racist incident to bring it all back out. That scared me, and it took me a while sitting alone at home to resume my composure. 'Much remains to be done,' I thought. But the question of what to do next was playing on my mind.

'The Liberal Democrats are encouraging me to run for parliament.' I broke the news to my friends over the table in Il-Barretto after I'd finished the story. 'We clearly need more diversity in Parliament, but without creating it artificially and so they're hopeful in people like me standing up to be counted.'

'Great news! What does your mother think?'asked Samir.

'She told me to stay away. She said my work must remain above *party*-politics, governing all of politics, in a way.'

'Then do as your mother says' came the voice of Fatima, 'She's right, and always has been'.

'No, no, don't listen to Fati, become an MP so that I can boast about it to my friends,' Samir insisted jokingly.

'I'd hope there's already quite a story to tell your friends!' I retorted.

The question was left unresolved, and the option left on the table. As I pondered my next move, my thoughts moved to Ammar. I see him every Saturday and keenly teach him what basic football skills I can offer. I smile to myself with satisfaction every time he cheers on Liverpool FC, just as his father had done over two decades earlier. *You can be whatever you want to be, Ammar. Don't ever let anyone tell you otherwise.* Returning again to the world he would be raised in, I thought of the work that lay ahead.

'But how much more can I do before I'm too old to be running around like this?' I asked.

'Maajid, you're only thirty-four. You have a whole life ahead of you to consider such things' came the laughing reassurance from Fatima. 'Right now the movement you're building needs your support. It won't grow just like that.'

'Yes, perhaps you're right,' I said. 'Maybe my next move can wait till I hit forty-two'.

Glossary of Arabic Terms

(except where indicated: Urdu/Punjabi)

Akhi (my brother)

'Alayhi salam (shortened Muslim prayer for Prophets: upon him be peace)

Al-Jabbar (The Compeller – one of the ninety-nine names of Allah)

Allahu akbar (God is great)

Allahu musta'an (prayer: help is sought from Allah)

Assalaamu alaykum (greeting: Peace be upon you)

Amir (leader)

Azan (call to prayer)

Beta (Urdu: son)

Bhai (Urdu: brother)

Bi iznillah (with Allah's permission)

Da'i (missionary)

Da'wah (mission)

Daris (student)

Dariseen (students)

Deen (religion)

Eeman (faith)

Fee sabeelillah (in the path of Allah)

Ghimamah (blindfold)

Habib (dear friend, beloved)

Halal (permissible)

Halaqah (private study circle)

Hizbi (a partisan)

Itnain (two)

Itnain wa arba'een (forty-two)

Kafir (infidel)

Khilafah (caliphate)

Kuffar (infidels)

Kufr (disbelief)

Muhajir (immigrants, plural *muhajiroon*. Also the name of a banned extremist group in London founded by Omar Bakri Muhammad)

Muraja'aat (revisions)

Mu'taqal (the arbitrarily detained, plural *mu'taqaleen*)

Nana Abu (Urdu: maternal grandfather)

Nani Ammi (Urdu: maternal grandmother)

Nikah (marriage ceremony)

Qiyadah (leadership)

Raqam (number)

Sall Allahu alayhi wa-salam (longer Muslim prayer for the Prophet: May Allah's peace and blessings be upon him)

Shahadah (martyrdom, testimony of faith)

Shaikh (learned man, religious scholar, old man)

Shari'ah (body of Islamic edicts)

Shaweesh (conscripted Egyptian guard)

Sohni (Punjabi: beautiful)

Subhan Allah (Muslim invocation: Exalted be Allah)

Tai Ammi (Urdu: wife to eldest paternal uncle)

Wahid (one)

Wallahi (oath: by Allah)

Wilayah (province)

Ya Allah (O Allah)

Zaabit (officer)

Zalim (tyrant, plural – *zalimun*)

Resources

1. Maajid Nawaz debating Anjem Choudary on BBC *Newsnight*
   http://www.youtube.com/watch?v=2BrueU4xd2w

2. *Telegraph* article about the arrested coup-plotters in the
   Pakistan army http://www.telegraph.co.uk/news/worldnews/
   asia/pakistan/1440284/Pakistan-army-officers-arrested-in-
   terror-swoop.html

3. Transcript of an exchange between Maajid Nawaz and Dr
   Sa'ad al-Din Ibrahim after the former's release from prison
   http://www.bushcenter.com/downloads/theInstitute/human-
   freedom/wave-of-freedom/A_Conversation_with_Dr_Ibrahim.
   pdf

4. Maajid Nawaz and John Cornwall Amnesty International
   promotional video http://www.youtube.com/
   watch?v=GpNzOBhvtoA

5. Profile of Gita Sahgal http://en.wikipedia.org/wiki/Gita_Sahgal

6. Maajid Nawaz's BBC *HARDtalk* interview with Sarah
   Montague, during the last of his HT days http://news.bbc.
   co.uk/1/hi/programmes/hardtalk/4931416.stm

7. Quilliam website http://www.quilliamfoundation.org/

8. BBC *Newsnight* featuring Maajid Nawaz's journey from HT
   and Islamism

   part 1: https://www.youtube.com/watch?v=HYtP-4r4OE8

   part 2: https://www.youtube.com/watch?v=2yLZRONdIa0

   part 3: https://www.youtube.com/watch?v=CM4pkRqL0c0

9. Lord Ashdown's remarks at the Quilliam launch https://www.
   youtube.com/watch?v=5KfLQ6olnwA

10. Jemima Khan's remarks at the Quilliam launch https://www.youtube.com/watch?v=oN0QBNXMjxQ

11. Survivor of 7/7 Rachel North's remarks at the Quilliam launch https://www.youtube.com/watch?v=5BbXckInd8Q&list=UU7fkP6rdeoTbrzlr7oXK3Vw&index=77&feature=plcp

12. Seumas Milne's far-left criticism of Quilliam http://www.guardian.co.uk/commentisfree/2008/jul/17/islam.race

13. Glenn Beck's right-wing criticism of Maajid Nawaz and Quilliam http://www.youtube.com/watch?v=O_gr6FOBwOg

14. BBC *Doha Debate* Maajid Nawaz hosted by Tim Sebastian arguing against politicised Islam http://www.thedohadebates.com/debates/player.asp?d=42

15. Intelligence Squared debate Maajid Nawaz and Zeba Khan defending the faith of Islam from anti-Islam rhetoric against Ayan Hirsi Ali and Douglas Murray http://www.intelligencesquared.com/events/islam-is-a-religion-of-peace

16. Maajid Nawaz interviewed on *Larry King Live* http://www.youtube.com/watch?v=IF_A02IF4Bc

17. Maajid Nawaz interviewed in-depth by al-Jazeera's Riz Khan http://www.youtube.com/watch?v=4z1Eps1wJjQ

18. Maajid Nawaz profiled on CBS *60 Minutes* http://www.cbsnews.com/video/watch/?id=6711907n

19. Maajid Nawaz's facebook public page https://www.facebook.com/MaajidNawazFanPage

20. Maajid Nawaz's twitter page https://twitter.com/#!/MaajidNawaz

21. Maajid Nawaz testifies in the US Senate

    part 1: http://www.youtube.com/watch?v=4XJLkdCgHQc

    part 2: http://www.youtube.com/watch?v=HCF2dhtfy7k&feature=related

22. Maajid Nawaz's video blog response to Sayyid Qutb's *America that I Saw*

    part 1: http://www.youtube.com/watch?v=Q0qdURg4Qz0

part 2: http://www.youtube.com/watch?v=7mX6A27D5g0

part 3: http://www.youtube.com/watch?v=y3JqAKi2FTU

23. Maajid Nawaz testifies in UK parliament http://www.publications.parliament.uk/pa/cm201012/cmselect/cmhaff/uc1446-i/uc144601.htm

24. Prime Minister Brown cites Maajid Nawaz among reasons for not banning HT in the UK http://www.publications.parliament.uk/pa/cm200708/cmhansrd/cm071114/debtext/71114-0005.htm

25. Analysis of HT activity within the Pakistani army http://www.ctc.usma.edu/posts/hizb-al-tahrir-a-new-threat-to-the-pakistan-army

26. Khudi website http://www.khudipakistan.com/

27. Maajid Nawaz on the TED stage launching the idea for a counter-extremism social movement http://www.ted.com/talks/maajid_nawaz_a_global_culture_to_fight_extremism.html

28. BBC *Newsnight* tour of Maajid Nawaz to Pakistan

part 1: http://www.youtube.com/watch?v=yixGca6zZg4

part 2: http://www.youtube.com/watch?v=3unCtnLVZ-4

29. Pakistan Lawyer's Movement http://en.wikipedia.org/wiki/Lawyers%27_Movement

30. Khudi youth magazine *Laaltain*'s website http://www.laaltain.com

31. Maajid Nawaz at Google Zeitgeist http://www.zeitgeistminds.com/videos/impact-of-ideology

32. Maajid Nawaz interviewed by *Newsweek*'s Christopher Dickey at Goa's THINKFest http://www.youtube.com/watch?v=rKBE9Bm8aCI

33. News on Bangladeshi military thwarting an HT coup attempt http://newagebd.com/newspaper1/frontpage/49718.html

Acknowledgements

The book would not have been possible without the help of the key people who made it happen. Firstly, I would like to thank my agent and friend Neil Blair and his colleague Zoe King at The Blair Partnership. Neil, despite us initially meeting for an entirely unrelated purpose, you immediately saw the importance of my work and supported me above and beyond the call of duty. Thank you. Thanks also go to Jonathan Blair for suggesting that I abandon the large, corporate US agencies and consider instead his twin brother. It worked. I am indebted to the publishing director of the Virgin and WH Allen imprints at Ebury, Ed Faulkner, a visionary who saw me on the TED stage and instantly became enthused about the need to get my story out there. I'd also like to thank Yvonne Jacob for being so proactive in spotting my story in the first instance, and Caroline Newbury, Sarah Bennie and the entire publishing team for their support and backing. Thanks to my co-writer, Tom Bromley, for the hours spent conducting interviews, transcribing my words and picking my brains so that he could provide the structure I could build upon for this book. Thank you to Faye Husain, wife of Ed Husain, for fearlessly telling me to get more emotionally engaged with my rather stoic first draft, despite her husband's belief that 'It would do'. Thanks to Fatima

Mullick for reading through my words so diligently, and putting me in my place when I was sounding too grandiose. Thanks to my son Ammar for reading the prologue and telling me it sounded really 'cool'. Ammar, now you can read on. Thank you to my family for being so patient while I worked endlessly on this book. A special mention for my mum, who ensured that the facts about my family history were correct and for my newborn niece Nusaybah, who I didn't see enough of while I was busy writing.

This story would not be complete were it not for my many early supporters: Iqbal Wahhab, Jemima Khan, Ruth Turner, Evelyn Rothschild, Hazel Blears, Dougie Smith, Dean Godson, Catherine Fieschi, Jonty Feldman, Michael Gove and Yonca Brunini. From the US, I would particularly like to thank Chad Sweet, Farah Pandith, Juan Zarate, Michael Davidson, Bailey Cuzner and the GenNext team, Frank K, Jared Cohen, Dan Sutherland, Tim C, Paul D'Agostino, Truman Anderson, Mauro Lorenzo and Michael Murray.

Finally, my thanks to the tireless staff at Quilliam, especially Noman and Harriet, who expertly handled things for me while I was away compiling this story, and the brave team at Khudi Pakistan: Imran, Ali, Shabbir, Rab Nawaz and Umair, for building the dream.